Mountain Biking British Columbia

2nd Edition

FOR MY FAMILY
* * *

This is a Rip It Up publication.
All rights reserved.
Copyright © 2001 by Rip It Up Publishing, North Vancouver, BC, Canada
Printed in Canada by Transcontinental Printing Ltd.

For information contact:
mountainbikingbc@hotmail.com

Mountain Biking British Columbia
Second Edition

Cover design by Kinetix (www.kinetixweb.com) / Steve Dunn
Typesetting, Maps & Layout by Mathew Hoffman, Vancouver, BC

Cover Photos:
Riders at bottom left & bottom right by Chris Rollett (chrisrollett@home.com)
Rock rider (center) by Ian Hylands (www.photo-x.com)
Grizzly Bear & Totem Pole courtesy Tourism BC
Background photo of 800 year old cedar tree bark by Steve Dunn
Back cover photo courtesy Comox Valley Tourism

CANADIAN CATALOGUING IN PUBLICATION DATA

Dunn, Steve, 1971-
Mountain biking British Columbia

Includes index.
ISBN 0-9680342-2-5

1. All terrain cycling—British Columbia—Guidebooks. 2. Bicycle trails—
British Columbia—Guidebooks. 3. British Columbia—Guidebooks. I.
Polischuk, Darrin, 1966- II. Title.
GV1046.C32B75 2001   796.6'3'09711   C2001-911056-1

Mountain Biking British Columbia

2nd Edition

4

table of contents 5

introduction

Darrin Polischuk

Back in the early nineties I packed up the VW van, stuffed it full of bike gear and headed out to ride the western US. It was kind of my "Easy Rider" adventure with lycra, mountain bikes, and power bars. Enroute I stumbled across more then a few trail maps and assorted guides. Three months later I returned home and realized the riding in BC truly is the best and that nothing had been printed to show folks the way. Hmmm?

My first effort was a local guide book for the Okanagan Valley, and the following year came the first edition of *Mountain Biking BC*, complete with rambling essays on the stoke I felt for the sport. Self published and self financed, it had more than a few typos and misguided maps. The old guide is now more of a mountain biking time capsule than anything else. Nevertheless it served its purpose and got more than a few riders stoked on the sport.

That was 1996 when Lycra and titanium bar ends ruled and downhill riding was the domain of the racers only. Since that time a few things have changed. Bikes improved, trails got crazier and more creative, local riders became film stars and BC has become the undisputed center of modern mountain biking.

Yet, despite all the radical terrain that has been sculpted for your riding enjoyment and advances in equipment, the basics of riding your bike in the woods remains the central draw to this wonderful sport. Keep it simple, ride more and be careful.

To publish this second edition I drew on the services of my good buddy Steve Dunn. After migrating out west from Nova Scotia, his overall stoke for riding grew as the scars on his body multiplied. Our passion for mountain biking and desire to share this information with others created an improved guide, guaranteed to fill your weekends. Take it away Steve…

Steve Dunn

I want to ride my bike.... a lot. This simple desire has changed very little since I was three. Around that time, I got my first bike, which was a hand-me-down from my older brother. I felt like I had learned to fly when I wobbled out of my driveway and down the sidewalk. Since those days, my bike has allowed me to see and do many things. It has taken me over countless kilometers of trails, allowed me to meet some cool people, kept me fit, sane and even allowed me to save a little money. My bike has no emissions, (although sometimes the rider does) and it's even a whole lot of fun. I believe it has to be one of the most practical things ever invented by humans.

Now my bike is allowing me to exercise my brain by updating *Mountain Biking BC.* Plus, I get to share the passion I have for cycling with as many people as possible. Riding throughout BC I've realized that it's a paradise for the adventurer. For its size and sheer diversity of landscape, no other place in the world can match my adopted home province. No matter what your riding ability you're sure to find a trail that will inspire, or move you in some way. If you're lucky, you'll even find some of the special places that can only be seen and fully appreciated from the saddle of a mountain bike. If you haven't been on your bike in a while, or ventured somewhere new recently, read the back cover of this book right now! and make plans to explore. You and your bike *do* deserve it.

"The best bike in the world is the one you're riding." -Dag

8 acknowledgements

This book is a result of the hard work and assistance of many people. Countless details were faxed, re-faxed, e-mailed and re-e-mailed to make this book a reality. The project may have ground to a halt at any moment without the continued support of the people whom I've worked with and rode with:

Simon from Simon's Bike Shop (www.simonsbikeshop.com) has been a great supporter of cycling in Vancouver for years, many thanks for his support and enthusiasm for this project. Thanks to Darrin for his inspiration and reminding me to "keep it simple, Stupid", Steph for always being there for help, Blair Polischuk for his ability to steer in a storm of confusion and to Matthew Hoffman for his dedicated and detailed work on maps and layout. Merci beaucoup to Carys Evans for her inspiration, support and meticulous editing, Stan Rogers for giving me something to sing about, Chris Rollett for photographic assistance and overall stoke, my family for their long distance encouragement, and Bean for setting a killer pace.

A big "Muchas Gracias" to Chris Fewell at www.kinetixweb.com for his great work on the cover, Kareem & Jed for their sometimes tardy but always effective tech support, Digger for starting the craze, the boys at On Top for keeping me on the trails, Donald Ehman at www.freeriders.org for all the Kamloops pics, Bob Marley, Lyle Knight for Lillooet pics, Ian Hylands for the cover shot, Blake Goodman at Trails-Kamloops, Klaus Gattner, Vernon Tourism, Buddha, Smithers Chamber of Commerce, Comox Valley Tourism, all of the advertisers who supported the book, Tourism BC, BC Rockies Tourism, Whistler Mountain for the pics, my guitar, Larry "aioli" Falcon for his garlic dip and guiding services, Graham Keurbis for showing amazing strength and tenacity, Peter Dolman for making me ride my bike, Triple J for keeping my energy wire-tight, Olafson's Bagels, Blair Mercer for the 'therapy hikes', and those guys who gave me a tube on Grouse Mountain.

acknowledgements

The compilation of the latest trail information was a burden that was borne by many helpful folks at bike shops and forestry offices around BC. My thanks to all whom I've pestered for maps and trail information:

Thanks to the South Island Mountain Bike Society (www.simbs.com), Trevor at Westshore Bikes in Victoria, Peter Kelly for Millstream maps, Bob at Pacific Rim in Nanaimo, Kebble & Martin at Arrowsmith Mtn. Cycle in Parksville, Tig Cross of Hornby Island Cycle, Robert Baron for bringing Cumberland to my attention, Les at Black's Cycles in Comox, Dan at the Urban Lemming in Campbell River, Dean at Taw's Cycle in Powell River, Doug Deitweiller for being the driving force behind Sprockids and one of the great friends of mountain biking on the Sunshine Coast, the folks at Wenting Cycle in Mission, Spuzzum Bike Emporium, Kevin Bell at D.N.V, Peter Dorey at Olympia Cycle in Vernon and Robin Baycroft at Silver Star Mountain for putting up with my persistent nagging and especially Dag Abbey for building the best network of trails around, Mark at the Sacred Ride in Nelson, Eric at the Ski Base in Fernie, Mark at Red Shred's in Williams Lake, Gary O. for his insight on Williams Lake, Rob at McBike in Prince George, Peter at McBike in Smithers, Jim Maybee of Skookum Cycle in Salmon Arm, Dale from Dizzy Cycles for Burke & Eagleridge info., Jerome & Jeremy at Summit Cycle in Golden, James at Java Cycle in Kamloops, Frank at the Silver Barn in Grand Forks, Bob at Wildways in Christina Lake, Kevin at High Country Cycle in Revelstoke, Bob at the Ridge in Port Moody, Jim Richardson of the Kelowna Mtn. Bike Club, Pat Ansdell of Gravity Fed Adventures in Lillooet, Lyle Wilson of www.nipika.com for the Invermere info., Brian Smart Sunshine Coast Forest District for the great help with maps, Kurt Flaman at Freedom Bikes in Penticton for the maps and all the others whom I'm sure I've forgotten.

Special thanks to everyone that has ever reminded my why I ride a bike, whether you knew it, or not.

Mountain biking is a great way to enjoy the outdoors, and continues to gain in popularity. When you are trail riding, it's important to be aware of and follow certain rules, especially as more and more people use the trails. The following rules of trail etiquette have evolved over the last decade to take into account the various needs of the different types of trail users: hikers, horse riders, motor bikers and mountain bikers. For the safety of both you as a rider and of others on the trail, please respect these rules.

be aware

Be aware of other trail users. Always anticipate a horse or hiker around a blind curve and slow down. Prevent the sudden and unexpected encounters made possible by a bike's quick and silent approach; use a bell or friendly greeting to let others know of your presence.

yield the trail

Yield to hikers and horse riders. When encountering hikers, slow down to their speed, or stop and pull over. When encountering an equestrian from the front, ALWAYS stop. Move to the lower side of the trail to let horses pass, because they are less easily spooked by an object lower than themselves. A clearance of two or three meters is recommended between you and the horse, depending on the terrain.

From the rear, follow passing directions given by the horse rider.

In general, cyclists going uphill have the right of way. Yield to other cyclists you encounter.

ride, don't slide

Learn how to minimize damage to trails through proper riding techniques. Don't skid. It's neither a safe of efficient way to ride; it will erode the trail surface, and will eventually cause the trail to be closed to bikes. Take that turn slowly, or if it's a

Photo: www.Trails-Kamloops.com

tight switchback, dismount and walk it. Feather your brakes down steep descents to hone your riding skills and prevent skidding.

Avoid extremely muddy areas. Wait for trails to dry out in the spring or after rains. Riding wet and muddy trails is hard on your bike and on the trail. Tire ruts will become pathways for water erosion. If you must negotiate a puddle, ride straight through it, rather than widening the trail around it. Stay on the designated trail. Meadows are easily damaged by fat tires. Carry your bike over fallen trees and obstacles. Don't create a new trail around the obstacle. Don't short-cut switchbacks and corners.

be courteous

User conflicts can lead to trail closures. Cyclists are the newest group to use trails – in a dispute, we are the first to go. Respect private property and "No Trespassing" signs. Leave gates as you find them. DO NOT LITTER. Carry out what you bring with you and if you have room, carry out any garbage you find.

be prepared

Carry a spare tube and pump, tools, adequate food, water and clothing, small first aid kit, etc. A short cycle in is a long walk out if something goes wrong with your bike. Check the weather forecast and inquire about trail conditions and closures before you go. Let someone know where you're going and when you'll be back. Most important of all, wear your helmet and cycle safely. A successful trip is one without injuries.

Printed with permission from CYCLING BC (604) 737-3034 (#3137)

This guidebook is designed to serve as a general resource for mountain biking in British Columbia. It is by no means a definitive guide for the province's profuse system of trails and roads. Its purpose is to inspire the reader to travel to the many beautiful places that BC has to offer, and encourages the reader to seek more detailed information on each area visited. Because of the very accurate and current local knowledge possessed by riders in each individual community, it is highly recommended that you seek counsel in a local bike shop before venturing into the hills. Most shops welcome the opportunity to impart their wisdom to keen riders who have traveled great distances to enjoy their coveted singletrack. In fact, in some instances, you may find it difficult to stop the barrage of details and "fishing tales" that some friendly shops will churn out. Talking about mountain biking is as much a part of the sport as riding is. Enjoy every opportunity you get to exchange information or excitement about this great sport, whether it's over a pint, a coffee or other substances on the trail.

It should be noted that the author has endeavored to make this publication accurate. However, due to the nature of the sport, trails, trail conditions and access may change at any time without notice. The author and publisher will not be held legally responsible for any errors that may occur herein or for any injuries, loss or damage incurred while using information found in this guide. If you notice errors or glaring omissions in this guide, please alert us to the changes or share your insights by contacting us at: mountainbikingbc@hotmail.com.

MOUNTAIN BIKE TRAIL GRADING SYSTEM:

The trail grading system used in this guide is subjective and by no means scientific. Common sense should be exercised when choosing a trail. Due to the mountainous nature of British Columbia's trails, this rating system may not be accurate for riders from the flat places of the earth. Use common sense and ride within your limits.

EASY	basic riding skills and average fitness required
INTERMEDIATE	mountain bike experience and good fitness recommended
DIFFICULT	technical singletrack skills necessary and excellent level of fitness specific to cycling advantageous
VERY DIFFICULT	excellent cycling fitness and very advanced skills required, (insanity is helpful)

REQUIRED EQUIPMENT:

A bike in good working order, basic first aid kit, CSA approved helmet, lots of water, pump, spare tube (or patch kit), tire levers, a small selection of tools, cycling gloves, (body armour on some trails), comfortable cycling shorts with chamois, a good attitude (or a Rastafarian Medical Kit) and trail ethics.

WHAT DO YOU THINK?

Did we show you a little piece of paradise? Did we get you lost? Did we miss out on a great singletrack stash? Did we zig when we should have zagged? Drop us a line and let us know just what you think. Tell us what we can do to make this a better guidebook. Whether it's scathing criticism or just to let us know about a great ride you had, we want to hear it. Feel free to send along photos or stories of rides both memorable and horrible.

Or if you have a trail or an area that you think is worthy of inclusion in subsequent editions of this guide, please share the wealth and enlighten us.

Address all correspondence to:
mountainbikingbc@hotmail.com

British Columbia - west

British Columbia - east

Photo: Steve Dunn

vancouver**island**

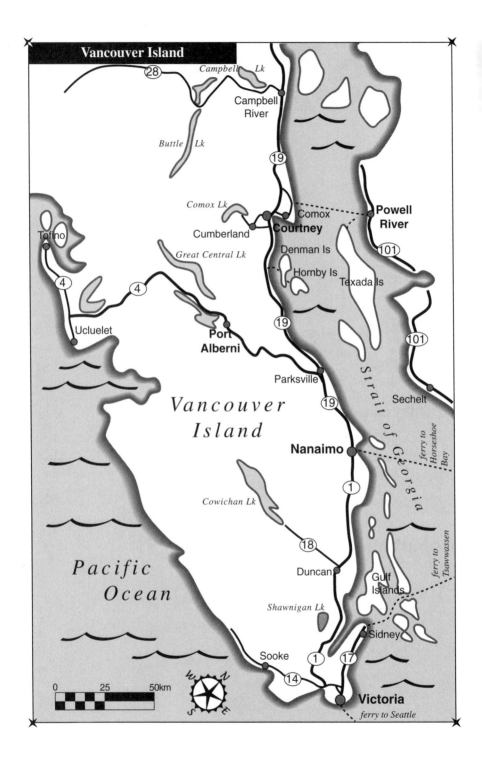

Vancouver Island

28

Campbell Lk

Campbell River

Buttle Lk

19

Comox Lk

Cumberland

Courtney

Comox

Powell River

101

Denman Is

Hornby Is

Texada Is

Great Central Lk

Port Alberni

Tofino

4

4

Ucluelet

19

Parksville

Sechelt

101

Strait of Georgia

Vancouver Island

19

ferry to Horseshoe Bay

Nanaimo

1

Cowichan Lk

18

ferry to Tsawwassen

Duncan

Gulf Islands

Pacific Ocean

Shawnigan Lk

Sidney

Sooke

1

17

14

Victoria

ferry to Seattle

0   25   50km

N E S W

what to expect

The capitol of BC is a unique riding destination that combines great single track within close proximity to a huge variety of off the bike attractions. The Mediterranean-like climate of Victoria is the warmest average temperature in the country, giving it the most consistent year round riding conditions in Canada. It's also the home training ground for the Canadian National Cycling Team. Cycling is a huge part of life in Victoria. The coffee shops buzz with keen riders fueling up early in the morning, roadies are seen buzzing around town in their shiny lycra and the overall cycling vibe is one of the best in the province. It truly is one of the most beautiful cities in Canada and what better way to see it than from behind bars (handlebars, that is).

Victoria was first established as a Hudson's Bay Company fort and this connection to the past is preserved through the many historic buildings and museums in the area. A walk through some of its downtown streets conjures up images of colonial days gone by.

The mountain bike community in Victoria is well organized and dedicated to improving & maintaining their extensive trail network. The South Island Mountain Bike Society (SIMBS) was successful in creating a mountain bike park with the help of volunteers and the local government and the result is found at Hartland / Mt. Work. This 500-hectare park is only 20 minutes from Victoria and has enough sweet singletrack to keep you busy all day.

trail descriptions

HARTLAND (BEGINNER TO DIFFICULT)

The South Island Mountain Bike Society (SIMBS) has struck a major blow for mountain biking. With the help of the Outdoor Club of Victoria, and many others, they have managed to create a 'sanctuary' where mountain bikers will be able to grow and flourish in the wild without the threat of fines or reprimand.

The 210 hectare Hartland / Mt. Work Mountain Bike Park is located adjacent to the municipal landfill, but don't let this deter you from riding here. Rarely does it smell bad; this progressive landfill is much easier on the senses than you'd expect. Ample parking, washrooms and a bike wash down facility are among some of the parks amenities.

Imagine this park as a gigantic singletrack buffet. You've got your fresh salad (easy climbs and beginner singletrack), your meat and potatoes, (intermediate singletrack), and your sweet, sweet desserts, (technical downhill singletrack with stunts & drops). It's all you can eat for the low, low price of a short smooth climb.

Individual trail descriptions are spared here due to the plethora of lucid signage at the trailheads.

The park is only a 20 minute ride from Victoria, and makes for a great warm up. To access the park from the ferries, take Patricia Bay Hwy. (17) south to the royal Oak turn off and turn right at the lights onto Royal Oak Dr.. Turn right on West Saanich Rd. and follow it along to Hartland Ave. turn left.
From up-island, take the Helmecken turn off left to West Saanich Rd. where you go left, then left again onto Hartland Ave. From Victoria, travel north on Blanchard St., which becomes the Patricia Bay Highway. After taking the Royal Oak exit, go left at the lights onto Royal Oak Drive. Turn right onto West Saanich Rd. then left onto Hartland Rd., go to the end, the parking lot is on the right. From up-island (north), head south on Highway One (Island Hwy.). Take the MacKenzie exit and follow signs to Hwy. 17 (ferries) north. Then take the Royal Oak exit and from there, follow the directions above from downtown Victoria.

MILLSTREAM HIGHLANDS (INTERMEDIATE TO DIFFICULT)
Although the riding in the Highlands can be somewhat rootier and occasionally muddy, it does have a great stash of trails to keep you busy for a long time.

Novice and intermediate riders will want to ride to the tip where the trails are generally smoother and faster. To access the top, you'll want to head up the main powerline road and veer left at the 'dirt mound'. The climb gets a

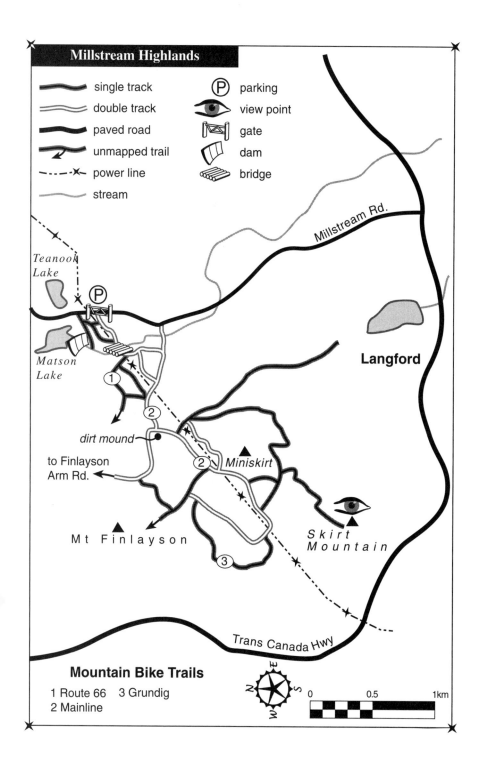

Millstream Highlands

Legend:
- single track
- double track
- paved road
- unmapped trail
- power line
- stream
- ⓟ parking
- 👁 view point
- 🚪 gate
- dam
- bridge

Teanook Lake

ⓟ

Matson Lake

① Route 66

② Mainline

dirt mound

to Finlayson Arm Rd.

②

Miniskirt

▲

Langford

Millstream Rd.

Mt Finlayson ▲

③

👁

Skirt Mountain ▲

Trans Canada Hwy

Mountain Bike Trails
1 Route 66   3 Grundig
2 Mainline

N E S W

0   0.5   1km

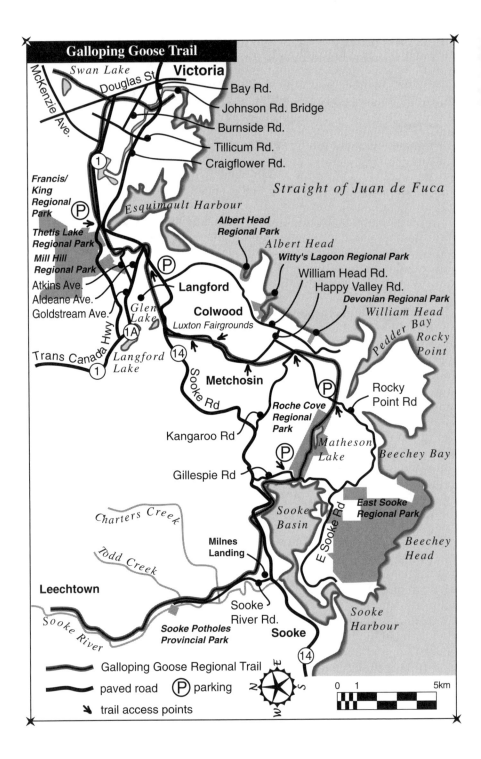

Galloping Goose Trail

Swan Lake
McKenzie Ave.
Douglas St.
Victoria
Bay Rd.
Johnson Rd. Bridge
Burnside Rd.
Tillicum Rd.
Craigflower Rd.

Straight of Juan de Fuca

Francis/ King Regional Park
Ⓟ
Esquimault Harbour
Albert Head Regional Park
Albert Head
Witty's Lagoon Regional Park
William Head Rd.
Happy Valley Rd.
Devonian Regional Park
William Head
Pedder Bay
Rocky Point

Thetis Lake Regional Park
Mill Hill Regional Park
Atkins Ave.
Aldeane Ave.
Goldstream Ave.
Ⓟ
Langford
Colwood
Luxton Fairgrounds
Glen Lake
1A

Trans Canada Hwy
1
Langford Lake
14
Metchosin
Sooke Rd.
Roche Cove Regional Park
Ⓟ
Rocky Point Rd
Matheson Lake
Beechey Bay

Kangaroo Rd
Ⓟ
Gillespie Rd
Sooke Basin
E Sooke Rd
East Sooke Regional Park
Beechey Head

Charters Creek
Todd Creek
Leechtown
Milnes Landing
Sooke River
Sooke River Rd.
Sooke Potholes Provincial Park
Sooke
14
Sooke Harbour

Galloping Goose Regional Trail
paved road   Ⓟ parking
⬊ trail access points

N E S W

0   1   5km

little steeper here, and riders will want to veer left after crossing the powerline, and get onto the maze of top trails. Give yourself about 30 minutes to climb to the top. Exploring these moderate grade climbs will bring you to a viewpoint on top of Skirt Mountain. If you find yourself on a descent away from the powerline, be aware that you will be climbing out before you get carried away. Most of the trails dropping southeast have climbs that connect with the powerline road.

The singletrack on the lower slopes are generally more difficult because of their northern exposure. These moist, more rooted trails are quite technical with plenty of sidehills, tough obstacles, and steeper pitches. These trails provide a contrast with the open fast singletrack on the top. Weekly fun looney races have been held on the lower slopes of the Highlands. The suburbs are spreading out into this area soon, so ride these trails before they become the paved home of the mini-van people.

THE GALLOPING GOOSE (BEGINNER)

The Galloping Goose is a multi-use trail that was created in 1989, giving Victoria 60 km of friendly gravel paths to ride, hike or run on. The easy rail grade of 'the Goose' is not really what I consider mountain biking to be, but the length, history, and beauty of this trial makes it worthy to mention and map in a mountain biking book. Furthermore, all mountain bikers will enjoy riding it.

The Galloping Goose Railway owes its existence to the pursuit and extraction of gold and timber. The railway was built to connect the resource-rich Leechtown area with Sooke and Victoria. The name came from the image of a wobbly, gas-powered rail car loaded with trees heading down to Sooke. Today, the 'rails to trails' project, affectionately referred to as 'the Goose', takes people away from the buzz of the city into the countryside that is in spots only meters away from the concrete of Greater Victoria. Do the whole ride, or explore sections as time permits.

Mountain Bike Trails

1 Regional Trail	13 Inventive
2 Crossover	14 Skull Trail
3 South Ridge Trail	15 Little Face
4 Fun Trail	16 Rock Bottom
5 Green Ribbon Trail	17 Extension Ladder
6 Say Ahhhh...	18 Breathless
7 Hot Cherry	19 Twister
8 Emergency Two	20 Lemmings Run
9 Dave's Line	21 Daves Dementia
10 Birth Control	22 Snakes & Ladders
11 Centerfold	23 Sidewinder
12 Switchback Trail	24 Step Ladder

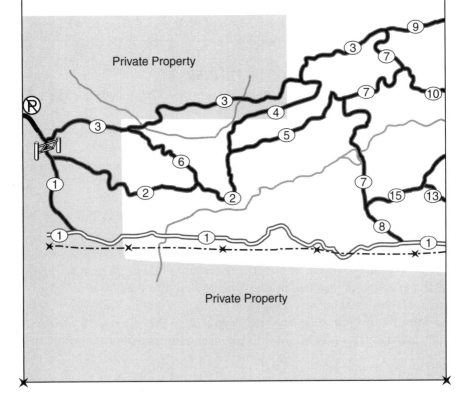

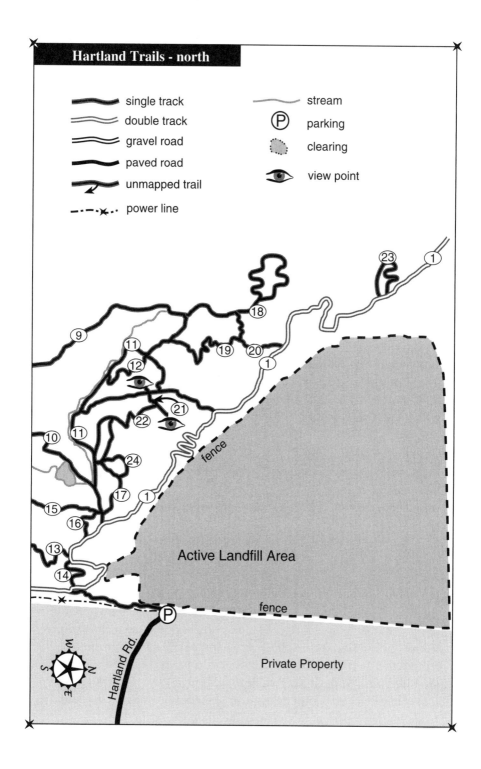

BURNT BRIDGE (INTERMEDIATE)

This is the site of the Burnt Bridge International Classic Cross Country race, a classic of classics. Trails criss-cross this area like lines on George Burns' face. They're everywhere. The Burnt Bridge Race loop is the best sample of the rides in this area. Up the road to Eagle heights is another area that is loaded with trails, too numerous to map. Go explore.

To get to the Burnt Bridge area from Victoria, go north on Hwy. 1 (Malahat Drive) and turn left at Shawnigan Lake R. (south end). Next, turn left at West Shawnigan Lake Rd. and left again on Renfrew Rd. Continue onto the gravel road and park at the 3-way intersection near the bridge.

Photo: Chris Rollett   *Rider: Kim Steed*

To access the Race Loop, follow the wide road to your left after crossing the river. You'll go over a small bridge and ride under the power lines before turning right about 4 km from the start. As you ride under the powerline again, veer left and then take an immediate right onto a trail that narrows. Soon you'll be screaming down and over a log jump onto a dismount at a log bridge. Go right after the bridge and remember to veer left as you climb to the top ridge of a cut-block. Follow this rim trail around the Wild Deer Creek drainage until a steep descent shoots you into the forest back to the main road near the bridge. The left fork gives you more singletrack as it goes through an intermittent creek and back to the road. Simply, a perfect mountain biking loop.

CAN-AM TRAILS (INTERMEDIATE)

These trails are located below the main forest service road and skirt near the Koksilah River. Go right after the burnt bridge and veer right at the first fork, about 2.5 km from the start. Follow along this double track until you see the singletrack on the left. This trail plummets down. Go left at the intersection and down to a nice lookout of the Koksilah River. Return back on the same trail and take the left fork back to the main road.

local knowledge

tasty bites & frosty pints

The Cheesecake Café, 910 Government St., (250)-382-2253
Indian Curry House, 102-506 Fort St., (250) 361-9000

camping / shelter

Thetis Lake Campground, 1-1938 West Park Lane, (250) 478-3845
Markham House B&B, 1853 Connie Rd., Victoria, (250) 642-7542

off the bike in victoria

Victoria is such a beautiful city that it's definitely worth taking a day to check it out. The heritage buildings that line the streets and the tall ships in the inner harbour make it a photographic dream. There are plenty of options for rest days around here. Number one on your list should be the Royal British Columbia Museum and the National Geographic Theatre; expand your mind, (don't worry, your helmet will still fit). There is always something interesting on exhibition there, ((250) 356-7226).

Try horseback riding through the trails of the Saanich Peninsula with panoramic views of the Gulf Islands and Mt. Baker, all just 20 mins. from Victoria. (Woodgate Stables (250) 652-0287). I'm sure an afternoon of sipping wine at a vineyard tour would be acceptable. There are several wine tours near Victoria, try Cherry Point Vineyards, (250) 743-1272. For more 'off the bike' ideas contact Tourism Victoria at (250) 414-6999.

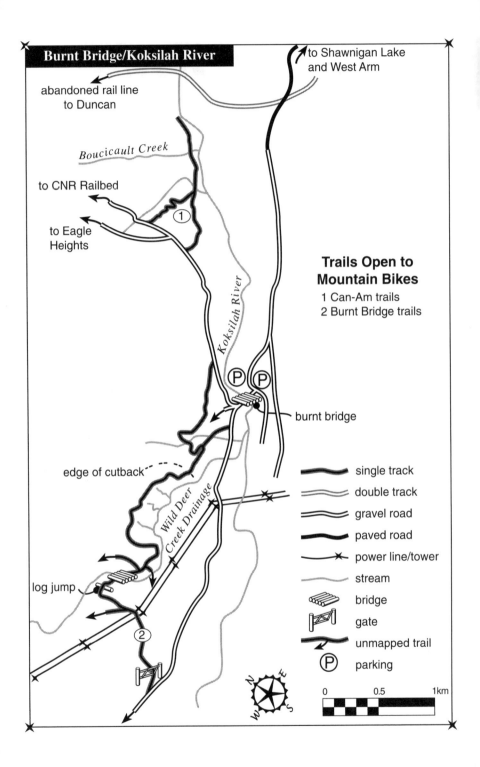

Burnt Bridge/Koksilah River

to Shawnigan Lake
and West Arm

abandoned rail line
to Duncan

Boucicault Creek

to CNR Railbed

to Eagle
Heights

Koksilah River

**Trails Open to
Mountain Bikes**
1 Can-Am trails
2 Burnt Bridge trails

①

Ⓟ Ⓟ

burnt bridge

edge of cutback

Wild Deer
Creek Drainage

log jump

②

single track

double track

gravel road

paved road

power line/tower

stream

bridge

gate

unmapped trail

Ⓟ parking

N E S W

0   0.5   1km

what to expect

I fell in love with the riding in Nanaimo on my first ride there. It was the world famous Abyss trail. Well, it might not be world famous, but it's a ride that many know and few forget. Most of the rides in this area are so sweet because they've been built by a dedicated and eccentric group of riders know as Team Resin. The Resin boys take their trails seriously because they build masterpieces, and I don't mean those short, "Wow, that was quick." sort of thing either. These guys build epics. One of the things that make this riding area so appealing is the ability to easily link up a series of trails to make a nice long and varied ride, much like a mountain bike amusement park. Grab your tickets and head on in. Steeps, stunts, thrills, chills, screaming fast, cross country technical or whatever else you can handle, you'll find it here. Carys Evans, one of BC's most hardcore female riders, (seen in the mountain bike movie, *Kranked*) learned to rip on these trails; maybe you can too.

trail descriptions

THE ABYSS (DIFFICULT)

The Ultimate Abyss has to be the most famous trail on Vancouver Island. It was named in 1989 by a couple of local hikers after its most distinguishing feature, a large crack in one of the huge rock slabs sections cause by an earthquake

Photo: www.freeriders.org

many years ago. Unfortunately, the Abyss is a victim of its own popularity. Because the trail is technically difficult, riders too often opt for an easier line, resulting in widening of the trail in its most gnarly sections. Please ride the correct line, or grab a slice of humble pie and walk it. Since the first publication of this guide in 1996, much work has been done on the Abyss. New sections have been added, stunts have been built and rock slabs cleaned. It all makes for an incredible cross-country circus.

To access the trail, head up Harewood Mines Rd. from Seventh St., past the overpass and park in the small pullout under the power lines. Mount up and ride southwest under the power lines for about 200 meters and take the short climb up to the right and into the forest. Welcome to the Abyss. There are many side trails that meander off the main one. Feel free to explore, but keep straight for the full Abyss experience. One option for returning is to turn around and ride the Abyss all the way back to the start. Or, when you've ridden the final smooth descent you'll be at a waterline access road. You can turn left (east) on this road and in five minutes you'll see a singletrack up on the left. This is HUMILITY, which you can ride back to the powerlines at the start of the ABYSS.

WESTWOOD LAKE LOOP (BEGINNER)

This is a great family type of ride on an easy groomed trail surface around Westwood Lake. The trail is either flat or slightly rolling on bark mulch or dirt surfaces. The trails and bridges are in good condition and signs will point you around the lake. Keep your ears and eyes on alert for the beavers that inhabit this human-enhanced, urban lake. This is the best lake in the city to visit; don't forget your swim trunks and some Scooby snacks for the post ride.

This is a Regional District of Nanaimo maintained area with picnic facilities and washrooms. To access the trail, drive up Jingle Pot Rd. onto Westwood Rd.

WESTWOOD RIDGE / ROCKY ROAD / 3 CREEKS TRAIL (INTERMEDIATE)

This combination of trails makes for a great medium distance ride and gives the rider just the right mixture of all the stuff that makes mountain biking the amazing sport that it is. Expect some tough technical climbing and a few dismounts on the way up, but the long, fast descent makes up for the tougher than usual climb.

Start this combination ride at the northwest tip of Westwood Lake. When

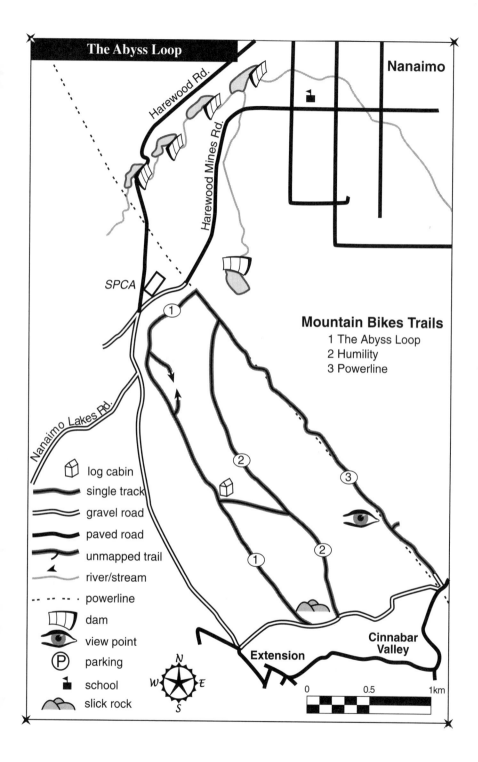

The Abyss Loop

Nanaimo

Harewood Rd.

Harewood Mines Rd.

SPCA

①

Nanaimo Lakes Rd.

Mountain Bikes Trails
1 The Abyss Loop
2 Humility
3 Powerline

②

③

①

②

Extension

Cinnabar Valley

🏠 log cabin

〰〰 single track

── gravel road

━━ paved road

〰 unmapped trail

◢ river/stream

- - - powerline

🏠 dam

👁 view point

Ⓟ parking

▪ school

⛰ slick rock

N W E S

0   0.5   1km

the trail starts to go around the tip of the lake back toward Nanaimo, you go right, ending up under the power lines. Hiking groups have put up signs with different trail names at the beginning of the technical climbing. Once the trail becomes more forgiving, you will pass an old cabin site while riding an old creek bed. Once past this area, avoid your first major right and left. Continue to climb until you are along a fence line. This is the National Department of Defense land and shooting range, so obviously avoid it (unless you *really* want this ride to be over). At the sight of a shack, go right and up Rocky Road. Continue past all possible lefts and rights. Once you crest the climb you are on the 3 Creeks Trail. This 3.5 km descent has some fast, well established lines through creeks that range in depth from dry in the summer to hub-level rushing water in the spring and winter. Parts of 3 Creeks Trail have been logged and are now unrideable. Take Nanaimo Lakes Rd. to the power lines which will bring you back to Westwood Lake.

DOUMONT TRAILS (INTERMEDIATE TO DIFFICULT)

This area is a vast network of single and double track trails that criss-cross up and down the mountain. There really is a lot of high-quality riding here. There is so much, in fact, that it would detract from the riding experience to try and describe them all. The best way is to go and explore but use the map as a guide. Many of the trails are signed but even if they're not, it's difficult to stay lost for too long. PMS and Three Sisters are some great trails to check out.

To access the trails, go to the end of Dumount Rd. and park in the pullout at the end of the pavement before you reach the moto-cross track. Climb the logging road and pick your trailhead. They're everywhere.

Photo: Steve Dunn   Rider: Carys Evans

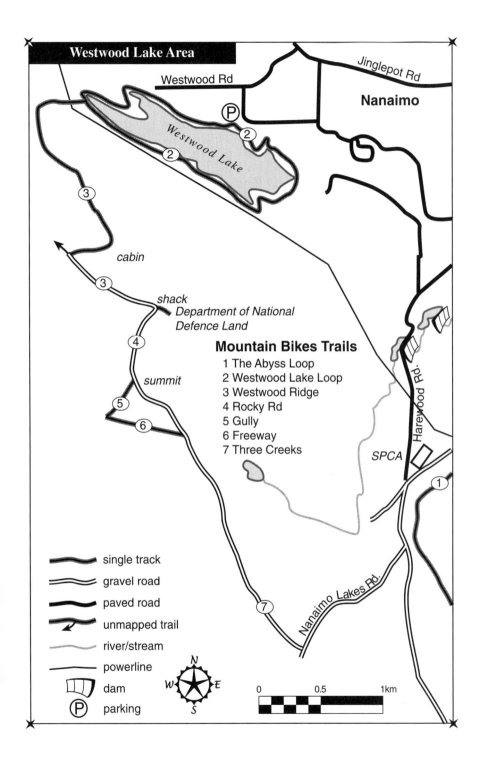

Westwood Lake Area

Jinglepot Rd

Westwood Rd

Nanaimo

Ⓟ

Westwood Lake

2

2

3

3

cabin

shack

Department of National Defence Land

4

summit

5

6

Mountain Bikes Trails
1 The Abyss Loop
2 Westwood Lake Loop
3 Westwood Ridge
4 Rocky Rd
5 Gully
6 Freeway
7 Three Creeks

Harewood Rd.

SPCA

1

7

Nanaimo Lakes Rd.

single track
gravel road
paved road
unmapped trail
river/stream
powerline
dam
Ⓟ parking

N
W E
S

0   0.5   1km

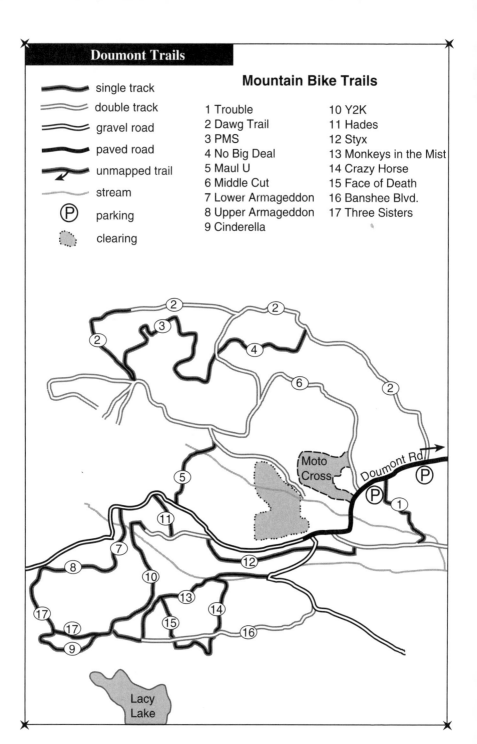

Doumont Trails

Legend:
- single track
- double track
- gravel road
- paved road
- unmapped trail
- stream
- (P) parking
- clearing

Mountain Bike Trails

1 Trouble
2 Dawg Trail
3 PMS
4 No Big Deal
5 Maul U
6 Middle Cut
7 Lower Armageddon
8 Upper Armageddon
9 Cinderella
10 Y2K
11 Hades
12 Styx
13 Monkeys in the Mist
14 Crazy Horse
15 Face of Death
16 Banshee Blvd.
17 Three Sisters

Moto Cross

Doumont Rd

Lacy Lake

local knowledge

tasty bites & frosty pints

Gina's Café, 47 Skinner St., (250) 753-5411
Crow & Gate Pub, 2313 Yellow Pt., (250) 722-3731, 10 minutes south of
Nanaimo (GREAT PUB!)

camping / shelter

Newcastle Island, 10 minute foot
ferry from downtown (no cars!)
very cool spot to camp while in
Nanaimo, beautiful, quiet and lots
of history.

off the bike in nanaimo

If you're driving between Victoria
and Nanaimo on your way to more riding or to catch a ferry, you'll be
driving right past one of North America's first bungee operations. The
Bungee Zone, (250) 753-JUMP, is a fine way to scare the hell out of
yourself for an afternoon without getting your bike dirty. Being situated
next to the water and mountains has its advantages, in particular being able
to have your pick of recreation opportunities. Kayaking, sailing, hiking,
climbing, swimming, fishing are a few ideas you can work with here.

what to expect

Parksville is a quiet retirement community with a gorgeous stretch of beach that attracts tourists in the summer. However, for mountain bikers in BC, it is the home of the 'season opener' for the BC Cup race series. The Hammerfest racecourse is a challenging network of trails that will keep the muddy grin on your face all day long. Nearby, the Top Bridge Mountain Bike Park is one of the few designated riding parks in the province. This is a super fun way to spend a day; whether you're learning to ride or looking for a self-contained dirt circus. Most of these trails were built and are maintained by the Arrowsmith Mountain Bike Club, (250) 248-5575. You're bound to bump into some really stoked riders on these trails. It's not hard to figure out why they feel that way: beautiful, uncrowded trails that ride like a dream.

trail descriptions

A.M.C. TOP BRIDGE MOUNTAIN BIKE PARK

The Arrowsmith Mountain Bike Club has done a tremendous job of creating an area designated for mountain biking. The Parksville area has many great rides outside the park, but many of them are confusing and usually require a guide to ensure a positive experience. The A.M.C. Top Bridge Mt. Bike Park, on the other hand, offers up some great singletrack in an area that is easy to navigate although going in circles is a distinct possibility). Before the A.M.C. crew was given permission to develop the area, the only trails were Upper and Lower Reefer Ridge. Years of riding have smoothed out these trails, but fun rideable obstacles keep these originals on everyone's 'must ride' list. Since receiving official permission to build trails, the area has flourished with new rides.

To access the park, head to the south (Nanaimo bound) weigh scales and Kay Rd., then turn onto Chattell Rd., and follow it past the gun range to the park. All of the on and off ramps may be confusing, but a bit of common sense will see you through this concrete mess.

The locals recommend jumping off the nose into the Englishman River to cool off after a hot day on the trails. Make sure you take the time to check out the First Nations rock carvings on the river rock, just a little reminder who originally lived here.

The first trail built was the Ragin' Ravin which follows the ridge high above the Englishman River. Built in 1995, the trail is a nice rough contrast to the buffed up Reefer Trails, and gives those craving a more technical ride their needed fix. The B-Trail, or Berm Trail is a fast, short, but extremely fun descent to look for as well.

New trails in the park include a beautiful dual slalom track with big berms and jumps. It will eventually run the full length, from top to bottom.

HAMMERFEST RACE COURSE

This is the perfect site for some early season racing and riding. An all-new downhill course with loads of jumps has recently been built as well as a kid's racetrack and scores of other trails linking existing ones. The course and trails are located at Englishman River Falls Provincial Park near Parksville. To reach it, take the Alberni Highway inland, and follow the signs toward the park. There are washrooms and campsites nearby with hot shower and flush toilets. The trails are on MacMillan Bloedel land, so the next time you curse the giant forest companies for their mandate, try to mitigate your nasty thoughts with memories of the great riding and the permission you had to ride on their property.

The course starts with a short climb onto the Burnt Ridge singletrack. Once you negotiate Big and Little Rock climbs, the course goes back to the main gravel road climb. Next, you jump onto Pete's Power Line Express, a steep climb that brings you to the first summit 4.2 km into the course. A left into Fern Gully awakens you from the view back to some exciting downhilling. The Enchanted Forest leads you across the main road into the short and twisty Rotten Trail. Climbing up the power lines you are actually on the old downhill course. Continue to grunt upward on the last climb of the loop, which rises a leg-searing 140 meters in 1.3 km. Finally, the climbing ends and some fresh singletrack called Extreme Dream escorts you down the mountain in fine island style. The single track hooks up with the faster main road of the old downhill course. A left onto a new gravel road completes the loop.

off the bike in parksville

It seems BC is full of towns that could be considered multisport havens. However, the east coast of Vancouver Island seems to have the monopoly on oceanfront towns that do a fantastic job of marrying ocean and mountain.

If you want to relax here, hit the beach, dude. The waterfront in this area is remarkable. There's plenty of sand for everyone, enough, in fact to host the annual Sandcastle Competition, which draws builders from around the world every summer. So play nice and don't throw sand. For more activity ideas, contact the Oceanside Tourism Assoc. in the Qualicum Beach Train Station, 174 Railway Street in Qualicum Beach.

local knowledge

tasty bites & frosty pints

Boar's Head Pub, 1025 Lee Rd, French Creek, (250) 248-3713
Fish Tales Café, 3336 Island Highway W, Qualicum Beach, (250) 752-6053

camping / shelter

Englishman River Falls Provincial Park, 13 km southwest of Parksville, off Hwy 4, (250) 954-4600
Tranquility Woods, 2080 Errington Rd., south off Hwy. 4A near Englishman River Falls Park Parksville, (250) 954-1661

Photo: Chris Rollett

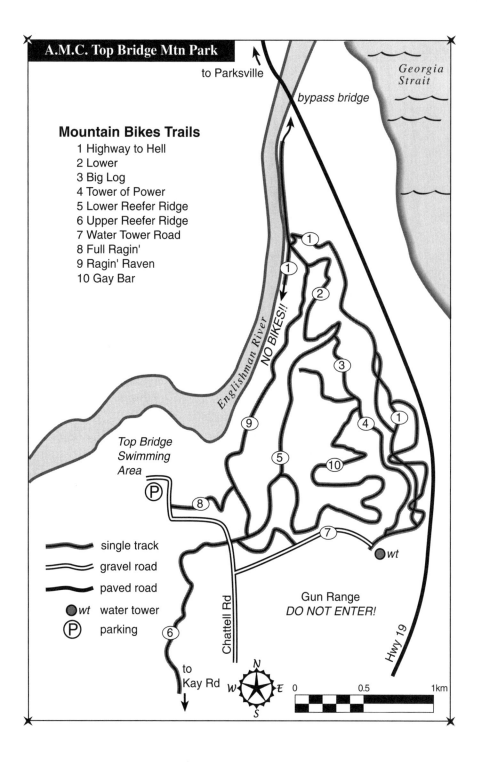

A.M.C. Top Bridge Mtn Park

Georgia Strait

to Parksville

bypass bridge

Mountain Bikes Trails
1 Highway to Hell
2 Lower
3 Big Log
4 Tower of Power
5 Lower Reefer Ridge
6 Upper Reefer Ridge
7 Water Tower Road
8 Full Ragin'
9 Ragin' Raven
10 Gay Bar

Englishman River

NO BIKES!!

Top Bridge Swimming Area

ⓟ

single track

gravel road

paved road

●wt water tower

ⓟ parking

Chattell Rd

Gun Range
DO NOT ENTER!

Hwy 19

●wt

to Kay Rd

N
W E
S

0   0.5   1km

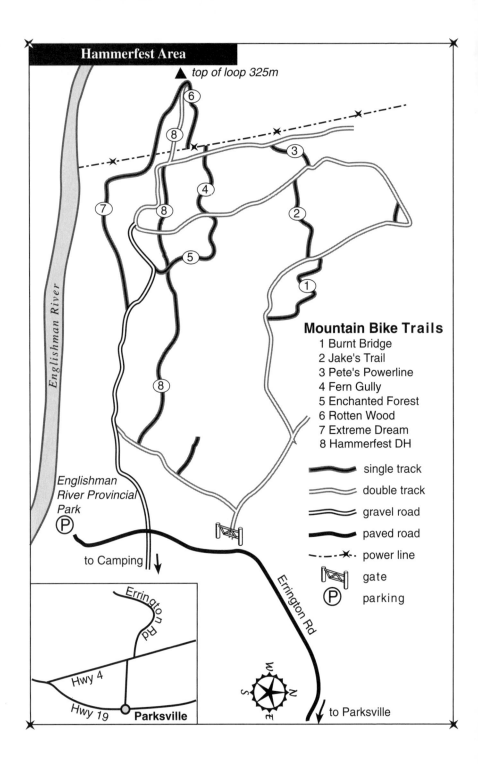

Hammerfest Area

▲ top of loop 325m

Englishman River

Englishman River Provincial Park

Ⓟ

to Camping

Mountain Bike Trails
1 Burnt Bridge
2 Jake's Trail
3 Pete's Powerline
4 Fern Gully
5 Enchanted Forest
6 Rotten Wood
7 Extreme Dream
8 Hammerfest DH

single track

double track

gravel road

paved road

power line

gate

Ⓟ parking

Errington Rd

Hwy 4

Hwy 19   Parksville

to Parksville

Errington Rd

what to expect

The trees begin to bend around your narrow cone of focus as your bike accelerates easily on the smooth, twisting singletrack. Time ceases to pass when you're riding "in the zone" on Hornby, in fact, it ceases to pass there, period. The riding is so sweet on Hornby Island, that many of the locals have never ridden anywhere else. "Why?" is the usual response when questioned. I tend to agree. Why leave heaven? The riding is fast, the pace of life is slow and the view of the Vancouver Island mountains from the top of the Rim Trail is one you'll never forget. Hornby Island is a very special place indeed. Far removed from the mainland by the 3 ferries needed to get there, it hosts an enclave of artists, artisans, hippie love-children and some soulful riders. You can hit all of the gems in a day, but you'll want to spend a week there. The trick is to ride the Byzantine network of trails in sections so you're always on new ground. Talk to Tig or Vern at Hornby Island Cycles (250) 335-0444 and they'll set you up real good.

trail descriptions

Because of the cornucopia of mind blowing single track on the island, I've included directions for only two trails. The best Hornby experience involves taking a map and getting into the thick of things. It's very difficult to get lost here, if you somehow manage to do that…congratulations! People have been trying to lose themselves on Hornby since it was first settled.

THE SPIT TRAIL (BEGINNER)

The Spit Trail connects Fords Cove with the ferry terminal. The trail can be ridden in either direction and is the fastest way across the island. The trailhead is located on your right when you come off the ferry, or on your right while approaching Fords Cove off the paved road. The trail is essentially a beginner ride but has some tricky sections to keep you on your toes.

THE BENCH TRAIL (BEGINNER)

The Bench Trail is an out-and-back trail that can be ridden in either direction. The easiest access for newcomers to Hornby is off of Mount Rd., which is close to the ferry terminal. From the parking area at the trailhead, a smooth single track awaits with views that seem to get better the further you ride. At one point the trail splits and rejoins about 500 meters later. Mountain bikers who take the right fork SHOULD DISMOUNT as the trail is VERY EXPOSED and dangerous, the views are better when you're off your bike anyway. The Bench Trail is a smooth well worn hiking trail that can be very busy during the summer so be on your best behavior; and don't ruin someone else's day by riding too fast or out of control.

local knowledge

tasty bites & frosty pints

Jan's Café, (250) 335-1487, next to Hornby Island Cycles
Hornby Island Resort, 4305 Shingle Spit Rd, (250) 335-0136

camping / shelter

Tribune Bay Campsites, Sheilds Rd., (250) 335-2359

off the bike in hornby

If you've lost your 'Zen-like' focus for riding, a good spot to start looking for it is Hornby Island. If you're just plain lost, just keep riding; you'll eventually end up somewhere familiar. If you're feeling like you're stuck for something to do…you're just not getting it, you're on Hornby. Relax. Check out the interesting notices on the bulletin board at the Hornby Community Centre. I once saw an ad that read, "I will hypnotize your cat and tell you what it was in its past life." And what a bargain at only ten bucks. Hornby Ocean Kayaks, (250) 335-2726, offers kayak rentals and guided tours around the island. How about firing up the campfire and cooking the 15 lb. salmon that you caught on the boat this afternoon? Inter Island Charters, (250) 335-2321, can be the expediter of your fishing dreams and can show you one hell of an afternoon on the water.

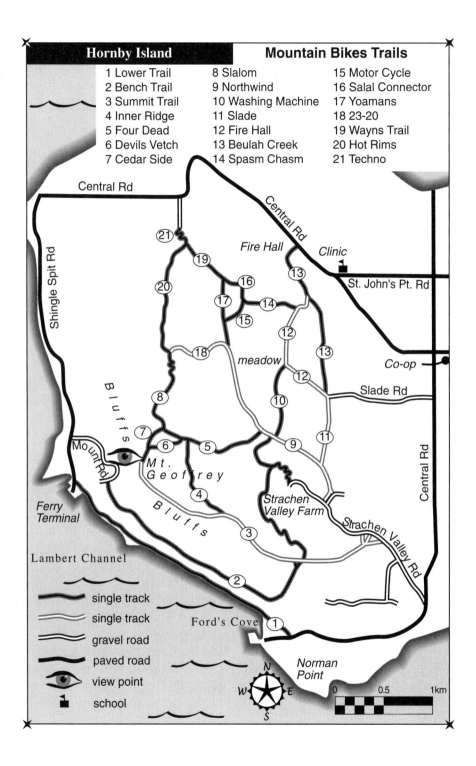

Hornby Island

Mountain Bikes Trails

1 Lower Trail
2 Bench Trail
3 Summit Trail
4 Inner Ridge
5 Four Dead
6 Devils Vetch
7 Cedar Side

8 Slalom
9 Northwind
10 Washing Machine
11 Slade
12 Fire Hall
13 Beulah Creek
14 Spasm Chasm

15 Motor Cycle
16 Salal Connector
17 Yoamans
18 23-20
19 Wayns Trail
20 Hot Rims
21 Techno

Central Rd

Central Rd

Fire Hall

Clinic

St. John's Pt. Rd

Co-op

Slade Rd

Central Rd

Shingle Spit Rd

meadow

B l u f f s

Mount Rd

Mt. Geoffrey

B l u f f s

Strachen Valley Farm

Strachen Valley Rd

Ferry Terminal

Lambert Channel

Ford's Cove

Norman Point

single track
single track
gravel road
paved road
view point
school

N
W E
S

0   0.5   1km

44 cumberland

what to expect

The roots go deep into the old coal mines that run underneath this "Village in the Forest", 9 kms west of Courtenay. Some of the finest coal in the British Empire was discovered here in the late 19th Century. The mines brought men from China, Japan, USA, Central Europe, Britain, and Italy to settle in this booming little town. Railways were built connecting the port at Union Bay all the way up through Cumberland to the head of Comox Lake.

Following mining, forestry became the main drive of the local economy. Cumberland's forest supplied the wood for some of the historical buildings and houses still found standing today in Cumberland. Also remaining from this industry are many old roads and horse and footpaths built by men working with nothing but their very own hands.

Eighty years later, the forest has grown up again, covering most of the evidence of these once prosperous industries.

In the early 1990's the first "mountain bike trails" were built by a group of local mountain bikers on the foundation of these forgotten roads and railway beds. A network of connecting trails began to form and to this day the network continues to grow into trails loved by all.

trail descriptions

MAMA BEARS TRAIL OF TEARS (BEGINNER)

A wide single-track that accesses the lower entrance to Buggered Pig and Two and a Juice. It's a nice way to hook up to the China Town Railway to get to Comox Lake for a swim. Don't expect any huge adrenaline rushes but do expect to see some beautiful west coast forest, big trees and good 'ol brown dirt. The trail ends at a gravel pit that is the property of the rod and gun club. Respect the targets and pass through quietly. Pedestrians have the right of way on this one.

CHINA TOWN TRAIL (BEGINNER)

This trail is actually a railway grade that runs through the old china town site. The trail passes some beautiful marsh area and is an excellent spot to check out waterfowl. It's a good ride to take the kids on as the trail also passes some coal hills that provide some fun little woopdee-doos.

TWO AND A JUICE (INTERMEDITATE)

This trail was built to create a loop with Buggered Pig for the original Rasta Roosta XC racecourse. This trail could be ridden both ways but is best ridden from the look out road to connect with Buggered Pig or Ewoks Drop. A fun quick trail with a fun downhill section at trails end. Expect the usual West Coast trail commodities such as roots, rocks and many a log to kachunk over.

BUGGERED PIG (INTERMEDIATE)

Buggered Pig is a trail that can be ridden both ways. It's a consistent singletrack that contains some logs and lots of roots. Ridden from the top (China Creek), the trail is moderately downhill and ends at Mama Bears. Ridden from the bottom the trail is a tight and twisty climb that leads to the lookout road. This trail presents no dangerous stunts or big drops so any one wanting to try out some tight single track could give this trail a go.

BIG LOG (INTERMEDIATE)

Named after the log ride, is a connector between the two roads that run up to the pump house. Nothing crazy just a nice fun piece of trail in beautiful woods.

BRONCO'S PERSEVERANCE (INTERMEDIATE)

This trail follows the original Perseverance Trail and was named after Bronco Moncrief, Cumberland's mayor for the last thirty years. A great trail to ride both ways or to incorporate into a loop with other trails. Don't forget to stop and appreciate the sweet views of Perseverance Creek on the way down.

BIKE GOD (DIFFICULT)

Named after the valley's mountain biker Methuselah, Bike God is a classy trail to test any true mountain biker. A grueling climb to the trailhead is the only way to access this bad boy. The entrance is sort of hidden as it is above the road level. The trail starts with a quick downhill but turns on itself to climb up to the highest point. Check out the view at the top of the singletrack climb! The remainder of the trail is all downhill and quite tight. It would be a good idea to wear some armour for the decent if you are not overly confident on woodsy steep trails. Not recommended on wet days due to skidding.

BROADWAY (DIFFICULT)

Some biking Bettys and a guy built this trail. It's a tricky technical trail that has some nice steep sections and a phat log ride at the bottom. A good trail to hit while still buzzin from the bucket of blood.

CUMBERLAND CRUNCHER (VERY DIFFICULT)

The original dodge descent built by Booker. This is an awesome old-school trail. A real ripper of a descent followed by a lung burning technical singletrack climb (a six pack of lucky to the guy/gal who can clean the climb w/o dabbing). Hook up with Pity the Fool for a continued decent or follow the Cruncher to get out.

BUCKET OF BLOOD (VERY DIFFICULT)

"The Bucket" is as technical as you want to make it. The beauty of this trail is that anyone can ride it. The ramps have "chicken lines" around them for the less extreme crowd. The trail is a bit of a grunt to access but is well worth the climb. Expect some log rides bridges, boardwalks and big wheelie drops. Interesting point of the trail is the name, it used to be the name of the Waverly Pub in the 'Ol Cooty mining days.

Photo: www.freeriders.org

access detail

The best place to park your car and access the trails is at the local Cumberland Recreational Centre parking lot at the end of Dunsmuir Avenue.

Follow Cumberland's main street, Dunsmuir, to the sign directing you to turn left to go to Comox Lake. You will see the Recreational Centre parking lot on your left. Head out the parking lot and follow the signs directing you to the Comox Lake. As you are heading down the Comox Lake road you will see the road turn sharply to the right and directly in front you a yellow gate heading onto a gravel logging road. This road is where the fun begins. Enter onto this gravel road. Big Log is straight ahead and to your left. The other trails are to your right. This road is known as the Lookout Road and gives you access to all the trails found on this map.

This also marks the beginning of private property, so you alone are responsible for your own safety and well being.

local knowledge

tasty bites & frosty pints

Babe's Café, 2702 Dunsmuir Ave, (250) 336-2763
The Cumberland Hotel, 2714 Dunsmuir Avenue, (250) 336-8844

camping / shelter

Cumberland Lake Park, 1100 Comox Lake Rd., (250) 336-2144

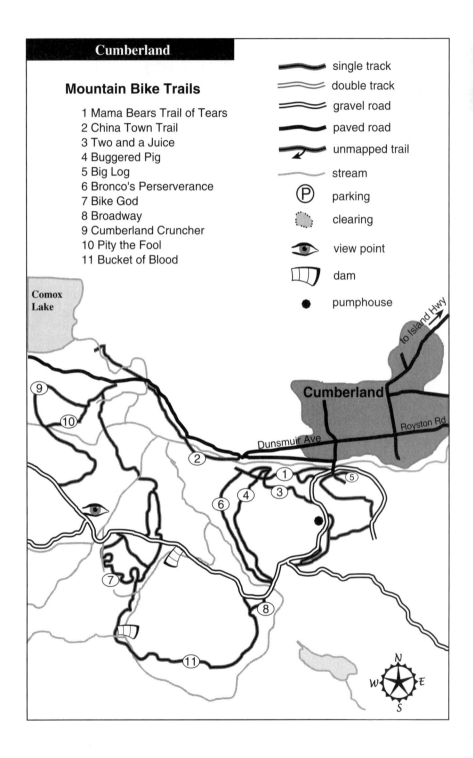

Cumberland

Mountain Bike Trails

1 Mama Bears Trail of Tears
2 China Town Trail
3 Two and a Juice
4 Buggered Pig
5 Big Log
6 Bronco's Perserverance
7 Bike God
8 Broadway
9 Cumberland Cruncher
10 Pity the Fool
11 Bucket of Blood

single track
double track
gravel road
paved road
unmapped trail
stream
P parking
clearing
view point
dam
pumphouse

Comox Lake

Cumberland

to Island Hwy

Royston Rd

Dunsmuir Ave

N
W E
S

what to expect

If you're into big trees, great singletrack, incredible glacier views and all that Super Natural BC stuff, then this beautiful valley, known as the 'Gateway to Strathcona Park' is just what you're looking for. The Comox / Courtenay area is a collection of small communities between the mountains and the ocean with excellent riding opportunities that range from the serene beauty and gentle riding of Seal Bay Park to the sky-high 'Monster Mile Downhill' at Mt. Washington and all points in between. It has stunning views of the glacier-capped peaks of the BC mainland across Georgia Straight as well as glimpses in to the interior peaks of the amazing Strathcona Park. It's also home to mountain bike Olympian Geoff Kabush. Geoff finished in the top 10 in cross-country at the Sydney 2000 Olympics.

trail descriptions

SEAL BAY (BEGINNER)

Seal Bay Nature Park is a 168 hectare forested area witin a short drive or ride from Comox/Courtenay. The trails are maintained under the supervision of the Comox-Strathcona Natural History Society. The Comox Indian Band, called the area Xwee Xwhy Luq, which means "lace of serenity and beauty". This area is a nature park and should be treated as such by mountain bikers. In other words, the trails are really meant for peaceful walks and not ripping fast rides. Take it easy and enjoy the flat single track. This is one of the best places for a new mountain biker to enjoy singletrack riding and progress in skill level in a beautiful, non-threatening environment.

To access the trails, go left on Anderton Rd. off Comox Rd. Follow Anderton to Huband, right on Waveland, and left on Bates Rd. The trailhead area has signs, parking and toilets nearby. There are NO bikes allowed on the trails east of Bates Rd., so if you want to go down to the ocean, walk your bikes, or lock them up and hike it, it's worth it!

TOMATO CREEK (DIFFICULT)

Riders can expect 2 steep logging road climbs to the start of the trail along Comox Lake Main. Once on the trail, there are steep single track climbs

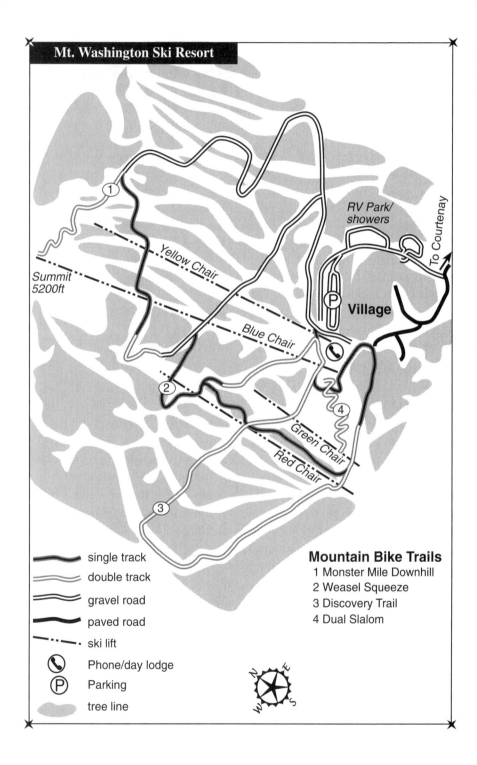

Mt. Washington Ski Resort

RV Park/ showers

To Courtenay

Summit 5200ft

Yellow Chair

Blue Chair

Village

Green Chair

Red Chair

1

2

3

4

P

single track
double track
gravel road
paved road
ski lift
Phone/day lodge
Parking
tree line

Mountain Bike Trails
1 Monster Mile Downhill
2 Weasel Squeeze
3 Discovery Trail
4 Dual Slalom

N E S W

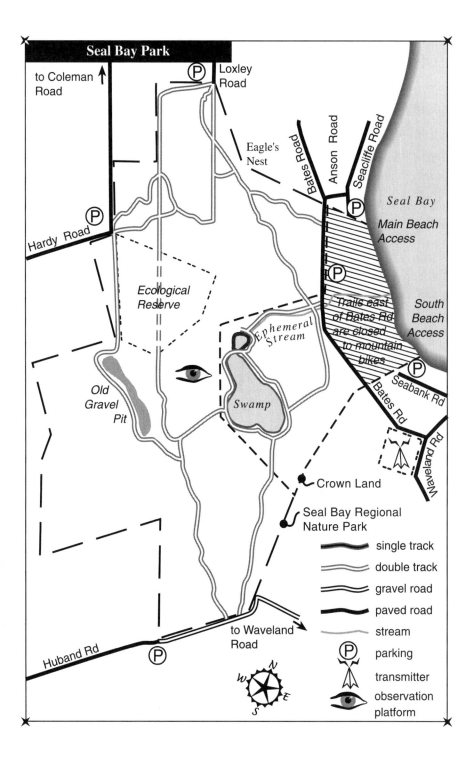

of approximately 15 minutes. Expect to encounter slick rock faces and climbs with a technical single track downhill.

SALAMANDER (BEGINNER)

The trail begins at the Hydro Dam Park. There are 2 trailheads beside each other. Take the left hand trail, or the one with the outhouse. The other trail is Bears Bait. Salamander is on of the easier and shorter trails in this area, and a great place to bring new riders.

BEARS BAIT (INTERMEDIATE)

This trail can be accessed at two points; the Hydro Dam Park, or the Fish Hatchery. The trail follows Puntlage River and offers a little bit of everything in the recipe book of good riding. There is technical single track with logs o' plenty, and rolling terrain.

NYMPH FALLS (INTERMEDIATE TO DIFFICULT)

The trailhead is located along Duncan Bay Main at the yellow gate, on the left side of the road, just before the crossroads of Forbidden Plateau Rd. and Duncan Bay Main. This is a very technical single track that scoots along to a popular swimming hole. The trail continues until the fish hatchery where you can hook up with Bears Bait. Although the trail does not have any climbs, its overly technical assault on your body makes the riding more tiring than you would expect from such a flat trail.

BEVAN TRAIL (INTERMEDIATE)

This is a point-to-point trail that is accessible from two points. One entrance is located on Comox Lake Main just before the Dam Park where the yellow gate is. The trailhead is on the right side of the road before the bridge that crosses the edge of the lake. The other trailhead is located off Bevan Rd. and follows the river on the other side from Bears Bait. This trail is tight single track with logs and other technical challenges.

BICS (INTERMEDIATE)

Bics is located off B21 and drops you from sub-alpine scrub to lower elevation rain forest on a short challenging trail. You can access this trail from the top or bottom of B21. There are some rock face drop-offs and other coastal trail delights.

ARBUTUS (DIFFICULT)

This trail lies adjacent to Bics and is more difficult that its next door neighbor. This is a bit of a psycho downhill and should scare the crap out of some of you. Expect the basic menu of scary stuff like steep chutes and drops that remind you of gravity's power. Although the trail isn't very long, it is very intense.

off the bike in comox / courtenay

This area is a remarkable meeting of mountains, ocean and forest and thus provides residents and visitors alike with endless recreation opportunities. That's a long-winded way of saying 'this place rocks'. Jacques Cousteau rated the waters near the Comox Valley as the second best cold water diving destination in the world. There is unlimited paddling, sailing and fishing on the waters in the area as well. If you're not into the water scene or even the beautiful beaches, Strathcona Park is only a short drive away. It provides you with some of the most beautiful alpine scenery in BC. Simply put, the

Photo: Steve Dunn

Comox / Courtenay area is an outdoor recreation paradise. Try some of these options:
Comox Valley Kayaks, 1-888-545-5595

local knowledge

tasty bites & frosty pints
Bar None Café, 250 6ᵗʰ St., Courtenay, 334-3112
Black Fin Pub, 244-4ᵗʰ St., Comox, 339-5030

camping / shelter
Strathcona Provincial Park offers several campsites throughout the park. For reservations for this or any other provincial park phone 1-800-689-9025.

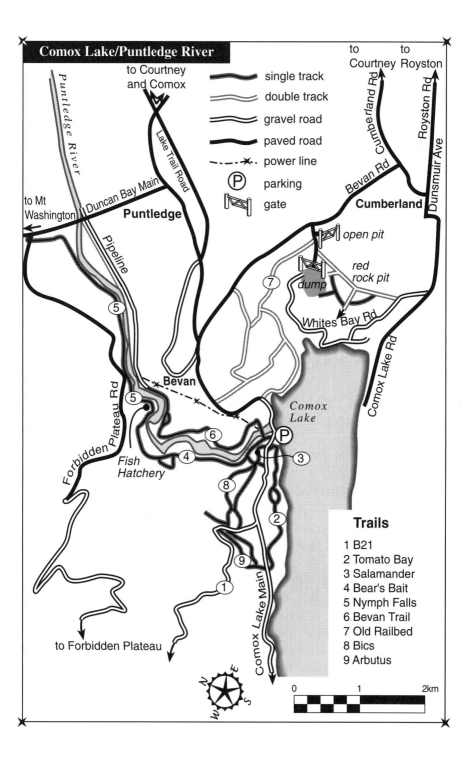

Comox Lake/Puntledge River

～～～	single track
～～～	double track
～～～	gravel road
━━━	paved road
─·─×─	power line
Ⓟ	parking
⊟	gate

to Courtney and Comox

to Courtney   to Royston

Puntledge River

Lake Trail Road

Cumberland Rd

Royston Rd

Bevan Rd

Dunsmuir Ave

to Mt Washington

Duncan Bay Main

Pipeline

Puntledge

Cumberland

open pit

dump

red rock pit

Whites Bay Rd

Comox Lake Rd

Forbidden Plateau Rd

Bevan

⑤

⑤

Comox Lake

Fish Hatchery

⑥

④

⑧

Ⓟ

③

②

⑨

⑦

①

Comox Lake Main

to Forbidden Plateau

N E S W

0   1   2km

Trails

1 B21
2 Tomato Bay
3 Salamander
4 Bear's Bait
5 Nymph Falls
6 Bevan Trail
7 Old Railbed
8 Bics
9 Arbutus

what to expect

Old logging roads in the Campbell River area have shaped the riding style by allowing great access to singletrack as well as providing excellent doubletrack tours of the surrounding mountains. Also, many of the trails in the area are actually overgrown logging roads, which makes for some great, fast riding.

The Snowden Demonstration Forest has endless kilometers of trails to keep even the keenest riders happy for a long time. There's a new riding area south of town in the Woods Creek area that doesn't even have a map yet. Ask Dan at the Urban Lemming (286-6340) about it and he may be willing to divulge some secrets.

trail descriptions

PUMPHOUSE (BEGINNER)

The Pumphouse trails are a 10 minute ride from town. This is a small riding area where riders can freely explore at will without any fear of getting too lost. These trails are not overly difficult and roll through rock bluffs and forest.

SKIDMARKS (DIFFICULT)

The name of this area probably relates to the tire tracks left on the ground, and the stains in your underwear. Riders can expect a 30 minute climb from town into this area. This is difficult riding on a single track downhill.

SNOWDEN DEMONSTRATION FOREST (INTERMEDIATE)

The Snowden trails are a 30 minute ride from town. This is the area in Campbell River that is filthy with trails. At last count there are approximately 50 km of trails that connect moderate single track with old rail grades, and old roads. Riders can expect the full spectrum of moderate mountain biking without any major climbs. The Snoden trails are part of the Demonstration Forest and maps of this area are available from the Forest Service office or at The Urban Lemming bike shop (286-6340). New trails are constantly being added so ask Dan for some updates.

OLD RAIL GRADES (BEGINNER)

The area north of Campbell Lake, off Brewster Lk, Rd. was logged by rails years ago. The old rail grades and trestles remain and mountain bikers can enjoy exploring the flat, easy terrain.

local knowledge

tasty bites & frosty pints

Willows Neighborhood Pub, 521 Rockland Rd., (250) 923-8311
Baan Thai Restaurant, 1090B Shoppers Row, (250) 286-4853

camping / shelter

Buttle Lake Provincial Campground – Strathcona Park Hwy 28, west of Campbell River, (reservations) 1-800-689-9025 anywhere in BC

off the bike in campbell river

Want to try something really different? Something you wouldn't expect to find in a mountain bike guidebook? How about walking into the bowels of the earth to explore a labyrinth beneath the mountain? There exists under these mountains, miles of fascinating caves carved over the eons by rushing water. Local outfitters will take you on a journey within like no other. Contact the Cave Guiding Association of BC at (250) 923-1311 to find information on tours.

Climbers wanting to get their hands on some rock for a change of pace should check out Crest Lake in Strathcona Park. This area boasts over 100 routes and some beautiful crags in old growth forests.

The waters of Discovery Passage, just off Campbell River, have been called one of the premiere dive destinations in the world. It was rated second only to the Red Sea by the Jacques Cousteau Society (and we all know 'ol Jacques knew a thing or two about diving, right?) The abundance of marine life and clarity of the water makes it a diving experience you'll be dreaming of long after you've left.

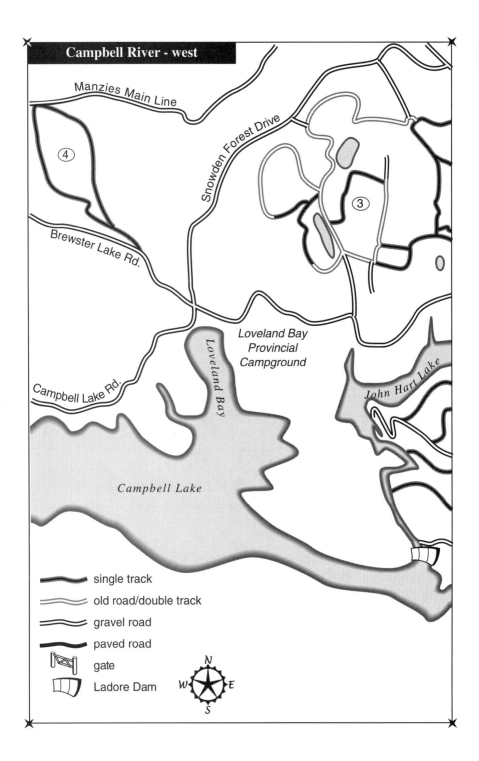

Campbell River - west

Manzies Main Line

Snowden Forest Drive

④

③

Brewster Lake Rd.

Loveland Bay
Provincial
Campground

Loveland Bay

John Hart Lake

Campbell Lake Rd.

Campbell Lake

single track
old road/double track
gravel road
paved road
gate
Ladore Dam

N
W   E
S

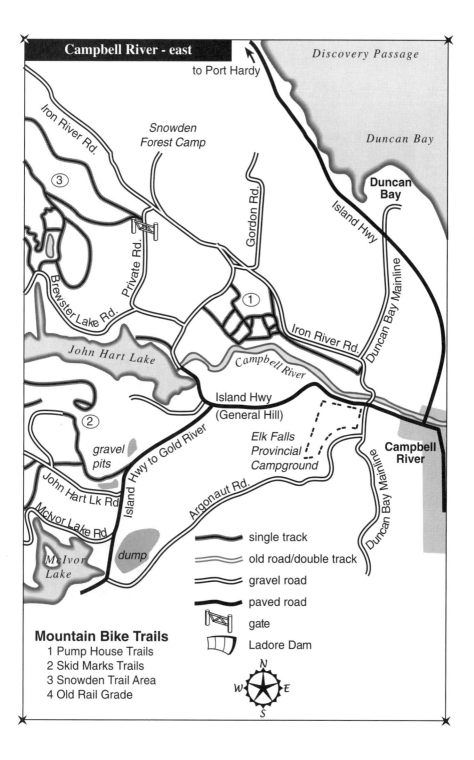

Campbell River - east

Discovery Passage

to Port Hardy

Iron River Rd.

Snowden
Forest Camp

③

Gordon Rd.

Duncan Bay

**Duncan
Bay**

Island Hwy

Private Rd.

Duncan Bay Mainline

Brewster Lake Rd.

①

Iron River Rd.

John Hart Lake

Campbell River

Island Hwy
(General Hill)

②

gravel
pits

Island Hwy to Gold River

Elk Falls
Provincial
Campground

**Campbell
River**

Duncan Bay Mainline

John Hart Lk Rd

Argonaut Rd.

McIvor Lake Rd

McIvor
Lake

dump

Duncan Bay Mainline

single track

old road/double track

gravel road

paved road

gate

Ladore Dam

Mountain Bike Trails
1 Pump House Trails
2 Skid Marks Trails
3 Snowden Trail Area
4 Old Rail Grade

N
W E
S

Photo: Chris Rollett   *Rider: Dave Watson*

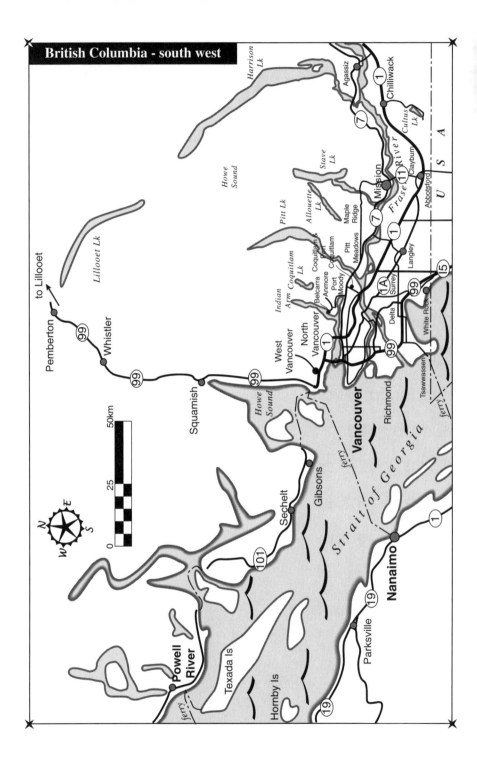

British Columbia - south west

what to expect

The North Shore is to mountain biking what the Banzai Pipeline is to surfing, or Alaska is to skiing and snowboarding. It is simply the 'next level', period! It is a bizarre combination of steep, rooted terrain, man-made ramps, bridges and teeter-totters conceived by a committed crew of fanatics whose desire to build scary trails is eclipsed only by their desire to ride them. All of this twisted creative genius has spawned its own riding style that we now simply call 'The Shore'. Just like the Banzai Pipeline in Hawaii or the Chugach Range in Alaska, the North Shore can humble, maim and destroy bones, egos and your gear. However, it can also exhilarate you and deliver a rush like you've never imagined, which makes the North Shore a way of life for many.

The Coast Mountains on the north shore of the Burrard Inlet are perfect for this kind of adventurous riding. They're steep and covered in stumps, logs, boulders and slimy, gnarled roots. As if that were not difficult enough, along came The Digger and his shovel. He, along with a few other inspired riders, began building the first trestles, ramps and log bridges over Mother Nature's obstacles in the late 80's. Many others have taken up shovels and hammers since then and have built a network of trails spanning three mountains, which is considered to be one of the best in the world. Since those early days in the 80's, this style has spread its scary grasp throughout this book and much further abroad. If you're coming to the Shore to ride for the first time, it's a very good idea to ride with someone who's been here before because they know how to make a splint with twigs and bike tubes. Although most are quite technical, there are excellent trails for all levels of riders, including novice.

Photo Courtesy Dangerous Dan

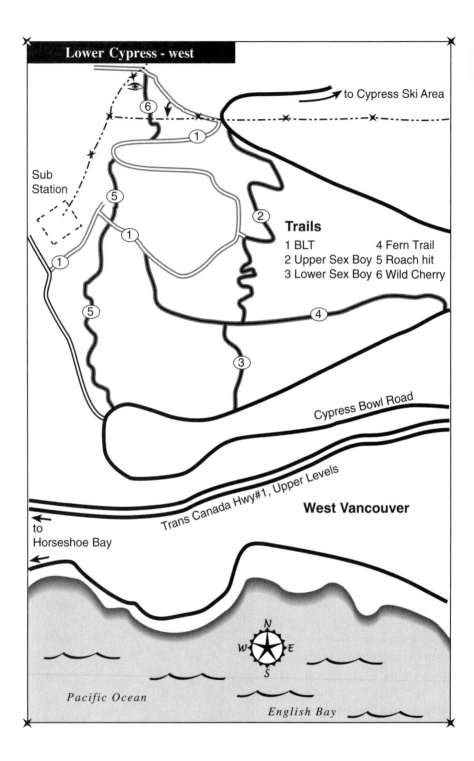

Lower Cypress - west

to Cypress Ski Area

Sub
Station

Trails

1 BLT   4 Fern Trail
2 Upper Sex Boy 5 Roach hit
3 Lower Sex Boy 6 Wild Cherry

Cypress Bowl Road

Trans Canada Hwy#1, Upper Levels

West Vancouver

to
Horseshoe Bay

Pacific Ocean

English Bay

N
W E
S

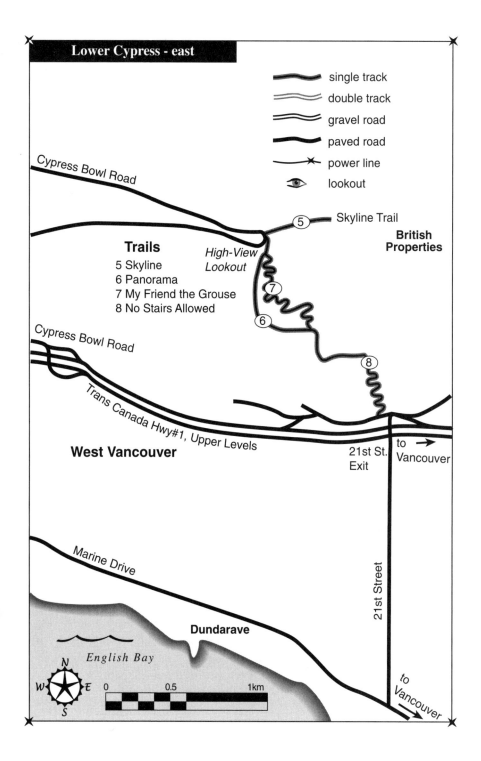

Recently, the North Shore trails have been under attack. Because most of them are on either the District of North or West Vancouver lands, there are some rather large liability issues that have come to light. On one dark day in 1999, the District of West Vancouver destroyed every man-made obstacle on the Cypress Mountain trails due to liability scares. It became known as the "West Van Chainsaw Massacre". Many of the remaining trails elsewhere on the North Shore are still threatened. With the growing number of people donating time and resources to trail maintenance days, the future of these trails is a little brighter. However, the only way we'll be able to enjoy them for years to come is with the continued support of those who ride them. Please donate some of your time to maintaining your trails, because they just might not be there tomorrow if you don't. Contact the North Shore Mountain Biking Association at info@nsmba.bc.ca for information on trail days, membership and more. However, the only way we'll be able to enjoy them for years to come is with the continued support of those who ride them. This isn't achieved by shuttling everyday and assuming the trails will always be there. Please donate some of your time to maintaining your trails, because they just might not be there tomorrow if you don't.

trail descriptions

CYPRESS MOUNTAIN TRAILS

Most of the trails on Cypress Mountain remain "officially" closed to mountain biking. In the past, the District of West Vancouver has turned a blind eye to all the stunts and singletrack. That was until "The West Vancouver Chainsaw Massacre", as most riders now know it. That was the day nearly every man-made stunt on Cypress Mountain was cut down due to liability issues. As of 2001, there are no man-made obstacles on any of the Cypress trails; however, the trails do remain "unofficially rideable". A task force is studying the option of re-opening a few of them, however, they would be a shadow of their former selves.

The trails cross a number of property lines. The British Pacific Properties, BC Parks and the District of West Vancouver are all stakeholders in the trail debate. Although there has been some action toward recognition of

mountain bike trails on Cypress, nothing official has happened to date.
These maps merely point out where the most traveled routes exist. There
are many more trails here than these maps indicate. Drop into On Top
Bike Shop on Lonsdale for the details. Please remember that all riders must
assume responsibility for their own actions and to ride responsibly because
you're on someone else's property.

SEX BOY (DIFFICULT)

Sex Boy remains a challenging, steep singletrack in the 'old school' style.
Steep rock drops, tight fall-line singletrack with that all-natural flavor.
Drop in & see him off the south side of the third switchback of the
Cypress Bowl Ski Road. It runs back down to the Cypress Bowl Rd. after
crossing the FERN TRAIL.

STUPID GROUSE (INTERMEDIATE)

This trail combination is a fun climb and an even better downhill. Recent
years have seen housing developments encroach upon this classic line, but
it remains in more or less the same old form. It links the High View
Lookout at the second switchback on Cypress Bowl Road and the 21st St.
exit on Hwy 1. Drop in from the Cypress Bowl Rd. and battle through the
scree to the singletrack below. When you reach the clearing for the housing
development, keep left and follow your wheel, it will know the way.

BLT (INTERMEDIATE)

The BLT (Boulders, Logs & Trees) is the only official mountain bike
trail in Cypress Provincial Park. This may change soon. The real value
of BLT is to provide an alternative to the road for climbing the
mountain. It's much more challenging due to its steep, boulder strewn
doubletrack. It climbs from the first switchback all the way to the
Cypress Bowl parking lot, with access to Fern Trail, Sex Boy and other
trails in this area. From the first switchback on the Cypress Bowl Rd.,
head left on the gravel road for about 1 km until you reach a junction.
Take a right on the old, rocky doubletrack and climb, climb, climb.
Quite steep at times, you'll be amazed at how much vertical you wil
gain in a short time. It can be used as access to FERN TRAIL,
ROACH HIT and WILD CHERRY, but the main road is best.

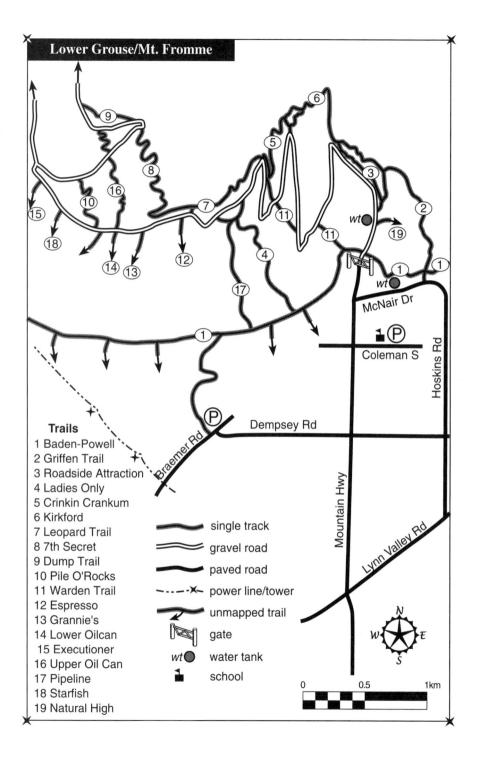

Lower Grouse/Mt. Fromme

McNair Dr

Coleman S

Hoskins Rd

Dempsey Rd

Braemer Rd

Mountain Hwy

Lynn Valley Rd

Trails
1 Baden-Powell
2 Griffen Trail
3 Roadside Attraction
4 Ladies Only
5 Crinkin Crankum
6 Kirkford
7 Leopard Trail
8 7th Secret
9 Dump Trail
10 Pile O'Rocks
11 Warden Trail
12 Espresso
13 Grannie's
14 Lower Oilcan
15 Executioner
16 Upper Oil Can
17 Pipeline
18 Starfish
19 Natural High

~~~ single track
═══ gravel road
▬▬▬ paved road
—··—×— power line/tower
~~~ unmapped trail
⊠ gate
wt● water tank
▟ school

N
W E
S

0   0.5   1km

FROMME MOUNTAIN (GROUSE MTN.) TRAILS

This is where it all began in the early 80's when Digger and others began to build some of the best mountain bike trails in the world. If you've never ridden here before, pad up, head over to the gate at the top on Mountain Highway and ask to tag along with some of the locals. Most are quite willing to play tour guide in their world-famous playground.

Although it's difficult to get *really* lost, it is very possible to get *really* hurt. The suggested plan would be to try PIPELINE first. This is one of the less severe rides on the mountain, although it can still pack a punch. If that has whetted your appetite, move on to LADIES ONLY and progress your way through the ranks of the legendary singletrack of the North Shore. Trails like EXECUTIONER and UPPER OIL CAN are some of the best trails around for pure flow and enjoyment.

Man-made obstacles are very much a part of most of the trails on Fromme Mountain. Bridges, teeter-totters, ramps and discombulators (multiple teeter-totters strung together) among other things, will be encountered in the beautiful second growth forest of Fromme Mountain. These trails range from DIFFICULT to EXTREMELY DIFFICULT, and there are even some rated STUPID, so beware and have fun.

To access these trails, ride to the top of Mountain Highway in North Vancouver. If you're driving, parking and noise are big issues here so do the locals a favor and park in the school lot on Coleman St., just a few blocks down the road. Once at the top of Mountain Hwy. Climb past the yellow gate and continue up the gravel road. Trailheads are visible all along this road, most dropping off the low side, which make their way down the mountain. The trails above the sixth switchback deposit you back on the same gravel road, some bring you to the lower neighborhoods and a few will reach the BADEN-POWELL TRAIL, which serves as a singletrack freeway running east-west. These trailheads are difficult to distinguish from one another and signage has only begun to be posted on some of the trails. They are difficult to describe so the following should be verified before you drop in.

Once you've begun the climb on the gravel road, you'll notice a number of trailheads on your right. NATURAL HIGH is a great little romp through the forest that features some ramps and smaller stunts. It drops in to the right just below the large green water tanks. Just past the tanks, you can drop in to the right and follow ROADSIDE ATTRACTION, which parallels the main road up to the first switchback. There is a great little network of trails that descend below the first switchback that used to be part of the North Shore Loonie Race series. After the first switchback, the main options descend from the third and fifth switchback, until you reach LADIES ONLY and PIPELINE.

About 600-700 meters after the fifth switchback, you'll round a small corner and there will be a noticeable clearing or widening of the road. On your left, you'll notice two trailheads; the lower one is LADIES ONLY, and just a few meters up is the trailhead for PIPELINE. If you continue climbing, the next noticeable (somewhat) trailhead is ESPRESSO, and further still, next to a large boulder is GRANNIE'S. LOWER OILCAN begins further up on the left next to a twisted, gnarled root system of an upturned tree. When you come to a trailhead up a little higher that has an old wash machine next to it, you've found STARFISH. This is a great trail that is very challenging, even for the pros. About 20 meters before you round the sixth switchback, you should see the trailhead for EXECUTIONER. This is one of my old favorites because of its steep pitch and fantastic flow. Continuing on up towards the seventh switchback, the obvious trailheads should come at you in this order: PILE O' ROCKS, UPPER OILCAN and

Photo: North Vancouver Tourism

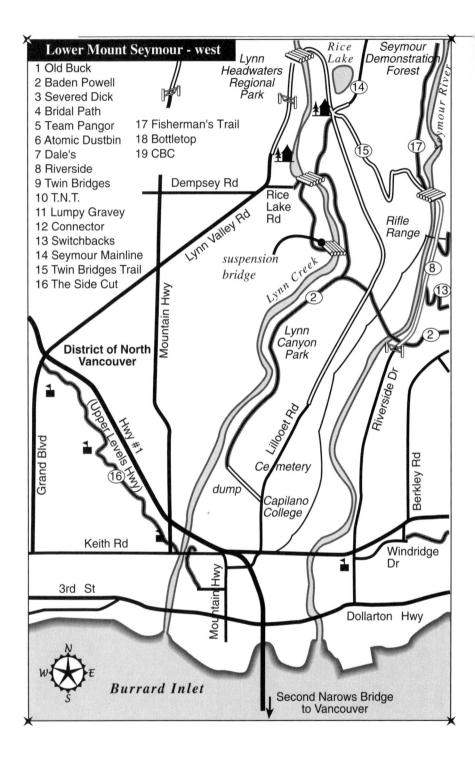

Lower Mount Seymour - west

1 Old Buck
2 Baden Powell
3 Severed Dick
4 Bridal Path
5 Team Pangor
6 Atomic Dustbin
7 Dale's
8 Riverside
9 Twin Bridges
10 T.N.T.
11 Lumpy Gravey
12 Connector
13 Switchbacks
14 Seymour Mainline
15 Twin Bridges Trail
16 The Side Cut

17 Fisherman's Trail
18 Bottletop
19 CBC

Rice Lake

Seymour Demonstration Forest

Lynn Headwaters Regional Park

Seymour River

Dempsey Rd

Rice Lake Rd

Lynn Valley Rd

Mountain Hwy

suspension bridge

Lynn Creek

Rifle Range

Lynn Canyon Park

District of North Vancouver

(Upper Levels Hwy)

Hwy #1

Lilloeet Rd

Cemetery

dump

Capilano College

Riverside Dr

Berkley Rd

Grand Blvd

Keith Rd

Mountain Hwy

Windridge Dr

3rd St

Mountain Hwy

Dollarton Hwy

N
W E
S

Burrard Inlet

Second Narrows Bridge to Vancouver

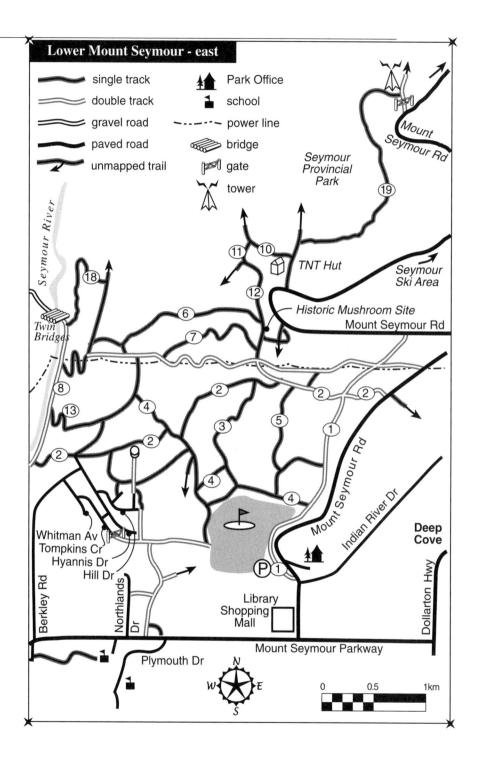

Lower Mount Seymour - east

Legend:
- single track
- double track
- gravel road
- paved road
- unmapped trail
- Park Office
- school
- power line
- bridge
- gate
- tower

Mount Seymour Rd

Seymour Provincial Park

(19)

Seymour River

(18)

Twin Bridges

(11) (10)

TNT Hut

(12)

Seymour Ski Area

Historic Mushroom Site
Mount Seymour Rd

(6)

(7)

(8)

(13)

(4)

(2)

(2) (2)

(3)

(5)

(1)

(2)

(4)

Mount Seymour Rd

Indian River Dr

Deep Cove

(4)

Whitman Av
Tompkins Cr
Hyannis Dr
Hill Dr

Berkley Rd

Northlands Dr

P (1)

Library
Shopping
Mall

Dollarton Hwy

Mount Seymour Parkway

Plymouth Dr

N
W E
S

0   0.5   1km

Photo: Steve Dunn

the classic of classics, THE SEVENTH SECRET. (You may spot a faint trailhead just before you reach SEVENTH, if you didn't know it was there already, I suggest you walk away from the FLYING CIRCUS and count yourself lucky. This one is for experts who make the mountain bike movies you buy. It's best to have a guided tour of something like this, as it would be very easy to find yourself in way over your head.) If you don't feel confident in these directions, you can always ask someone on the climb up the road.

MOUNT SEYMOUR TRAILS

The trails of Mount Seymour wind through a lush, green rainforest that spends most of the year shrouded in fog and mist. Gnarled roots, big trees and twisting singletrack cover the mountain and add to its rich character. One of the benefits of living in Vancouver is to have a riding season that spans the twelve months of the year. My favorite time to ride Mount Seymour is in the middle of the long, wet rainy season because I'm seeing the rainforest in its natural state: green, wet and beautiful.

Car shuttling seems to be overtaking real riding on Seymour these days, which is a sad statement. The "mountain coasters" (you're not really mountain bikers) wouldn't be such a bad thing if more than 1% did any trail maintenance. It's quite obvious that increased traffic on these trails is due for the most part to shuttling. If this is to continue, and if the trails are to survive, they must be maintained on a more consistent basis by the regular users. Don't forget what it's like to pedal your bike up a hill, it can be quite satisfying.

trail descriptions

OLD BUCK (EASY)

This was the old access road for the ski area in the 50's. The OLD BUCK climb continues to be the main human powered freeway to the top, aside from the paved road. This is a multi-use trail and is really meant as an access climb. From OLD BUCK, you can either turn left at the intersection of the BADEN POWELL or continue along until you reach the paved road, and climb up to the next switchback trailhead off of this road. If you go left onto the BADEN POWELL, you can access trails like TEAM PANGOR, THE BOOGEY MAN, and SEVERED DICK. It is a little-ring grunt all the way up, but it gets you up the mountain faster than a mountain goat on acid.

NED'S ATOMIC DUSTBIN (INTERMEDIATE)

Ned's is an old North Shore classic. It was one of the original mountain bike trails on Mt. Seymour. Today, it remains one of the more popular trails in the area because of its relatively easy singletrack. It can be a great rainy day option or an exciting downhill run anytime.

To access Ned's, climb the Old Buck trail past the BADEN-POWELL TRAIL, until you reach the Mt. Seymour Road. Climb the road to the next switchback and drop into the trailhead behind the concrete barrier on the left. Ride straight down the bumpy, wide track and hang a right at the major intersection. Follow this wide singletrack to its end and you'll see the trailhead just ahead and to the right. This small clearing at the intersection is known as the Mushroom Site. It served as the end of the line for the Old Highway that climbed to Mt. Seymour and as an information board. Above this point, a bus used to carry skiers to and from the ski area.

For an alternate route down to Ned's, take the immediate left after dropping in from the Mt. Seymour Road. This is CORKSCREW, which is a more technical, yet much more fun approach to Ned's and other trails in this area. It will drop you onto the same wide track that leads directly to the Ned's trailhead.

BOTTLETOP (INTERMEDIATE)

Bottletop is a great natural extension of Ned's Atomic Dustbin. You've reached the end of Ned's when you've hit a "T" intersection. Take a left to reach the Powerline downhill to the Seymour River or keep right to finish off the ride with some exciting, ridgeline singletrack on Bottletop. After turning right at the end of Ned's, the obvious trailhead for Bottletop is on the left after about 100 meters or so. This is a fine piece of singletrack that takes a clever line down to the Riverside Trail next to the Seymour River.

DALE'S

This is an old, steep line down the slopes just below Ned's. Reach it by taking a left from the Old Mushroom site, near the trailhead for Ned's. Trail condition vary with the weather. The real Dale now runs Tyax Tours out of Whistler, where they fly you to a mountain lake and you can ride out.

SEVERED DICK

This is one of the original mountain bike downhill trails in the area. To this day, it can still serve up a scary ride to the bottom. After climbing to the top of the wide track portion of the BADEN-POWELL from OLD BUCK, it drops left into some singletrack again. The trailhead for SEVERED DICK is a short way down on the left. This is part of the old Hell of the North race course, not your average cross-country mountain bike race.

CBC (INTERMEDIATE - DIFFICULT)

This is a relatively new trail on Mt. Seymour and will be the focus of a study of the impact of riders on the trails on the mountain. Not only trail conditions will be studied, but the riding community's commitment to its upkeep. If you've ridden it, and liked it, pitch in to help preserve it. It passes through some truly beautiful forest, winding through some trees that are estimated to be almost 1300 years old.

To access this trail, ride to the fourth switchback, where you'll see two large towers in the vicinity. Two roads exit the left side of the highway. Take the upper one with the green gate. Ride past the gate and access the trailhead for CBC on the left, just as the road begins to veer right. CBC

RIVERSIDE TRAIL (EASY)

This is actually a doubletrack road, not a singletrack; however, it is definitely worth checking out if you've never seen the Seymour River Canyon: a 100-foot deep chasm with the powerful river cutting through it. The Riverside Trail starts at the north end of Riverside Dr., off of the Seymour Parkway. It follows the Seymour River for a few kilometers before crossing it at Twin Bridges. This road continues up the hill to the Seymour Demonstration Forest and on into Lynn Valley Headwaters Regional Park to make a great longer ride.

TEAM PANGOR (INTERMEDIATE – DIFFICULT)

This trail is a great introduction to steeper, trials-style riding. It has some great flow to it as well as a few ramps and drops that will school the uninitiated. The trailhead is on the left about 750 meters up the BADEN-POWELL from its junction with OLD BUCK.

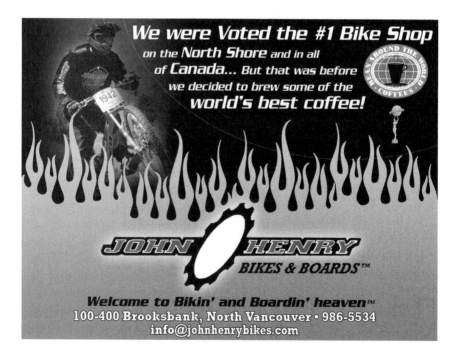

local knowledge

tasty bites & frosty pints
Bean Around the World Café, 1522 Marine Dr., West Van., (925-9600)
The Raven Pub, 1060 Deep Cove Rd.,
Deep Cove, (929-3834)

camping / shelter
Globetrotter Inn Hostel, 170 West Esplanade, North Van., (988-2082)
Contact Explore BC reservations for alternatives, (684-4386)Deep Cove, (929-3834)

camping / shelter
Globetrotter Inn Hostel, 170 West Esplanade, North Van., (988-2082)
Contact Explore BC reservations for alternatives, (684-4386)

off the bike on the north shore
The riding on the North Shore draws people from all over North America and beyond. Fortunately there is plenty to do if the infamous North Shore weather prevents you from riding:

North Vancouver boasts one of the best indoor rock climbing gyms in Canada. An afternoon at The Edge Climbing Center is one of the best ways to spend a day off the bike in North Van. Spend all day being a kid again, regardless of your climbing ability, (www.edgeclimbing.com) (604) 984-9080.

Hike to the 'Peak of Vancouver', Grouse Mountain and enjoy superb views of the city with a frosty pint and a great meal. There is always something happening up there: concerts, logger sports, or festivals. (604) 984-0661

A popular past time for mountain bikers in these parts seems to be hanging out at coffee shops telling 'fishing tales' of their riding exploits. The Lynn Valley Starbucks is the place to be if you've got a good one.

what to expect

Your long journey to Mountain Bike Mecca is over! Set up camp, buy the postcards and get ready to ride awhile. Squamish singletrack can lead you to the alpine bowls and back down to the ocean all in one amazing, unforgettable day. The town sits at the end of the long fjord of Howe Sound at the beginning of the wide valley that leads up to Whistler, Pemberton and into the heart of the Coast Mountains. Logging and mining has left a legacy of old roads and rail grades that grant us great access and screaming fast descents, but the real masterpieces in Squamish are the singletrack trails that are so abundant. Whether you're looking for an intermediate spin through the forest, a full-on downhill circus or a 4 hour alpine lung buster, Squamish has it. The Squamish Off Road Cycling Association (SORCA) as well as a host of other dedicated local riders has amassed a collection of trails in the area that could be considered the crown jewels of our sport. Combined with the trails of the North Shore, Whistler and Pemberton, the Sea to Sky corridor truly is the Mountain Bike Mecca of the world.

trail descriptions

POWERSMART (INTERMEDIATE / DIFFICULT)

This is one of the best long rides in Squamish because it offers fantastic singletrack from top to bottom. This beautiful trail was constructed with the generous support of BC Hydro and SORCA (Squamish Off Road Cycling Assoc.). Although the climb up the Diamond Head Road to the trailhead may be a little steep in some places, it is a great workout and warm up nevertheless. SORCA does ask that you not shuttle this trail because it is getting thrashed due to the rapid increase in traffic it causes.

To access this trail from Squamish, head north on Hwy. 99 and turn right on Mamquam Road, (Look for the BC Parks sign that reads 'Diamond Head'). Follow this FSR up the mountain for approximately 10 kms. At the last switchback before the Diamond Head Trailhead there is a small double track road that branches straight off the main road. Follow this for a short distance as it becomes narrower and levels out. Check out the

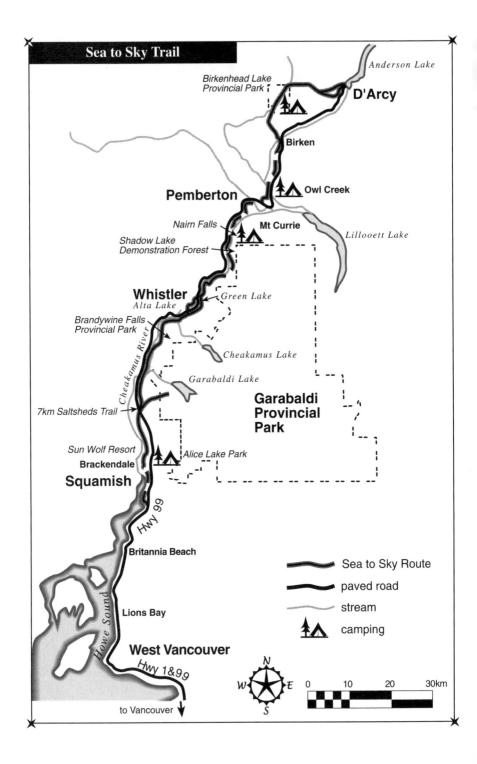

Sea to Sky Trail

Anderson Lake

Birkenhead Lake
Provincial Park

D'Arcy

Birken

Owl Creek

Pemberton

Nairn Falls **Mt Currie**

Shadow Lake
Demonstration Forest

Lillooett Lake

Whistler
Alta Lake

Green Lake

Brandywine Falls
Provincial Park

Cheakamus Lake

Garabaldi Lake

7km Saltsheds Trail

**Garabaldi
Provincial
Park**

Sun Wolf Resort
Brackendale

Alice Lake Park

Squamish

Hwy 99

Britannia Beach

Lions Bay

Howe Sound

West Vancouver

Hwy 1&99

to Vancouver

Sea to Sky Route

paved road

stream

camping

N
W   E
S

0   10   20   30km

amazing views to the valley 3000 feet below! This old road now drops to the left slightly and brings you directly to the Powersmart trailhead. Drop in and enjoy the descent.

You have the option to hook up with Skookum and then a range of other fantastic yet challenging trails like Homebrew, High & Dry, Pseudotsuga (sudo-suga), Another Roadside Attraction and Another Man's Gold. It's tough to choose from so many great options. If you choose to ride Powersmart to the bottom, you'll reach the powerlines, hang a left and endure a short, 5 minute hike-a-bike to get you back to the Diamond Head Road.

HOMEBREW / HIGH & DRY (DIFFICULT / VERY DIFFICULT)

Homebrew and High & Dry are both technically difficult trails. Homebrew is a short romp through the trees with some stunts, and High & Dry is a longer, more difficult high-wire act on fallen logs and bridges snaking through a cut block. The teeter-totter at the end of High & Dry will leave you shaking whether you've ridden it or not. These two great trails are easily accessed from Powersmart or by climbing the Diamond Head Road.

From Powersmart, follow the signs that lead to Skookum. Near the end of Skookum, cross the creek on the log bridge and then follow the logging road down through the clearing. Lower Skookum begins almost immediately on your right. Continue down the road through the cutblock to the far edge of it for Homebrew. It begins in the trees, at the far end of the clearing, just after the road re-enters the forest. Look for the trailhead on the right. It will drop you onto another logging road. Head right, up the short climb to the entrance to High & Dry in the middle of the cutblock. A short wheelie-drop begins this double black diamond trail that can boast it is more wood than dirt. Cue the circus music.

From the Diamond Head Rd., climb to the Ring Creek North FSR sign, go left. Keep right at the first fork and pass through an older cutblock before reaching the trailhead for Homebrew, on the left, just in the trees on the edge of the next clearing.

RING CREEK RIP (INTERMEDIATE)

This is a Squamish classic and an epic one at that. With stunning glacier views, a long climb and a 'ripping' fast downhill it proves itself worthy of the term 'epic'. Although it's not technically difficult, it is a long ride, and it is one that most riders can tackle provided they are prepared for an all day outing in the backcountry. This means bringing extra food, clothing, tubes and tools. The Ring Creek Rip takes you far into the mountains on the edge of Garibaldi Park. The downhill section follows the 10,000 year old lava flow, which emanated from Mt. Garibaldi. Very serious speed can be achieved on this downhill as you wind your way down this old, wide singletrack.

Photo: www.freeriders.org

To access this trail, climb the Mamquam FSR, which starts at Hwy 99 just past the main parking lot for the Squamish Chief. There is a smaller gravel parking lot here with bathroom facilities. This is a long, often steep logging road climb with remarkable views of the glaciers and peaks beyond. Over the 12 kms, you will climb and descend, eventually crossing 9 Mile Bridge at roughly...9 miles. Cross the Mamquam River and keep left at the first major fork. Climb Lava Flow hill to a small, flat clearing. On the left is the trailhead for the Ring Creek Rip. Near the end, you have the option to drop into The Powerhouse Plunge to finish up or continue down, cross the Ring Creek foot bridge and back to the Diamond Head Road. Try not to smile too much... you'll get bugs in your teeth.

FOUR LAKES / CHEEKEYE LOOP AT ALICE LAKE PARK (INTERMEDIATE)

The terrain around Alice Lake, named for the first white woman to see the lake in 1893, offers some excellent singletrack riding without having to endure super steep climbs. Here, a network of trails snake their way through a beautiful second growth forest that stretches from the park to Garibaldi Highlands in Squamish. The park can be very busy during peak summer months, and is best avoided on weekends. Once July and August have passed, Alice Lake comes alive with great riding, right into the early winter. In the spring the trails are often too wet to ride and are actually closed for that reason. Check at Corsa Cycles in Squamish for up to date information on spring trail closures.

To access the trails in Alice Lake, drive north from Squamish 9.5 km along Hwy. 99 to the Alice Lake turnoff. Turn right and drive a short distance to where the road splits at the main entrance to the park. I recommend going left, towards the RV sani-station, where a small parking lot sits near the Four Lakes trailhead. At this point, a small map will show you a rough idea of where you are going. The Four Lakes Trail lies entirely within the park boundaries, and is well marked with direction signs. The trail runs from the parking lot up to Stump Lake, where it splits, with a branch running along both shores. You can take either one, as they meet again at the far end of the lake. At this point a sign will indicate the route to the second of the four lakes, Fawn Lake. When you reach Fawn Lake, the singletrack pops out on a small dirt lot. From this point, signs will indicated that the Four Lakes Trail runs to the right, down the dirt road, but you should consider a small detour to the Cheekeye Loop before continuing.

THE CHEEKEYE LOOP starts at the end of the dirt lot, just beyond the boulders. The trail follows an old logging road through the forest for about a kilometer, until you arrive at a clearing under some powerlines. Continue past the powerlines, back into the forest. Immediately start to look on the right for a singletrack entrance. Follow it to the banks of the Cheekeye River. Here the trail turns left, and follows the river bank for awhile, until it reaches an old "corduroy road", so named because they were made by lying lengths of timber side by side. This road leads back to the powerlines, but the singletrack continues to the right. It follows the river a bit longer, and then heads back to close the loop under the powerlines. Turn right to head back to Fawn Lake.

Continue to follow the signs to the third of the four lakes, Edith Lake. Here you will have to make another decision: whether to continue to Alice

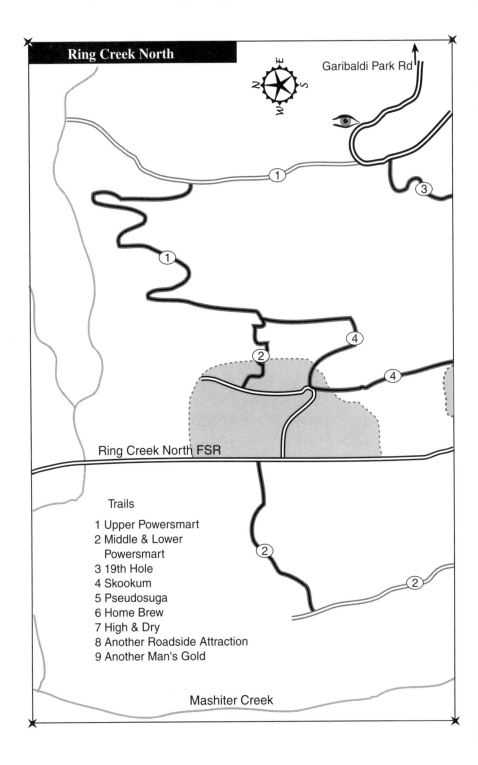

Ring Creek North

Garibaldi Park Rd

N E W S

① Upper Powersmart

①

③

④

④

②

Ring Creek North FSR

Trails

1 Upper Powersmart
2 Middle & Lower
   Powersmart
3 19th Hole
4 Skookum
5 Pseudosuga
6 Home Brew
7 High & Dry
8 Another Roadside Attraction
9 Another Man's Gold

②

②

Mashiter Creek

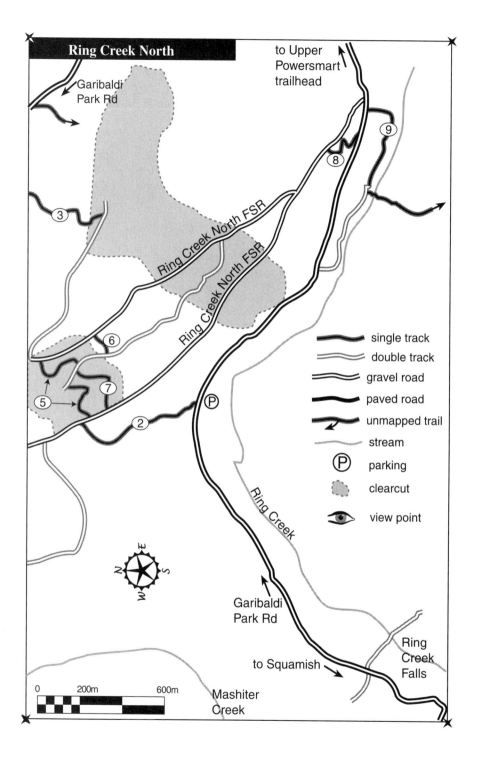

Lake, or head out of the park towards Garibaldi Highlands. If you choose to go to the Highlands, continue along the shore of Edith Lake and you will find yourself on another corduroy road. This short road is known as the TRACKS FROM HELL. Soon you'll reach a dirt road called the MASHITER TRAIL. Turn right and enjoy a gentle downhill toward Garibaldi Highlands. Further down the road, after crossing a bridge, look for a singletrack on the right at the crest of a small hill. This is ROLLER COASTER, and it is a beautiful descent through the moss covered forest to Garibaldi Highlands. Otherwise, continue straight for the "low-phat" version back to town.

DIAMOND HEAD ALPINE TRAIL (DIFFICULT – due to length of climb)

This trail is a high alpine ride and the only trail open to mountain bikers in Garibaldi Provincial Park. It is an out-and-back ride that follows an old jeep road and features stunning vistas of jagged peaks, hanging glaciers, Howe sound, and acres of wild flowers. You can expect about 2500 vertical feet of climbing from the parking lot or a whopping 5800 feet if you ride from the valley floor. This trail can be very busy in the summer, so keep your bike under control on the descent and try to plan your high alpine rice on a weekday if possible.

To access the trail from Squamish, head north on Hwy. 99 for about 4 km to the blue and white 'Garibaldi Provincial Park" sign reading 'Diamond Head 16 km'. Turn right and follow this road as it runs past the golf course and becomes hard packed dirt for 16 km to the parking lot. For most mortals, this ride will start from this lot, where relevant trail information will be posted. From the start, the trail switches up through old growth forest that steadily thins as you approach the treeline. Soon you will reach the Red Heather Hut, located at the treeline on the edge of the meadows. From here, the trail climbs into the alpine areas of Round Mountain. It is very important to stay on the main trail while in the alpine, and avoid riding on the side trails as the meadows are very fragile and can be easily damaged. As the trail reaches its crest on the flank of Round Mountain you are presented with a stunning panorama of the interior of

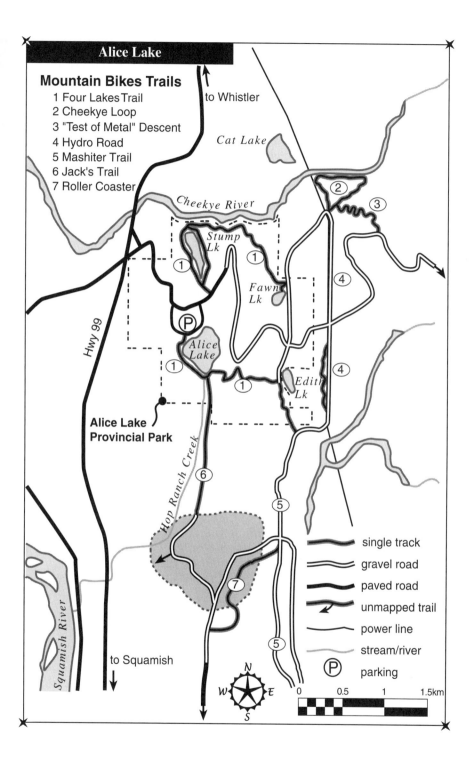

Alice Lake

Mountain Bikes Trails
1 Four Lakes Trail
2 Cheekye Loop
3 "Test of Metal" Descent
4 Hydro Road
5 Mashiter Trail
6 Jack's Trail
7 Roller Coaster

to Whistler

Cat Lake

Cheekye River

Stump Lk

Fawn Lk

Edith Lk

Hwy 99

Alice Lake

P

Alice Lake Provincial Park

Hop Ranch Creek

Squamish River

to Squamish

N
W E
S

single track
gravel road
paved road
unmapped trail
power line
stream/river
P parking

0   0.5   1   1.5km

Garibaldi Provincial Park. From this point, the trail continues for another 5 km or so t the Elfin Lakes Hut along the ridge ahead of you. The trail drops down to the cabin, requiring a short climb back out on the return trip. The legal bike route ends at the hut, but hiking routes extend further into the park. This is the beginning of a stunning ski traverse in the winter that takes you across the glaciers of the park to the mountains just south of Whistler. Retrace your steps back and be aware of other riders and hikers on the trail.

local knowledge

tasty bites & frosty pints

Howe Sound Brew Pub, end of Cleveland Ave, (604) 892-2603
Quinn's Café, 38105 2nd Ave., (604) 892-5560

camping / shelter

Stawamus Chief Prov. Park, under the 2000 ft. rock face, you can't miss it.
Alice Lake Prov. Park, Off Hwy. 99, just north of Squamish.

off the bike in squamish

The obvious choice for riding alternatives in Squamish is rock climbing. You're surrounded by one of the best climbing destinations in North America, second only to Yosemite Valley, California. There are outfitters in town that offer one day courses, guiding and rentals to make it easy for anyone to go out and pull on some of the best granite in the world. (Squamish Rock Guides, 604-898-1750) That towering hulk of stone is not the only rock playground there is in the area. The Smoke Bluffs, just above town, is a vast array of smaller crags with pleasant climbs for all abilities. If climbing is not your bag, there are myriad other options to keep you satisfied. The name "Squamish" is actually a native word that describes the "strong winds" the valley. The windsurfers figured that one out years ago. They can be seen skimming across the surface of Howe Sound daily. Lessons and rentals are for hire in town. (Sea to Sky Ocean Sports, 604-892-3366) Squamish is an outdoor recreation paradise; it's tough to be bored here.

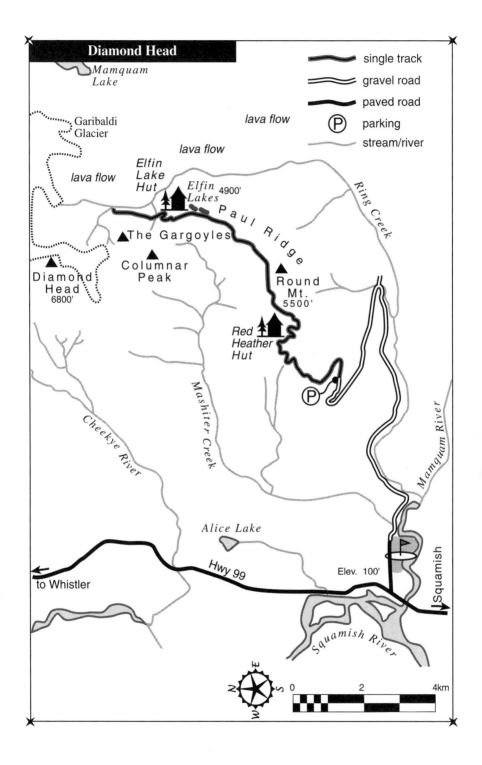

Diamond Head

single track
gravel road
paved road
Ⓟ parking
stream/river

Mamquam Lake

Garibaldi Glacier

lava flow

lava flow

lava flow

lava flow

Elfin Lake Hut

Elfin Lakes 4900'

Paul Ridge

Ring Creek

The Gargoyles

Columnar Peak

Round Mt. 5500'

Diamond Head 6800'

Red Heather Hut

Ⓟ

Mashiter Creek

Cheekye River

Mamquam River

Alice Lake

Squamish

Hwy 99

Elev. 100'

to Whistler

Squamish River

N E S W

0   2   4km

what to expect

Welcome to your fantasy. On your left is your dream trail, stretching on forever. On the right, an ideal mountain bike park, complete with gondola. Straight ahead, a high, skinny log bridge with a 90-degree bend over a rock pile. You can have all of this with an urban flair or a peaceful mountain village feel, it's your choice. The reason Whistler has become the "Disneyland in the mountains" is in many ways due to the inexhaustible efforts of trail builders. The Whistler Valley boasts an impressive network of trails that stretch from Function Junction south of the town to Green Lake and further north. Both sides of the valley have rides that are some of the best in the province. On the east side, the KHYBER PASS is an epic known for its sheer length and altitude. On the west side, A RIVER RUNS THROUGH IT is a very popular and accessible trail that has both technical and easier sections.

Whistler is North America's premier winter resort destination but summer doesn't necessarily mean quieter times for the country's only 'Resort Municipality'.

There really is no such thing as an 'off-season' in Whistler. The summer means events, concerts, weekend crowds, great parties and warm lakes. Perhaps the best time to visit Whistler is in the fall. The valley is warm, the trails are dry and buffed and the locals are riding hard with a gleam of winter anticipation in their eyes.

Photo: www.freeriders.org   Rider: Steve Mitchell

TRAIL DESCRIPTIONS

BRANDYWINE FALLS (EASY)

This moderate ride follows old logging roads along the valley floor from the village of Whistler to Brandywine Falls Provincial Park and back. Most of the riding is technically easy, but includes a modest singletrack section just past the suspension bridge at the Cal-Cheak Forest Service Site. The route also traverses the Lava Lakes area above Brandywine Falls, on a great high-speed double track through stands of Lodgepole pine. This is a popular early season ride and is usually the first ride of any length to be free of snow.

To access the trail, ride south from the village on Hwy. 99 for 7.5 km past Whistler Creek to Function Junction, which is marked with a large wooden sign. Turn left into the Whistler Interpretive Forest and ride up the paved

Photo: Tourism Whistler

road towards the dump. After crossing the single lane bridge over the Cheakumus River the road splits. The left fork is marked as Westside Main and the right fork leads into the dump. Follow the right fork into the heart of the landfill. You will pass a building on your left, and on your right a road that goes deeper into the dump. Keep riding for about 100 meters and you should see another road on the right that leads away from the dump. A Brandywine Falls sign was there once, but may be missing.

Follow this road as it rolls through the hills south from the dump. There is a basalt quarry about 1 km from the dump so be aware of heavy vehicles. After a couple of kms, just past the crest of a hill, the road forks, with the right branch dropping downhill, while the main road continues off to the left. Take the right branch and begin the rough, rocky descent down the

Photo: www.freeriders.org

Cheakamus River. Along the way you pass another road heading left. Ignore it and keep descending to the bridge. After crossing the bridge the road rolls along to an area known as the Basalt Columns. This is a volcanic formation of hexagonal pillars just off the highway. Here you must ride down the highway a short distance to the Cal-Cheak Forest Service Campsite. The turnoff is on the left just before a bridge and is marked with a small sign. If you reach the for land section of highway, you've gone too far. After entering the Cal-Cheak site, which is named for the confluence of the Callaghan Creek and Cheakamus River, ride past the first campsite down to the hydro lines. The entrance to the suspension bridge is through the second campsite on the right. Once across the bridge there is a section of singletrack that follows the riverbank for about 1 km. This trail emerges briefly beside some railway tracks.

From here the trailheads back into the woods, but don't ride it if you want to get to the falls, as it becomes unrideable beyond this point. The route for mountain bikers crosses over the railway tracks and briefly along a dirt road to the hydro lines. From here, a doubletrack runs up into the pine trees on the left beside the powerlines. This section is known as Lava Lakes. This entire area is an ancient lava flow, and in the depressions, rainfall collects forming many small ponds. This section of trail is slightly downhill and is great fun. Be aware of a short, steep section just before the entrance to the park. This hill has a nasty drop-off on the right, so be careful. The park, with plenty of hikers and the beautiful Brandywine Falls, awaits. Retrace your steps back, or ride the highway back to Whistler.

Photo: www.freeriders.org

WHISTLER INTERPRETIVE FOREST (EASY)

The Whistler Interpretive Forest is a working demonstration forest in the upper Cheakamus Valley, at the southern boundaries of Whistler. In the past few years a fantastic network of multi-use trails has been developed, providing some great riding. While some of the trails are quite technical, the majority are wide, fast and smooth.

To access the trails, ride or drive 7.5 km south from the Village, to Function Junction, which is marked with a large wooden sign. Turn left off of the highway, away from Function Junction, and you will immediately see a large information sign and a small parking lot. If you drove, park here and begin the ride; if you rode, check out the maps on the info sign and then begin the ride.

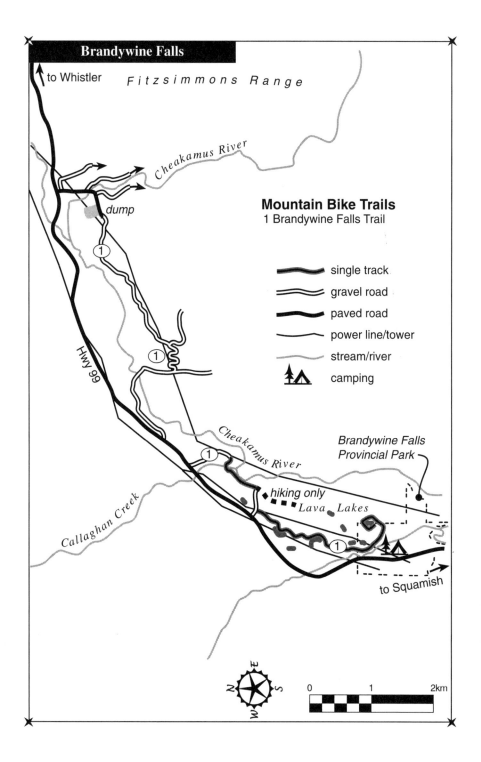

Brandywine Falls

to Whistler

Fitzsimmons Range

Cheakamus River

dump

(1)

(1)

Hwy 99

Mountain Bike Trails
1 Brandywine Falls Trail

〰〰〰 single track
〰〰〰 gravel road
〰〰〰 paved road
─── power line/tower
〰〰〰 stream/river
🏕 camping

Cheakamus River

(1)

*Brandywine Falls
Provincial Park*

♦ *hiking only*
Lava Lakes

(1)

Callaghan Creek

to Squamish

N E S W

0   1   2km

There are trails leading directly from the parking lot that lead to the bridge over the Cheakamus River Cross the bridge, and immediately on the left another trail will be seen. The Riverside Trail follows the river up the valley for several kilometers, with occasional sections along the Eastside Main road. Eventually you will arrive in a dirt parking lot, from which trails head in several directions. The Riverside Trail continues to parallel the river, while directly across the road a gated road climbs steeply up to Logger's Lake and the Ridge Trail Also across the road a new trail heads off below the cliffs of the Crater Rim (Logger's Lake sits in the crater of an extinct volcano) until it reaches the Basalt Spur Road.

At this point there is the option of continuing on the single-track, directly across the road (it climbs up to meet the Eastside Main road again, then continues up the valley to Helm Creek), or turning right on the Basalt Spur Road for a steep climb up the back of the crater to join the Crater Rim Trail. This technical single-track follows the narrow crater rim, and then descends to Logger's Lake. From the lake the Ridge Trail provides a fast, fun blast back to the dump, at the bottom of the hill.

On the other side of the valley, the Westside Main road climbs up to the Cheakamus Lake Trail, on of the few legal single-tracks in Garibaldi Provincial Park. Along the way several new loops have been cut that drop down to the river, then back to the road. There is also a short trail with a long title, the Biogeoclimatic Loop Trail. The Interpretive Forest is still under construction, and new trails are being added all the time, so be sure to check the maps at the trailhead.

RUNAWAY TRAIN (INTERMEDIATE)

This is a fun trail with a bit of history in the middle of it. A train wreck from the 1950's is still heaped in the forest among the giant cedars. The trailheads south from Function Junction until it reaches the wreck, then takes a logging road back to the highway. A new section has been built to connect to the BRANDYWINE FALLS TRAIL. This trail can be accessed by following Hwy. 99 south from Whistler for 8 km, just past Function Junction to the BC Rail crossing. Ride south along the side of the tracks for about twenty feet and a singletrack will be visible dropping off to the right.

The trail crosses the tracks several times, usually just going straight across, however the last time you cross, you'll need to go south down the tracks for about 100 meters or so to find the trailhead again. After entering, you'll soon be in the old growth cedar grove and at the site of the old train wreck. You'll find yourself back on the tracks shortly. You can ride back the way you came or hang a left and ride the tracks to a clearcut and take the road to the right back to Hwy. 99 and then back to the village.

KHYBER PASS / BABYLON BY BIKE / TUNNEL VISION (DIFFICULT)

This is quite possibly the longest singletrack downhill in the Coast Mountains. This Whistler epic begins above treeline in West Bowl on Whistler Mtn. and drops down to the microwave towers then down to the valley floor. As the trail access is on Intrawest property, liability is an issue, and thus you will have to ask for more precise directions at a local bike shop. Be prepared for a 4000 foot climb, (and a 4000 foot descent!)

WEST SIDE TRAILS (INTERMEDIATE – DIFFICULT)

This amazing network of trails just keeps growing. At last count, there were over 750,000 km of trails on the west side of the valley (not including doubletrack). All of these famous singletracks can be branching off of a short section of Alta Lake Rd, which runs north-south on the west side of the valley, and parallels Hwy. 99. Most involve stiff climbs up old doubletrack; followed by fun, steep drops.

Several routes can be taken to Alta Lake Road. The one described utilizes the Valley Trail, the multi-use paved ribbon running the length of the valley. From the village, ride out on Whistler Way to the Hwy. 99 underpass. This underpass leads to the parking lot of the Whistler

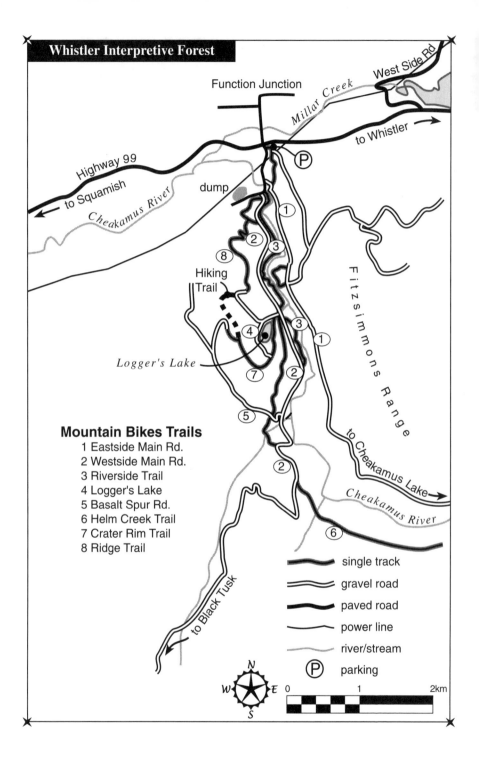

Whistler Interpretive Forest

Function Junction

West Side Rd

Millar Creek

to Whistler

Highway 99

to Squamish

Cheakamus River

dump

P

Fitzsimmons Range

Hiking Trail

Logger's Lake

to Cheakamus Lake

Cheakamus River

Mountain Bikes Trails
1 Eastside Main Rd.
2 Westside Main Rd.
3 Riverside Trail
4 Logger's Lake
5 Basalt Spur Rd.
6 Helm Creek Trail
7 Crater Rim Trail
8 Ridge Trail

to Black Tusk

single track
gravel road
paved road
power line
river/stream

P parking

N
W E
S

0   1   2km

Golf Club. The Valley Trail heads both north and south from here. Watch out for the rollerblade renters. Go north as the paved path skirts along the golf course. After passing the golf course, the path goes through Tapley's Farm, past the BC Rail station, over the River of Golden Dreams and forks. The right fork leads to Meadow Park Rec. Center. Take the left fork, a short climb up to Alta Lake Road. Across the road is the trailhead for Mel's Dilemma. Mel's climbs the mountain and turns into a maze of trails that loop back down to the road. Go south on Alta Lake Rd. to continue the tour.

A short way down the road, you'll see a gravel road on your left. Very shortly down this road is the well-worn trailhead for A River Runs Through It. This Whistler classic is not to be missed on a visit to the valley. It gains no altitude but manages to maintain a high level of difficulty by using beautiful, long log-rides, (one of which is the heart pounding 20 meter log ride over 21 Mile Creek) ramps and other super fun stunts. This trail rides like a circus in the forest. It has a couple of exit points, but eventually links up with Alta Lake Rd. further down.

About halfway along A River Runs Through It, you can exit on a gravel road to Alta Lake Road. Directly across the road is the entrance to Rebob. Head up Rebob as it follows along an old logging road that has been reclaimed by WORCA (Whistler Off Road Cycling Assoc.). There are many descents that drop off from the Rebob climb. Some are high speed, while others are slow, scary and technical.

After finishing River, go right on Alta Lake Rd. for about 500m and you'll see the trailhead for the Rainbow Trail on your left. Climb this trail to a point just past the small pump house, and then look for the marked trail that descends back to Alta Lake Rd. near Rainbow Park. This is Whip Me, Snip Me. It's fast and fun.

Thus ends your tour of the north end of Alta Lake Road. Go for a swim in Alta Lake or rejoin the Valley Trail back to the village. There's a lot more around here, just head into a local shop, buy something and maybe they'll tell you where to go.

GREEN LAKE / PARKHURST GHOST TOWN LOOP (EASY - INTERMEDIATE)

This loop is a great ride for the fit novice. It offers a bit of a road spin along Green Lake, stupendous views of the Rainbow Glacier and even a little history lesson as you pass through the old ghost town of Parkhurst on the shores of the lake.

Leaving Whistler, head north on Hwy. 99 and begin the 10 km road spin to the trailhead. This will take you past Green Lake and Emerald Estates, the heli-port and the municipal boundary. At the bottom of a long downhill, where the road and the Green River run parallel briefly, look for a road that branches right from the highway, over the railway tracks into a small parking lot at the provincial park sign for Wedgemount.

After turning right off of the highway, ride through the parking lot and over the bridge that crosses the Green River. The road forks here, the left fork leading to the Wedgemount hiking trail (not rideable), and the right fork heading back towards Whistler. Turn right and ride the first of the steep hills that characterize the Green Lake trail. After cresting this first hill the road drops down into a large open area that is the eroded remains of an old gravel pit. Continue along the road until you encounter a small creek that has washed out the road, (you may get wet feet or a wet ass depending on what season your riding here).
Cross the creek and go right off the main road, and ride towards the railway tracks. When you reach the tracks, turn left and follow them over the bridge and continue beside the tracks for about 200 meters until a singletrack on your left beckons you into the woods. This trail

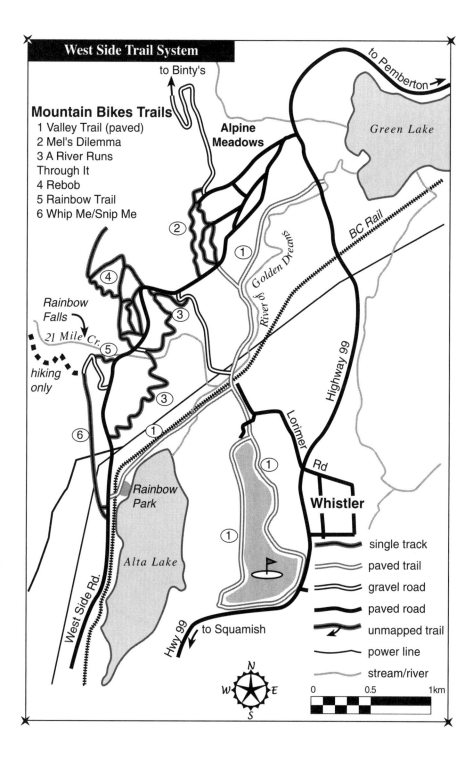

West Side Trail System

Mountain Bikes Trails
1 Valley Trail (paved)
2 Mel's Dilemma
3 A River Runs
Through It
4 Rebob
5 Rainbow Trail
6 Whip Me/Snip Me

to Binty's

Alpine Meadows

to Pemberton

Green Lake

BC Rail

River of Golden Dreams

Highway 99

Rainbow Falls

21 Mile Cr.

hiking only

Lorimer Rd

Whistler

Rainbow Park

Alta Lake

West Side Rd.

Hwy 99   to Squamish

single track
paved trail
gravel road
paved road
unmapped trail
power line
stream/river

N
W   E
S

0   0.5   1km

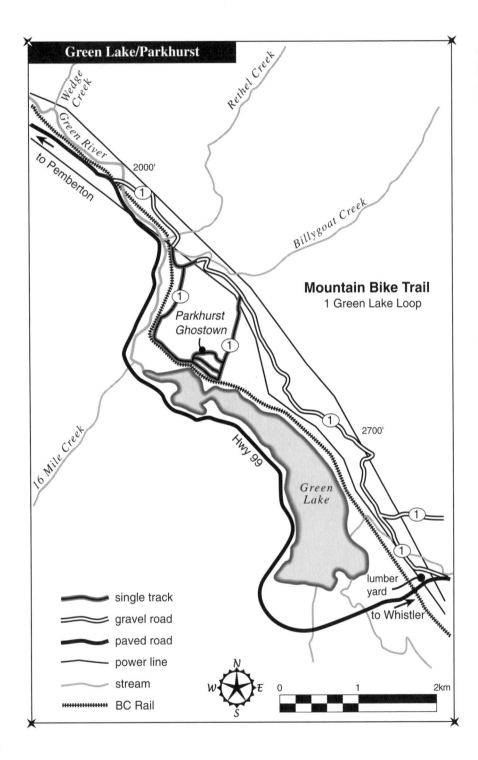

Green Lake/Parkhurst

Wedge Creek

Green River

Rethel Creek

to Pemberton

2000'

Billygoat Creek

Mountain Bike Trail
1 Green Lake Loop

Parkhurst
Ghostown

16 Mile Creek

Hwy 99

2700'

Green
Lake

lumber
yard

to Whistler

single track
gravel road
paved road
power line
stream
BC Rail

N
W · E
S

0   1   2km

soon widens, and you'll ride down a washed out spot. Keep to the right and shortly you'll see a road climbing to the right under the powerlines. From here the road begins a long, sandy climb, then a short descent to a flat section. Ride across the flats, and when the trail begins to climb again, look right for a well-worn singletrack. This is the Parkhurst Ghost Town Loop.

The Parkhurst trail is a short loop that branches off the main trail, and it is well worth exploring. After leaving the main trail, the Parkhurst trail drops down a steep rocky hill, crosses a small creek and then splits right and left. Take either fork, as the trail simply loops back to this point, and soon you will come upon the ghost town of Parkhurst. This small logging operation has been abandoned since the 1930's, though in recent years a few hardy individuals have fixed up some of the buildings. These folks appreciate their privacy, so please treat them with respect. When you have finished exploring Parkhurst, return to the main Green Lake trail by retracing your steps up the rocky trail you entered on. When you have rejoined the Green Lake trail, turn right and ride towards Whistler. From here the trail takes you high above Green Lake looking down on Emerald Estates. After a rocky descent, the trail ends at an intersection. The right fork leads to the Valley Trail and the left fork heads into the Lost Lake Trails. These trails are well marked and return to the village. Try Hydro Hill and stop for a swim.

ANCIENT CEDARS (EASY)

Surrounding yourself with the splendor found in a grove of old growth trees can quickly re-attach you to the natural world. The cappuccino bars and shopping frenzy of the village contrasts sharply with the atmosphere amid these quiet giants. After riding about 6 km up a logging road, the trail becomes a smooth singletrack that a rider can slowly glide along. These trees are estimated to be about 800 years old and are simply awesome. Bring some fishing poles and hit the Showh Lakes for a relaxing afternoon on the shore.

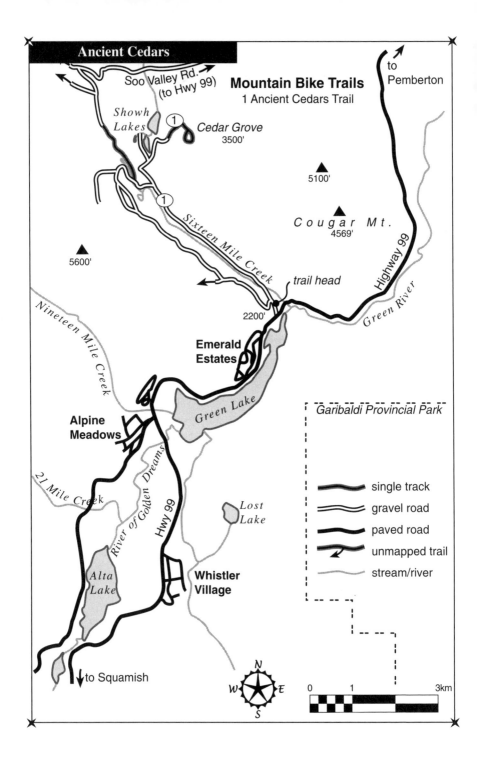

Ancient Cedars

Soo Valley Rd. →
(to Hwy 99)

to Pemberton →

Mountain Bike Trails
1 Ancient Cedars Trail

Showh Lakes

① Cedar Grove
3500'

▲ 5100'

① *Cougar Mt.*
4569'

Sixteen Mile Creek

▲ 5600'

trail head

Highway 99

2200'

Green River

Emerald Estates

Nineteen Mile Creek

Green Lake

Alpine Meadows

River of Golden Dreams

21 Mile Creek

Hwy 99

Lost Lake

Alta Lake

Whistler Village

↓ to Squamish

Garibaldi Provincial Park

〰️ single track
═══ gravel road
▬▬ paved road
↙ unmapped trail
〰️ stream/river

N
W ✦ E
S

0   1   3km

To access the trail, ride north about 6 km on Hwy. 99, past Green Lake and the Emerald Estates subdivision. Just past Emerald, look for a gravel road on your left with a brown sign reading "Cougar Mountain, Showh Lakes". This road has an easy, constant grade until it crosses the creek and starts to climb steeply up the north side of the valley. At the next fork take the right branch and continue climbing, around the switchback and up to the next fork, where you again take the right branch (the left branch heads to Showh Lakes, just a few hundred meters away). Both of these forks should be marked with Forest Service signs.

Please stay on the established trails, as the roots of the cedar trees are shallow and sensitive (just like my old boss).

local knowledge

tasty bites & frosty pints
South Side Deli, a Whistler landmark, across from the Husky station in Creekside - It's THE breakfast spot.
Auntie Em's, another great deli, located in Market Place Square, Village North.
Garibaldi Lift Co., a great pint at the base of the Whistler Gondola.

camping / shelter
Brandywine Falls Provincial Park, located 47 kms north of Squamish, just south of Whistler on Hwy. 99.
Nairn Falls Provincial Park, located 32 kms north of Whistler, campsites next to a beautiful waterfall.
Cal-Cheak Forest Service Campsite, located just south of Whistler off Hwy. 99

whistler

off the bike in whistler

Nowhere else in BC or probably Canada, for that matter, are there more attractions, or distractions for those who love the mountains. In the summer, the valley comes alive with bikes, boats, blades and bikinis. Luckily, the locals like to play hard and it's because of this, there is no shortage of things to do. Plans for a brand new bungee bridge near the Cal-Cheak Campsite south of Whistler are near completion. Whistler Bungee will dunk you into the deep pools of Callaghan Creek 180 feet below this magnificent bridge. There is also plenty of excellent rock climbing in the Whistler area. The crags in Nordic Estates are the closest and have some excellent climbs ranging from 5.8 to 5.12. With five lakes in the valley, swimming, paddling and wakeboarding are great hot weather options. Canoe and kayak rentals can be found on several of the local lakes. If you've missed winter, the glacier is open for most of the summer so you can head on up and get your fix. You'll be duking it out with all the ski camp kids for space though.

Photo: Janice Strong/Tourism Rockies   *Steeples Range - Cranbrook*

what to expect

Pemberton is the icing on the Sea to Sky mountain biking cake. It has one of the highest concentrations of great singletrack trails in all of BC right on its doorstep. The terrain here is like no other in the province. It is a unique mix of coastal and interior forests that makes for wide open cruising through pine forests or winding, technical lines through big cedars and firs. Just 35 km north of the year round playground of Whistler, Pemberton is a full 1500 feet lower in elevation than its trendy neighbor. This makes for a longer riding season and a very different riding flavor because it sits in the rain shadow of the Coast Ranges, creating a dry environment. Because Pemberton is at the southern tip of a large, unpopulated area, the likelihood of wildlife encounters is much higher here, than anywhere else in the Sea to Sky area. This can make for some even more exciting riding, so be sure to bring a camera! With that in mind, tread lightly, take only pictures and leave only footprints (no skid marks).

trail descriptions

MOSQUITO LAKE / McKENZIE BASIN TRAILS (INTERMEDIATE TO DIFFICULT)

On a small mountain above the Pemberton Valley, there is exists a network of trails that could be described at the best riding area in BC. Of course, this is open for debate; however, the mere fact that this claim would even hold water speaks volumes about the riding here. There are so many fantastic singletrack trails here that it is difficult to choose one. The climb up to the top is not too bad; so why not forget about shuttling and enjoy the view from the saddle. The view from the paraglider launch is something out of a Swiss postcard. It provides a great vista to take in while having a snack before the 2500 ft. descent to the valley floor. Access these trails by riding or driving about 2 km east from Pemberton on Hwy. 99 toward Mt. Currie. Take a left in the major right-hand curve in the highway by the log house. Park near the train tracks, or continue riding over them and begin the climb up Ivey Lake Road. The road climbs through a few sets of switchbacks and has its first major fork once you

reach the powerlines. Keep left if you want to reach the epic descents like COP KILLER, OVERNIGHT SENSATION, McKENZIE CRUISE and INDY 500. But beware, most of these trails cross private property and access can change at any time. Keep right to reach the Forest Service Site of Mosquito Lake and the network of singletrack that branches out from here. Rides like MOSQUITO LAKE TRAIL, THE RIDGE TRAIL and CRÈME PUFF offer incredible views of Mt. Currie, across the valley, as you descend through the open pine forest.

If you do keep right at this first major fork, you will reach a crest, then descend slightly and pass straight through an intersection. Pass straight through and climb another short hill, reaching a right branching road to Mosquito Lake (Forest Service sign). The main road ends a hundred feet further along. Ride down Mosquito Lake Rd. and soon you will see a trailhead for the Ridge Trail climbing up to your right. This trail climbs steeply up to the top of the ridge, and then drops down to the main Mosquito Lake singletrack descent. If you continue on the Mosquito Lake access road, it will turn to the right, and pass a cut block below on the left. Soon a gravel hydro road will appear on the left, and just past this, a fainter roadbed will be visible with a singletrack running up it. This is the Lake Loop, which climbs up under the hydro lines, then snakes through the trees behind Mosquito Lake back to the access road once more. Riding a little past the turn-off to the Lake Loop will lead you to Mosquito Lake itself. There is a picnic table, dock and a rope swing to monkey around on. Go ahead and take a plunge, but if you're riding here in May or June, remember that there is a reason why it is called Mosquito Lake. Sometimes it's best to just keep moving. Since 1996, many new trails have been created in this area. Some new trails connect existing ones, and others venture off into new parts of the mountain. Most are well maintained, technical and very fun. Drop in to the Pemberton Bike Co. (604) 894-6625, and they'll be sure to point you in the right direction.

BIRKENHEAD LAKE LOOP (INTERMEDIATE)

Birkenhead Lake Provincial Park surrounds a stunning mountain lake, which is set in some of the most striking mountains in the area. Along the way, you'll glide through untouched stands of Lodgepole pine along the

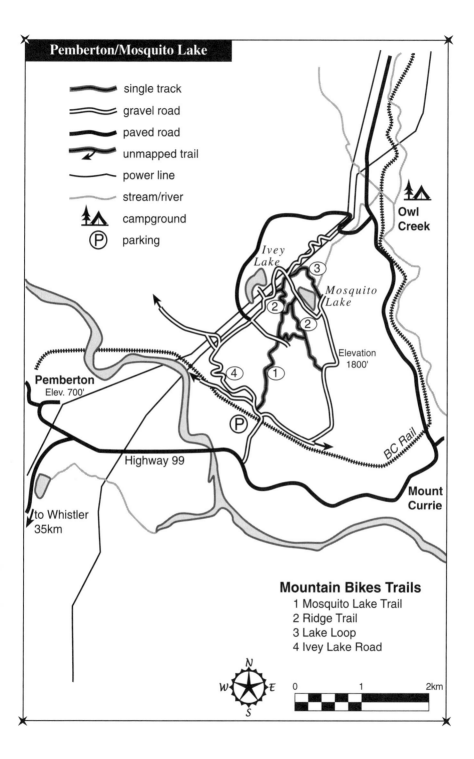

Pemberton/Mosquito Lake

Legend:
- single track
- gravel road
- paved road
- unmapped trail
- power line
- stream/river
- ▲ campground
- Ⓟ parking

Ivey Lake

Mosquito Lake

③

②

②

Owl Creek

Elevation 1800'

④

①

BC Rail

Pemberton
Elev. 700'

Ⓟ

Highway 99

Mount Currie

to Whistler 35km

Mountain Bikes Trails
1 Mosquito Lake Trail
2 Ridge Trail
3 Lake Loop
4 Ivey Lake Road

N
W E
S

0   1   2km

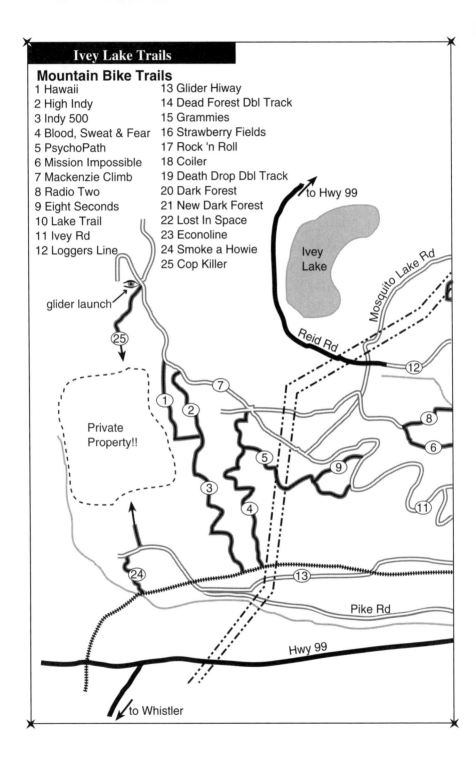

Ivey Lake Trails

Mountain Bike Trails

1 Hawaii
2 High Indy
3 Indy 500
4 Blood, Sweat & Fear
5 PsychoPath
6 Mission Impossible
7 Mackenzie Climb
8 Radio Two
9 Eight Seconds
10 Lake Trail
11 Ivey Rd
12 Loggers Line

13 Glider Hiway
14 Dead Forest Dbl Track
15 Grammies
16 Strawberry Fields
17 Rock 'n Roll
18 Coiler
19 Death Drop Dbl Track
20 Dark Forest
21 New Dark Forest
22 Lost In Space
23 Econoline
24 Smoke a Howie
25 Cop Killer

to Hwy 99

Ivey
Lake

Mosquito Lake Rd

Reid Rd

12

glider launch

25

8

6

7

1

2

Private
Property!!

5

9

3

11

4

24

13

Pike Rd

Hwy 99

to Whistler

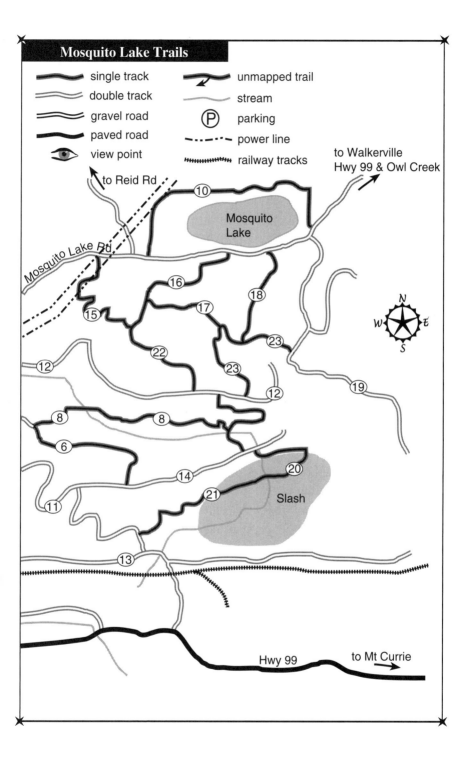

pemberton

west shore of Birkenhead Lake. This ride contains only one major climb, the 3 km hill up from the highway, the rest consisting of rolling hills and a final 7 km descent on a smooth dirt road. The trail is not technically difficult, however, you should make sure you've had your Wheaties before this one, because at over 50 km long, you'll need something to get you through. There are now numerous side trails being built, as part of the Sea to Sky Trail project. Contact Pemberton Bike Co., (604) 894-6625 to determine the latest trail status.

From Pemberton, drive east on Highway 99 approximately 6 km to the village of Mt. Currie. In Mt. Currie Highway 99 splits to the right, over the Duffy Lake Rd. to Lilooet, while the Portage Rd. continues straight through town, north towards D'Arcy. Drive north towards D'Arcy for about 17 km, at which point you should see a sign reading, "Birkenhead Lake Provincial Park Turnoff 16 km". It is important to note this spot, as you will be riding back down the highway to a turnoff at this sign.

Continue driving north, past Gates Lake, until you reach the main turnoff for the park, marked with a blue and white Provincial Park sign reading "Birkenhead Lake 17 km". Park at the bottom of this road and you are ready to begin the ride.

From your parking spot, backtrack south along the highway, past Gates Lake, for about 16 km towards that sign you passed earlier, reading "Birkenhead Lake Provincial Park Turnoff 16 km". You will know you are getting close when you pass the new subdivision called Poole Creek. Look for a spot where one of the large hydro lines crosses the road, and you should find a gravel logging road branching right (west) from the highway. Turn right onto the logging road, ride over the train tracks and you will see a sign reading, "Birkenhead Lake Forest Service Road", and another reading, "No Access to Birkenhead Lake". Don't sweat this second sign; it is designed to keep vehicles out of the park, not bikers. This road runs straight and flat for a short distance, then turns sharply to the left and begins the only big climb of the ride, a 3 km hill through a series of switchbacks. At the crest of the hill the road levels out and runs along the north side of the Birkenhead River valley.

Just past the crest another road branches to the right that leads to a section of the Sea to Sky Trail, marked, that parallels the main road. I've not yet ridden this, but they go to the same place, so the choice is yours.

The main road is signed with orange kilometer markers, and just past kilometer 8 you will come to a small bridge that crosses Taillefer Cr., at its confluence with the Birkenhead River. Shortly after crossing this bridge, you will come to a road that branches right from the main logging road. Head down this right branch and soon you will come to a gate marked "Private Property Birkenhead Lake Estates Ltd.". From this point a double-track road branches to the left, running through the forest parallel to the fence marking the private property. Follow this road and soon you will come upon several signs that mark the park boundary. Keep riding along this double-track until it makes a sharp left. At this point, look to your right and you will see a fainter road, blocked by a couple of large mounds, there to prevent motorized vehicles from entering the park. This is the main trail that runs along the west shore of Birkenhead Lake. If you miss this turn, the double-track will end at a gravel road; head back the way you came! After turning right onto the Birkenhead Lake trail, ride a short distance and you will find two trails branching to the right. The first returns to the private property; ignore it. The second provides a short detour down to a small campsite on the shore of the lake, a nice spot, perfect for a swim and a bite to eat. After taking in the sights, return to the main trail and continue the ride north around the lake. This section of trail gently rolls along, climbing up above the lake, then smoothly descending, for about 8-10 km, eventually popping out on the main park access road, right at the campsite and beach at the north end of the lake. Needless to say, this is another great spot to relax and go for a swim.

When you are ready for the final section of the loop, ride out onto the park access road and start the 17 km ride back to the highway. The first 10 km of this smooth, hard-packed sand road leads gently upwards, through

Photo: www.freeriders.org

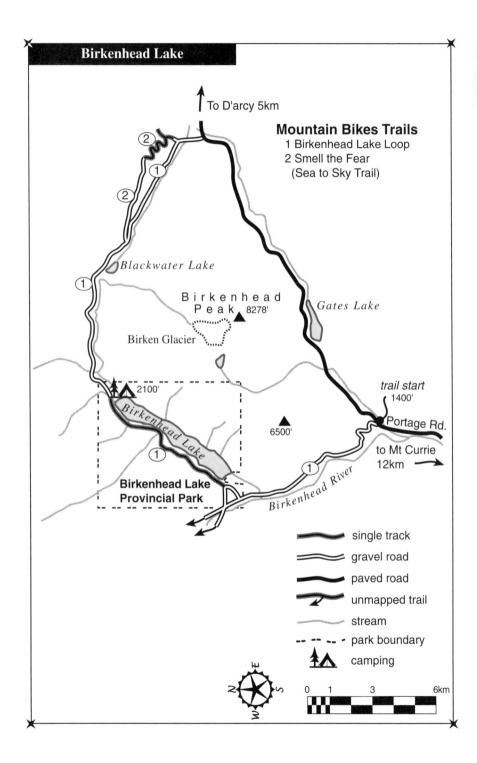

Birkenhead Lake

To D'arcy 5km

Mountain Bikes Trails
1 Birkenhead Lake Loop
2 Smell the Fear
(Sea to Sky Trail)

② ①

②

①

Blackwater Lake

B i r k e n h e a d
P e a k 8278'

Gates Lake

Birken Glacier

2100'

trail start
1400'

△ 6500'

Birkenhead Lake

Portage Rd.

to Mt Currie
12km

①

①

Birkenhead River

**Birkenhead Lake
Provincial Park**

single track

gravel road

paved road

unmapped trail

stream

park boundary

camping

N E S W

0 1 3 6km

rolling farmland towards the Forest Service recreation site at Blackwater Lake. Just after passing Blackwater Lake, the road begins a high-speed 1200-foot descent over the last 7 km, completing the loop at your parked car.

Just as the descent begins, there is an option to ride another section of the Sea to Sky Trail. Just after passing Blackwater Lake, look on the left for a road (it should be marked) and ride up a short distance to a fork. Take the right fork and follow the road as it climbs gently for about four kilometers. A single-track (aptly named 'Smell the Fear') branches to the right and begins a long, loose descent back to the Portage Road and the town of D'Arcy. The bottom sections of Smell the Fear branch in several directions, but all eventually reach the valley, and the signage should improve as the trail develops. Just keep going down. If you end up in D'Arcy, on the shore of Anderson Lake, you will have to backtrack down the Portage Road to your car.

BLOWDOWN CREEK (DIFFICULT – due to length of climb)

This epic out-and-back ride climbs from the parking area at 3500 ft. to its crest at an altitude of 7100 feet. The trail follows logging and mining roads high above the Duffy Lake Road. Blowdown Creek presents the rider with some amazing views, and a first class wildlife viewing opportunity. You can expect to see deer, mountain goats, and of course, bears. From Gott Pass, the road drops into South Cottonwood, which is part of the drainage system for the Stein Valley Park. You'll be heading into the LAST untouched watershed in southwestern BC. Recently granted protected status, the Stein Valley Nlaka'pamux Heritage Provincial Park is a truly pristine area that encompasses 107,000 hectares and has over 150 kms of hiking trails and routes. Please respect this beautiful area when you visit it.

To access the trail from Pemberton drive east to the village of Mt. Currie, then turn right onto the Duffy Lake Rd., at the mileage sign reading 'Lillooet 96'. The first 8 or 9 km follows the meandering Birkenhead River. Then the road begins its long, 4000 ft. climb up and out of the Pemberton

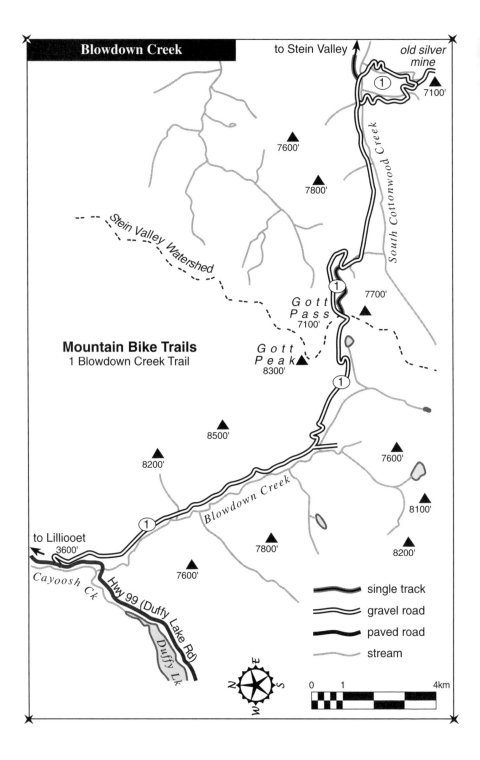

Blowdown Creek

to Stein Valley

old silver mine

▲ 7100'

▲ 7600'

▲ 7800'

South Cottonwood Creek

Stein Valley Watershed

Mountain Bike Trails
1 Blowdown Creek Trail

Gott Pass
7100'

7700' ▲

Gott Peak ▲
8300'

▲ 8500'

▲ 8200'

▲ 7600'

▲ 8100'

Blowdown Creek

▲ 8200'

to Lillooet
3600'

▲ 7800'

▲ 7600'

Cayoosh Ck

Hwy 99 (Duffy Lake Rd)

Duffy Lk

━━━ single track
━━━ gravel road
━━━ paved road
━━━ stream

N E S W

0   1   4km

Valley. Several Km after reaching Cayoosh Pass, you'll find Duffy Lake, and just after passing the lake, you'll drive over two small bridges. About 3 km past Duffy Lake you will reach a pullout beside a winter snow gate with a mileage sign just beyond it. Park at the mileage sign where the Blowdown Creek Road (marked 'Not A Through Road') climbs to the right.

From the Duffy, The Blowdown Creek Rd. climbs at a good middle-ring grade for about 45 minutes to an hour. The road is a smooth, double-track. Ignore all overgrown spurs. As you approach the end of the valley and the mountains are towering overhead, you'll reach a fork with the right one following the valley floor, and the rougher left one starting a steep, granny gear climb through an unlogged side valley to Blowdown Lake and Gott Pass. Head up the left fork and you'll find that this road is loose and rideable all the way into the alpine meadows and beyond. Just as you reach the treeline, the road switchbacks hard to the left, and from this corner a rough muddy track continues straight on through some marshy meadows to Blowdown Lake. If you want to explore the lake, walk it to avoid damage. The main road switchbacks once more then begins the final grind up Gott Pass. From this point, one can see down into South Cottonwood Creek and into the untouched watershed of Stein Valley Provincial Park. If you have the energy and time, you can explore this area as well.

The main road descends into South Cottonwood Creek, gradually wrapping around the left or north side of the valley, while a rougher road drops straight into the marsh below. These two trails eventually join, forming a short loop where you can descend the rougher trail, or ride down the valley on the main road and follow the old mining roads that run throughout the area. If you choose to ride into the South Cottonwood, be prepared because this is serious backcountry riding. The main road drops a long way into this valley, then turns and climbs back up to the treeline, before looping down to the main road again. Then you have to ride back up the pass, as there is no other way out. How about 6900 ft. of total climbing in one day! I get tired just thinking about it. When you are ready to descend, simply retrace your steps from the pass to Duffy Lake Road.

local knowledge

tasty bites & frosty pints
Pony Espresso, 100M past the Petro Can station, (604) 894-5700
Grimm's Deli, downtown Pemberton, (604) 894-5303

camping / shelter
Nairn Falls Prov. Park, Hwy. 99, 3 km south of Pemberton (with a 60m waterfall and campsites along the river)

Photo: Steve Dunn   *Downhill Dog*

lillooet 119

what to expect

Lillooet is B.C.'s little gold nugget. Situated along the banks of the mighty Fraser River, it has the beginnings of the semi-arid interior plateau to the east and the massive coast mountain range right at its back door. Lillooet was mile '0', the starting point for the Cariboo gold rush over a century ago. The gold has since run out but the adventure continues as people begin to rediscover this spectacular area rich in history and adventure. Outdoor recreational opportunities abound here with every imaginable activity available, but what sets Lillooet apart from all others is the amazing array of trails to ride your bike on.

The geography around Lillooet is vast, remote and littered with giant, pristine mountains, perfect for epic backcountry mountain biking. There are countless trails leading deep into the wilderness, many are well known (contact Lillooet Forest Service), but the true gold is in the hands of the locals. Ask at the sport shop, check with the tour operators or buy an old-timer a beer at the pub and you'll find that the local people, whether they're bikers or not, are very aware of where the gold is. One local who knows all about long, winding singletrack is Pat Ansdell. He runs Gravity Fed Adventures in Lillooet; which flys groups of mountain bikers to the summit of one of the local mountains for a full day, 7000 ft. singletrack downhill. You can also try a five day cabin-to-cabin backcountry ride. (250) 256-7947).

So maybe you're not the map and compass- " let's get lost"- type; don't despair, Lillooet has riding for people of every ability. There are old logging and mining roads, gentle trails near Seton and Fountain lakes, as well as trails built by local riders for all abilities. They've got everything from gentle cruises through the forest to North Shore type log rides, ramps and bridges. The weather in Lillooet is almost always perfect for riding. Because it's on the east side of the Coast Mountains the town is in a rain shadow resulting in a semi-arid climate, and coupled with its low elevation (650ft at town) the valley trails are rideable virtually all year long. So pack up your grubstake and get on the Goldrush trail to Lillooet.

trail descriptions

DELLA CREEK

This is a fantastic downhill above the mighty Fraser River with stunning views of the surrounding peaks and the river valley below. This is a fast, smooth and fun singletrack downhill with a 3500 ft. descent that will keep you smiling all day long.

From Lillooet, take the Texas creek road (on the west side of the Fraser River) past the sheep pasture golf course, past Texas creek FSR, traveling approx. 20 km to the start of the "Della Nesikep logging road" (sign at road). Hardcores can park there and begin the climb; downhillers and other lazy sorts leave one vehicle here and drive the second up the road 15km to a large pullout, there is a cattle guard and a yellow gate (usually open). Park here and gear up. Ride out to the ridge and find the trail leading along it. The trail is all singletrack, all downhill and all fun. It is a well-worn singletrack

Photo: Tourism Rockies

with stunning views but is unmarked so be aware of vague sections and tight corners. After a 3500ft descent you will pop out on the West Fraser road, an easy three kms from the start of the Della Nesikep logging road. When you are back at the truck hoist a cold one and salute our bovine friends who made this great trail.

local knowledge

tasty bites & frosty pints

Lillooet's Cookhouse Restaurant, 1237 Main St., (250) 256-0335
Lillooet Foods, 675 Main St., (250) 256-7114

camping / shelter

BC Hydro Campsite at Seton Lake, just south of Lillooet on Seton Lake

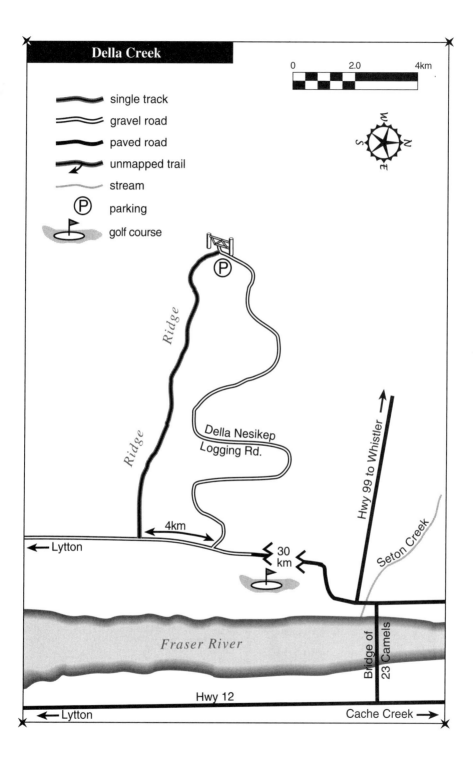

off the bike in lillooet

Lillooet has a very rich history that is evident today in the types of
activities offered here. Get in touch with its colorful mining heritage
by taking a tour of an old gold mine and while you're at it, try your
hand at gold panning. You just may come away richer than you
thought! (Spirit River Holidays Ltd., (250) 256-4417) Canoe down the
mighty Fraser River or on one of the local lakes with local guide, Hans
Meyer, (250) 256-4477. For the real Lillooet experience, I suggest a
tour through the grassy hillsides with one of the local adventure guides,
Red Rock Trail Rides (250) 256-4495.

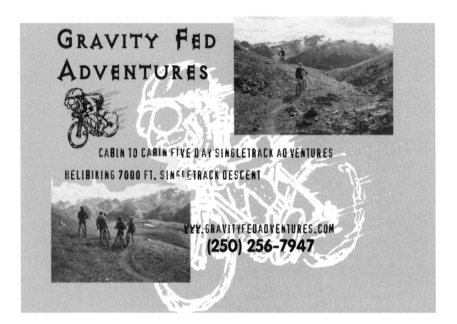

what to expect

This epic loop is probably deserving of the "best ride in the book", but I don't play favorites; they're all my babies. What this ride offers is views of endless mountain chains, backcountry solitude, and ample amounts of singletrack glee. You will travel through iron-rich mountains, which make for a very colorful landscape with red and orange hillsides in all directions. Many of these trails were created by miners in the 1930's who would hike over the high passes from one mining camp to another. There are incredible tales of adventure and hardship in these mountains that you may be able to coax out of one of the horseback guides on the trail. The backcountry riding in the Chilcotin area is unequalled in this guide or possibly any other for that matter and is sure to be a highlight of your riding summer.

The best way to experience the riding in this area is to have your camping gear and food flown into Spruce Lake for you, allowing you to do this epic loop in either two or three days. Contact Dale at Tyax Mountain Lake Resort on Tyaughton Lake, near Goldbridge (1-888-892-9288 or info@tyaxtours.com) and arrange for your camping gear to be dropped at Spruce Lake via floatplane.

With all this beauty and serenity comes a price. It may sound like a long disclaimer, but it may save your butt in the end. So be patient and read on. Because of the isolation during this ride, it has a sort of expedition feel to it that the true adventurers out there will love. Along with any adventure comes risks; this ride is no exception. Traveling in the backcountry on your bike requires preparation similar to a camping trip so you must bring ample warm clothing for unexpected weather as you will be climbing over passes that reach to 7500 feet. Extra food is a must due to the overall length of the trail. Anyone with a reasonably good fitness level can complete this loop in 2 or 3 days. As for safety precautions, you never think you need a first aid kit until you really need it, so pack a good one along for this ride because you're at least a day and a half from a hospital back there. Dale at the Tyax Resort has a satellite phone and radios available for rent, which is not a bad idea at all. It's worth mentioning that you should ride well within

your ability while in the backcountry because help is a long, painful hobble away. You are almost certain to encounter wildlife during this ride, so bring a camera and be bear smart. Please ride in control and at safe speeds at all times because you are sharing these wonderful trails with other users. The last thing a pack of horseback riders needs is some yahoo on a bike screaming around a corner at 50 km/h; "Plays well with others" is something that should apply all through life.

To access this trail from Vancouver, take Highway 1 to Horseshoe Bay then Highway 99 to Whistler; 35 kms after Whistler the road forms a "T" you turn left into the village of Pemberton (gas up). After crossing the railroad tracks the road forms a "T" again. You will come to a stop sign where you will turn right onto Birch Avenue. Follow this road, which will turn into Pemberton Meadow Road.

After 23 kms (14.4 miles) you will see signs for "Coast Mountain Outdoor School" and Gold Bridge, turn right at the pay phone. After 9 km, you will cross over a bridge and will see a sign "Hurley River & Gold Bridge", take this road uphill. This logging road starts out steep but flattens out on top. It then goes downhill into the Bridge River Valley. You will see a sign to the right, which says Bralorne, but follow the road towards Gold Bridge. After 60kms (35 miles) on this gravel road you enter a road that is seal coated. Turn right. You are now on Route 40. After 200 yards (1/4 kms) you see Gold Bridge on the right but stay on Route 40 and after 8 km (5 miles) you see the Tyax sign. Turn left and after another 8 kms you are at Tyax Resort. From Vancouver to Tyax is 255kms (160 miles). Total driving time: 4 – 5 hours.

trail descriptions

SPRUCE LAKE / GUN CREEK TRAIL DESCRIPTION (DIFFICULT)

After leaving the Resort at Tyaughton Lake, ride up the gravel road for a few kilometers (Dale offers a shuttle service to the start of the singletrack up the road which cuts out a logging road climb), taking the

3rd left fork at the three way intersection just after crossing North Cinnabar Creek at the big bend in the road. Begin to climb this road keeping right at the first spur and then keeping right at subsequent spur roads until you reach the wide singletrack above. The road narrows into a "motorcycle singletrack" size trail that climbs past the old Taylor Cabin, then an old mine and finally up and over El Dorado Pass. As you begin to drop into the incredibly beautiful Eldorado Basin, take in the sights, and avoid the old mining spur road on the right.

After dropping down from El Dorado Pass, you will get to another intersection; don't take the trail to the left down across the basin. Stay right and begin your climb up to windy Pass. This is a shorter grunt up to Windy Pass. At the pass, be sure to check out the view northwest to Castle Peak and beyond. From Windy Pass, it's a nice, long, mostly downhill run to Spruce Lake. This part of the ride is known as the High Trail. This trail will intersect with the Spruce Lake trail system, stay right and follow the trail around the lake. Your gear will be waiting on the dock at the recreation site at the north end. You can camp at Spruce Lake for one or two nights, doing day trips on other trails in the area, and your gear will be picked up by Dale and flown back to Tyax Resort for you when you're ready to leave. The Fishing is incredible in the lake so pack your fishing gear.

There are a number of great day-rides from Spruce Lake, but one of the highlights of this trip is the ride from the lake down to Tyaughton Lake following Gun Creek. You'll cover miles and miles of smooth, fast singletrack, passing through incredibly beautiful country. When you're leaving Spruce Lake, you'll pass by the High Trail intersection that you came in on, take the trail down to Gun Creek and generally keep left and continue to descend along side the creek. You will cross over the creek twice, but don't take the third crossing or you will end up at Gun Lake. Continue down the north side of the creek until you get to the end of Gun Creek Road

These days, there are more horses using these trails than miners, so please remember to control your speed and let the horses pass. This section of the trail is sensational. Right when you come upon Gun Creek Road, there is a logging road, which branches off to the left. Climb this through about five switchbacks, ignoring spurs until your climbing on the left side of an older cut block and the road forks, take the right fork, which climbs along the top of the cut block. This nice double track leads right back down to Tyaughton Lake and Tyax Resort. Although there are many spur roads along your way, if you stay on the most worn trail and continue to traverse the slope you should be fine. About half way across this bench you will cross Pearson Creek, please close the gate behind you and respect that this is a community water source. This double track will continue to get wider until you're back on the main Tyaughton Lake road, take a left and the lodge is just a short spin around the lake. Your gear will be waiting for you at the lodge.

Photo: Lyle Knight   *Spruce Lake Area*

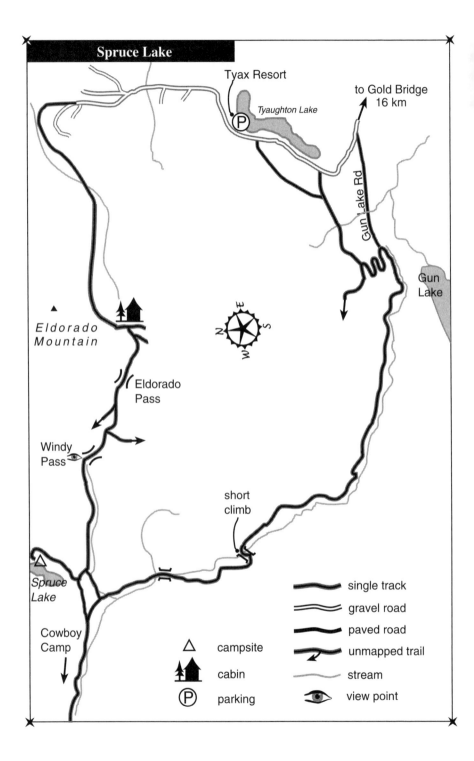

Spruce Lake

Tyax Resort

Tyaughton Lake

to Gold Bridge
16 km

Gun Lake Rd

Gun
Lake

▲
*Eldorado
Mountain*

Eldorado
Pass

Windy
Pass

short
climb

Spruce
Lake

Cowboy
Camp

single track

gravel road

paved road

unmapped trail

stream

△ campsite

🌲 cabin

Ⓟ parking

👁 view point

pacific**spirit**park

Cycling in a rainforest oasis sandwiched between Vancouver on one side and the Pacific Ocean on the other is a classic BC riding experience. As soon as you step off the pavement and into the cool moist air of Pacific Spirit Park (better known in Vancouver as The Endowment Lands) you really enter a different world. With almost 35 kms of trails ranging from wide gravel to sweet, flowing singletrack, the park is a piece of heaven amidst the urban sprawl. Start at any one of the dozen or so entrances and work your way through the maze of trails. You'll eventually end up where you started, but the journey will be a fun one. Spin over to the Museum of Anthropology, designed by Vancouver's master builder Arthur Erickson, and take a stroll among the giant totem poles. If you keep riding west, you'll eventually end up at the beaches where you'll be treated with a stunning view of Howe Sound and the glacier-draped peaks of the Tantalus Range; or you may catch a not so stunning view at Vancouver's only clothing optional "hang out", Wreck Beach.

A few years ago, the sometimes-shortsighted Vancouver Parks Board plotted to build a road around the entire headland of the park's coastline, changing it forever. UBC students literally sat down and blocked the bulldozers and effectively saved what you see before you. If you go

Photo: Tourism BC

exploring on this wild bit of coastline, you may stumble upon an old WWII gun tower with the bit of graffiti that seems to sum up the spirit of those who've helped preserve this gem: "Believe in what you feel, and act on that. When it comes from within, act on it."

The park itself is an amazing 763 hectares of beautiful, forested trails and beaches. The trails are generally a wide type of singletrack and are either

Photo: Steve Dunn   *Point Grey*

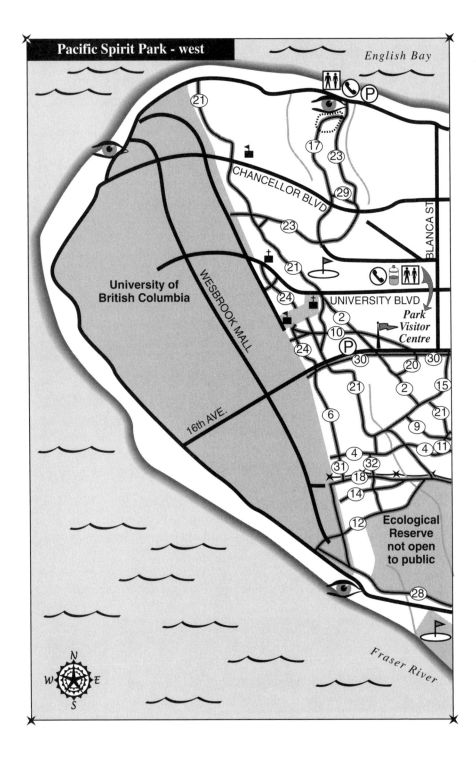

Pacific Spirit Park - west

English Bay

CHANCELLOR BLVD

BLANCA ST.

University of
British Columbia

WESBROOK MALL

UNIVERSITY BLVD

Park
Visitor
Centre

16th AVE.

Ecological
Reserve
not open
to public

Fraser River

N
W   E
S

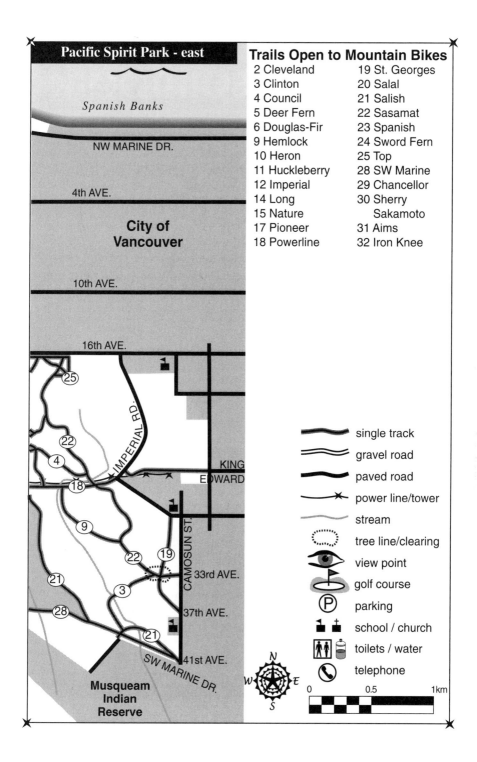

Pacific Spirit Park - east

Spanish Banks

NW MARINE DR.

4th AVE.

City of Vancouver

10th AVE.

16th AVE.

25

22

4

18

9

22

19

21

3

28

21

IMPERIAL RD.

CAMOSUN ST.

KING EDWARD

33rd AVE.

37th AVE.

41st AVE.

SW MARINE DR.

Musqueam Indian Reserve

Trails Open to Mountain Bikes

2 Cleveland	19 St. Georges
3 Clinton	20 Salal
4 Council	21 Salish
5 Deer Fern	22 Sasamat
6 Douglas-Fir	23 Spanish
9 Hemlock	24 Sword Fern
10 Heron	25 Top
11 Huckleberry	28 SW Marine
12 Imperial	29 Chancellor
14 Long	30 Sherry
15 Nature	Sakamoto
17 Pioneer	31 Aims
18 Powerline	32 Iron Knee

single track
gravel road
paved road
power line/tower
stream
tree line/clearing
view point
golf course
P parking
school / church
toilets / water
telephone

N
W   E
S

0   0.5   1km

flat or rolling. There are a few hilly sections, but no serious climbs. The only noteworthy ascents are the Spanish and Salish Trails, off N.W. Marine Drive. The gently, year-round riding in Pacific Spirit Park means that the area experiences a great deal of multi-use traffic. The park offers a welcome relief from the technical trails of the North shore, and has riders of all abilities enjoying the trials day and night.

Any mountain biker who uses the park must realize that this is a very sensitive area to ride in, with many other users, notably hikers and horses. Riding too fast around blind corners, or poaching hiking trails is just stupid. Ride like you're a guest here, because that's just what you are. It really is an amazing oasis amid the concrete desert, so if you're visiting Vancouver, make sure you get to ride it.

Photo: Steve Dunn

what to expect

In November of 1995, 820 acres of university land on Burnaby Mountain was transferred to the Province of British Columbia from Simon Fraser University, thus creating the Burnaby Mountain Conservation Area. Rarely do you find such a spectacular environment so close to a fast growing city. Within the park you'll find blacktail deer, bald eagles as well as a forest rivaling that of much larger and more remote areas. The trails of Burnaby Mountain have a serious, technical feel to them, yet they are not as severe as their North Shore neighbors. You may encounter steep drops and roots as well as nice, flowing singletracks that are perfect for a novice. Shuttling is definitely frowned upon on Burnaby Mountain. If you've been riding here more than once and have never climbed up from the bottom you're missing a great climb. It's just long enough to make the downhill feel well earned, but not too technical or steep to discourage the "just getting into shape" folks or those with heavy downhill rigs.

The best way to get a taste of the mountain is to park at or ride from the north end of North Road. From here, take the powerline climb up to Joe's Trial, finishing at the gas station. Go through the school toward Naheeno Park, and the access to Mel's Trail.

Photo: Chris Rollett   Rider: Peter Morin (60+yrs)

Mel's crosses Ring Rd. and begins to traverse across the slope. Shortly after the Water Pipeline downhill is the intersection for Nicole's. This is the best example of the singletrack riding on Burnaby Mountain. Other great trails include: Gear Jammer, a bit steeper than the others, and the flat but technical challenges of The North Road Trail. The lower portions of Burnaby Mountain have plenty of fun, un-named trails, but beware, some have been closed recently in an attempt to curb the unwarranted, and rogue trail building that has become a problem on the mountain.

A good rip around Burnaby Mountain can make you forget that you are surrounded by a throbbing city. Despite its urban flavor the trails are not a 'white bread', bark-mulch path sort of ride, but the real thing packaged into a confined area. There are trails with good technical challenges, but not so dangerous that at day's end you're bruises will out number smiles. Nevertheless, teeth have been lost and bones have been broken on the lower trails of the mountain, so be careful, ride with a partner and let someone know where you are. Try and stay out of the obituaries as long as you can.

Photo: Chris Rollett

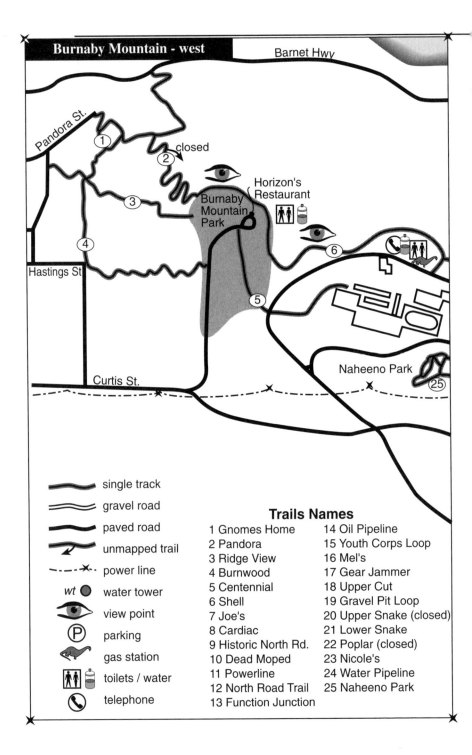

Burnaby Mountain - west

Barnet Hwy

Pandora St.

closed

Burnaby Mountain Park

Horizon's Restaurant

Hastings St

Curtis St.

Naheeno Park

Trails Names

single track
gravel road
paved road
unmapped trail
power line
wt water tower
view point
parking
gas station
toilets / water
telephone

1 Gnomes Home
2 Pandora
3 Ridge View
4 Burnwood
5 Centennial
6 Shell
7 Joe's
8 Cardiac
9 Historic North Rd.
10 Dead Moped
11 Powerline
12 North Road Trail
13 Function Junction

14 Oil Pipeline
15 Youth Corps Loop
16 Mel's
17 Gear Jammer
18 Upper Cut
19 Gravel Pit Loop
20 Upper Snake (closed)
21 Lower Snake
22 Poplar (closed)
23 Nicole's
24 Water Pipeline
25 Naheeno Park

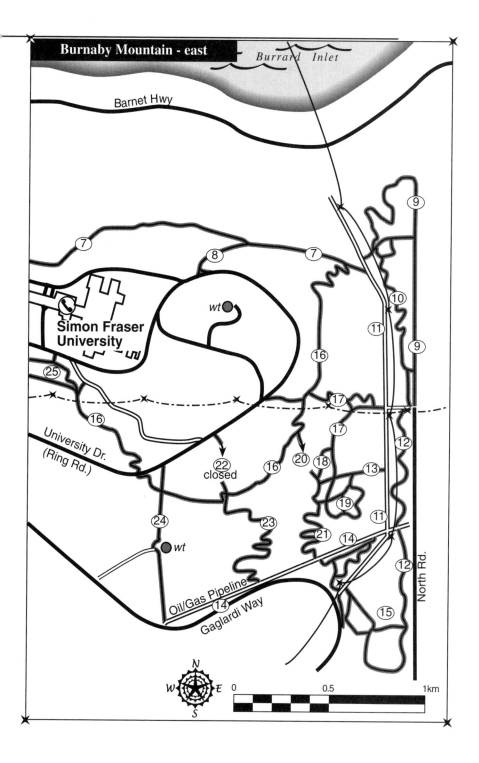

Burnaby Mountain - east

Burrard Inlet

Barnet Hwy

⑨

⑦

⑧   ⑦

⑩

wt

⑪

Simon Fraser
University

⑨

25   ⑯

⑰

⑯   ⑰

University Dr.   ⑫
(Ring Rd.)

⑳   ⑱

㉒   ⑯   ⑬
closed

⑲

㉔   ㉓   ⑪

wt   ⑭

㉑   ⑭

Oil/Gas Pipeline   ⑫

⑭

Gaglardi Way   ⑮

North Rd.

N
W   E
S

0   0.5   1km

what to expect

The trail builders on Eagleridge are a resilient bunch. After the amazing B&A was torn down to make way for new housing, the rumors spread that a new B&A was already in the works. Although it was one of the better trails on Eagleridge, there are plenty more similar trails just a short climb away. Eagleridge has everything you're looking for in a riding area: steeps, rolling singletrack, bridges & ramps. It is fast becoming a destination riding area, drawing many riders away from the overcrowding of the North Shore. One of the hardest things about riding on Eagleridge is deciding which trail to ride. New trails like Massage Therapy, Fat Bastard and Three Pigs bring the North Shore riding style to the valley. Check out our map to find these new treats but be sure to drop into see the folks at Blak Dog Bikes (604-942-3242, #105-2733 Barnet Hwy.) for the latest info on the area.

trail descriptions

Access to these trails is from Barnet Highway, and then north on Ioco Rd., to Heritage Mountain Blvd., which winds into Parkside Dr. and then into Forest Park Way. This runs into Panorama Drive where you'll see Noon's Creek Park on the left. This is a good place to park and begin the climb across the street. As this book was going to print, development was increasing in this area quickly; consequently, trail status may change quickly as well.

For riders who want to ride up from the Lougheed / Barnet Hwy., a fun technical climb call the BACKYARD TRAIL will bring you close to the good riding. To access the BACKYARD TRAIL, turn off the Barnet Hwy. at the Honda dealership toward Heritage Mtn. Blvd. / IOCO. As you go past the IGA mall onto Heritage Mtn. Blvd., look for a trail on your right just after the bridge, this is the trailhead for the Backyard Trail. It will literally bring you though people's backyards so refrain fro yelling at your bike or your legs on the climb up. You'll have no trouble finding your way if you just follow the tire tracks. As you enter the field at the top, you can continue until an intersection with the old paved road to the Hydro Station. This is the entrance to the WALL TRAIL. You'll be climbing right next to the housing development (and maybe even through it!) because houses sprout like mushrooms out here.

Once on the WALL TRAIL, be sure to veer right. Soon the powerline road brings you to the end of the WALL. Go left on the road and look for the entrances to THE GUTTER TRAIL and RANDY'S. These are great little technical descents. Another access point to the powerline road is via the ACADEMY TRAIL. This easier ride up is located off the first gravel parking lot on your right on the way to Buntzen Lake. Give yourself about 35 minutes to climb to the top of the ACADEMY TRAIL. From the top, a short ride on the powerline road will get you to the top of GUTTER / RANDY'S.

For those riders who want to access the higher trails like MASSAGE THERAPY or FAT BASTARD, follow the powerline road until it intersects the gas pipeline, located above the paved road. If you've climbed THE WALL, go right on the powerline road to get to the pipeline. This bumpy trail will get you to the pump station. Go around the pump station and look for a rocky left turn onto the LUNGBUSTER off the paved road.

The LUNGBUSTER is a bad-ass climb that requires power and skill to negotiate. Plenty of medium sized boulders bounce you around. The DENTIST is the first trail that beckons you off the bumpy climb with the SIDEWINDER coming shortly after a creek crossing. You can access SIDEWINDER about halfway down DENTIST on the left. DECAPITATOR is the next trailhead leading off the main climb. The climb continues, and if you go right on an old doubletrack, you'll see the trailhead for FOUR LOST SOULS and FAT BASTARD, which branch off just a short way into the trail. A further climb on the main road, and a left, gets you to the GREASER. This is all gnarly stuff that will curl the toenails of the weak. For those in the know and in great shape, MASSAGE THERAPY is up this road even higher. Its entrance may be concealed, so look around for the secret branch and pull it. The trail should open up for you.

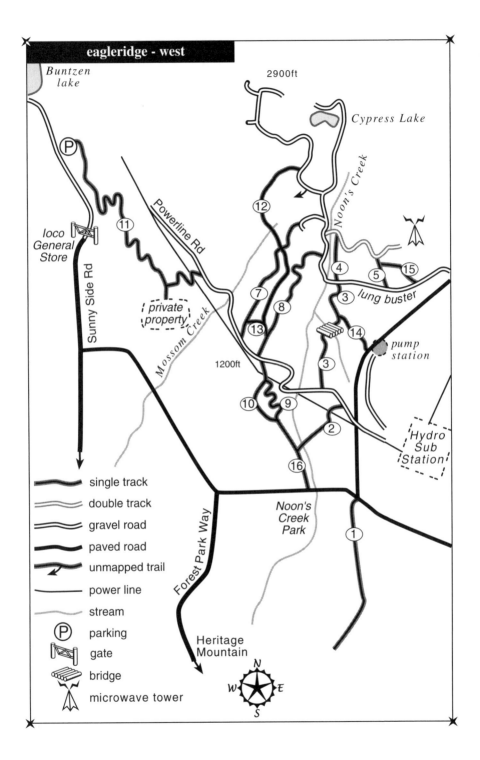

eagleridge - west

Buntzen lake

2900ft

Cypress Lake

Noon's Creek

(P)

loco General Store

⑪

Powerline Rd

⑫

④
⑤ ⑮

③ lung buster

private property

⑦

⑧

③

Sunny Side Rd

Mossom Creek

⑬

⑭

pump station

1200ft

⑩ ⑨

③

②

Hydro Sub Station

⑯

Forest Park Way

Noon's Creek Park

①

— single track
— double track
— gravel road
— paved road
← unmapped trail
— power line
— stream
(P) parking
gate
bridge
microwave tower

Heritage Mountain

N
W · E
S

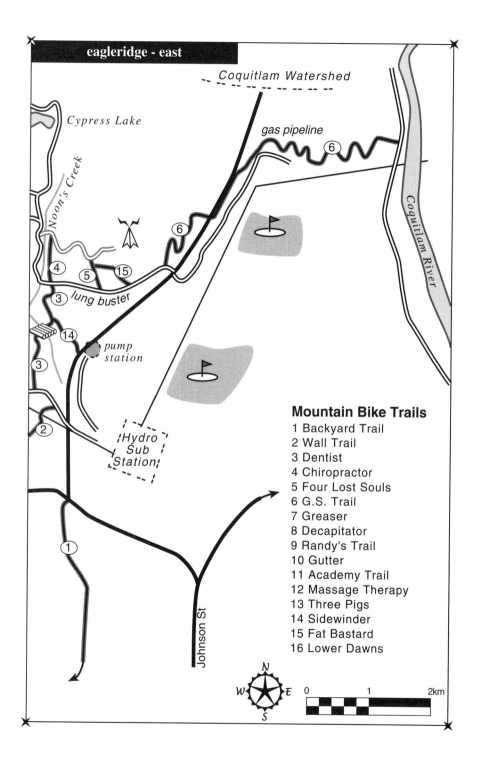

eagleridge - east

Coquitlam Watershed

gas pipeline

Cypress Lake

Noon's Creek

Coquitlam River

⑥

④ ⑤ ⑮

③ lung buster

⑭

pump station

③

②

Hydro Sub Station

Mountain Bike Trails
1 Backyard Trail
2 Wall Trail
3 Dentist
4 Chiropractor
5 Four Lost Souls
6 G.S. Trail
7 Greaser
8 Decapitator
9 Randy's Trail
10 Gutter
11 Academy Trail
12 Massage Therapy
13 Three Pigs
14 Sidewinder
15 Fat Bastard
16 Lower Dawns

①

Johnson St

N
W E
S

0   1   2km

142 burkemountain

what to expect

As far as backyards go, Coquitlam can't complain about Burke Mountain. It is one of the last vestiges of the 'Old School' style of riding in BC. You will not find any man-made stunts on Burke because these 'all natural' trails are steep and technical enough without ramps and bridges. You might think of Burke Mountain as being BC's "100% organic" riding area.

Part of the mountain has been made into a park, preserving the hiking and riding opportunities for years to come. Pinecone Burke Provincial Park was created in 1995 and its 38,000 hectares stretch from Garibaldi Park in the north to the southern slopes of Burke Mountain in Coquitlam. Some newer trails have been built in the area in the past few years but the number of people riding here has not increased dramatically as it has elsewhere. It's still possible to have a solo ride in these parts if you like, but when the riding is as good as it is here, it's always nice to share.

trail descriptions

WOODLAND WALK (EASY)

This trail serves as a feeder trail back to the parking area after riding SAWBLADE, but can also be a nice flat beginner ride. It quickly takes a rider deep enough into the woods that they forget they're in the city. A waterfall marks the end of the trail. From the parking area at the gate, take the first left. The trail should be signed. Continue on this main wide trail under the powerlines, to the turn around point at the watershed. Return the same way. Or hang a right at the last major intersection before reaching the gate. This is the LAST TRAIL and provides a fun run back to the start.

SAWBLADE (DIFFICULT)

The Sawblade trail is the result of over two years of trail building efforts in the early 90's from two serious, hard-core riders who simply wanted to have and off-the-scale, difficult trail in their backyard as an alternative to the typical North Shore scene. The result is a trail that will challenge all riders' technical skills and courage.

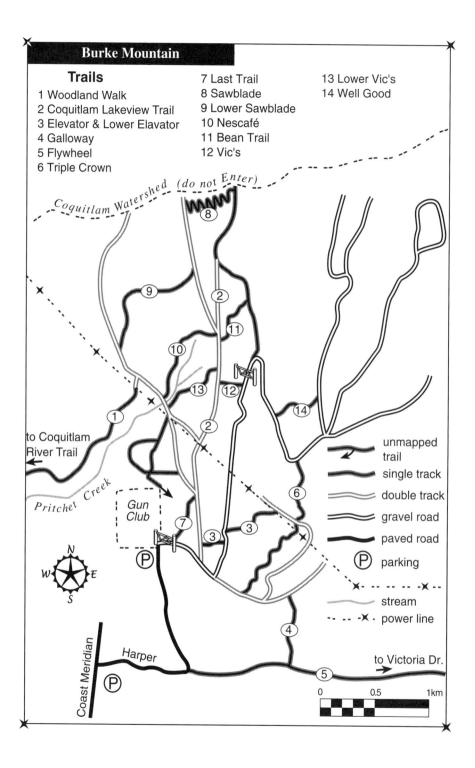

Burke Mountain

Trails
1 Woodland Walk
2 Coquitlam Lakeview Trail
3 Elevator & Lower Elavator
4 Galloway
5 Flywheel
6 Triple Crown
7 Last Trail
8 Sawblade
9 Lower Sawblade
10 Nescafé
11 Bean Trail
12 Vic's
13 Lower Vic's
14 Well Good

Coquitlam Watershed (do not Enter)

to Coquitlam
River Trail

Pritchet Creek

Gun
Club

N
W E
S

unmapped
trail
single track
double track
gravel road
paved road
P parking
stream
power line

to Victoria Dr.

Harper

Coast Meridian

0   0.5   1km

To access the Upper Sawblade, stay on the main old gravel road. This is not an easy climb due to its grade and rough, rocky surface. You will pass under the powerlines, then continued upward until the first flat spot and open space. The trail veers off to the left at the first switchback, and then begins to climb the brutal boulder field. Finding the actual entrance to Sawblade is not an easy task. While you're on the singletrack, at a small 'hump' on the trail you go left into the woods. The trail then slowly seems to disappear. Continue on and the trailhead will make itself apparent. From here, the trail drops to the Coquitlam Lakeview Trail. You'll know you've reached it when the tight, technical singletrack turns into a wider, smoother and faster roadbed. Turn left and follow this down, as the singletrack follows the old road for a while. Don't miss Lower Sawblade, which heads off to the right from the roadbed a little further down. This section of the trail is a nice, fast bit of singletrack that winds gently downhill through the forest eventually reaching the flat ground of the WOODLAND WALK. Go left, which takes you back toward the start of the climb. A short, fun diversion occurs after the powerlines on your right. Just prior to crossing Pritchet Creek, another trail goes down to the Coquitlam River along an easy path. The section of trail below Woodland Walk should not be ridden in very wet conditions, as it is an extremely sensitive trail during these times.

GALLOWAY (INTERMEDIATE)

The Galloway loop has some of the nicest rolling, slightly technical yet easy singletrack on Burke Mountain. To access the trail, begin at the gate, staying right at all intersections until you are climbing on an old skidder road. Start sniffing for the trailhead on your right. If you hit the powerlines, you've gone too far. The trail starts out steep, but soon settles into a winding trail that gently loses altitude in a mannerly fashion. You'll eventually hit Galloway Rd., where you can ride up on the pavement back to the start.

TRIPLE CROWN (INTERMEDIATE)

This is one of the longest trails on Burke. It has lots of steeps, and great flow. Although it is a bit of a longer climb, it is worth the extra effort. To access this trail, ride up the main road and take the first major left fork, being careful not to take the first left path, which is the WOODLAND WALK. Just after the Woodland Walk, the main road forks left. Climb past the powerlines, past the first switchback and look for the trailhead at the second switchback. The trail will drop down the south side of the mountain, crossing the powerline road and eventually returning you to the main road.

VIC'S (DIFFICULT)

Vic's has a steep start and then eases of a bit, blending in some great rock faces and cliff top singletrack. To access it, follow directions for Upper Sawblade. Look for the trailhead just after you leave the main road and begin climbing the boulder field.

BEAN / NESCAFÉ (DIFFICULT)

The Bean / Nescafé combination is destined to be a Burke Mountain classic. Bean starts you off with a more open, flowing ride before you reach the tighter, technical singletrack of Nescafé. To access these trails, follow the directions for Upper Sawblade, dropping into BEAN about 250-300 meters after entering the boulder field climbing section. It is the first left past the trailhead for VIC'S. When you reach the wide path that is COQUITLAM LAKEVIEW TRAIL, go right and NESCAFÉ should be a very short way along on the left. This will lead down to the WOODLAND WALK. A few options exist from this point; scan the map for the best choice.

Photo: Chris Rollett   *Cypress Provincial Park*

what to expect

Although Blue Mountain has not seen much in the way of trail development since 1995, it remains a popular area for its great singletrack downhills.

Photo: www.freeriders.org

To access the trails, drive through Maple Ridge eastward on Dewdney Trunk Rd., and turn onto McNutt Road. Follow McNutt until you see the sturdy gate at the bottom of Blue Mountain FSR. Park here. This main road is the way to gain elevation. The climb itself is challenging with plenty of cantaloupe-sized boulders to keep you on your toes when climbing. The omnipresent powerline is the other feeder trail, as well as a rocky double track that starts a few hundred meters above the powerline. All of these main roads, and a lower road, form the perimeter of most of Blue's good riding. There are dozens of additional trails that are not listed here; these represent some of the better rides. Blue Mountain Rd. continues to climb beyond the area mapped and plenty of fun and boggy, exploring opportunities await.

trail descriptions

HUMPHILL DOWNHILL (INTERMEDIATE)

This is a classic ride. It was the site of a downhill race in 1995 and continues to dish up the excitement today. Ride up the Blue Mtn. FSR past a couple of gravel parking lots. Just after you pass under the powerlines, there is a gravel clearing on the right. The trailhead starts at the end of this clearing and drops you down the mountain. Many side trails will call to you, be sure to keep left to remain on the

Humphill. Follow your front wheel, it will know. The bottom is fast, quite buffed and a bit wider than the top; perfect for a scary, fast downhill.

THE CHUTE / THE MUZZ (INTERMEDIATE)

There is some great riding further up the old double tracks of Blue Mountain. After climbing the Blue Mtn. FSR up past the powerlines, you will see an old logging road (resembling a creek bed) leading off to the left just past the gravel clearing. The Humphill Downhill starts in the gravel lot, but keep left and climb the double track to reach the

Photo: www.freeriders.org   *You want steep?*

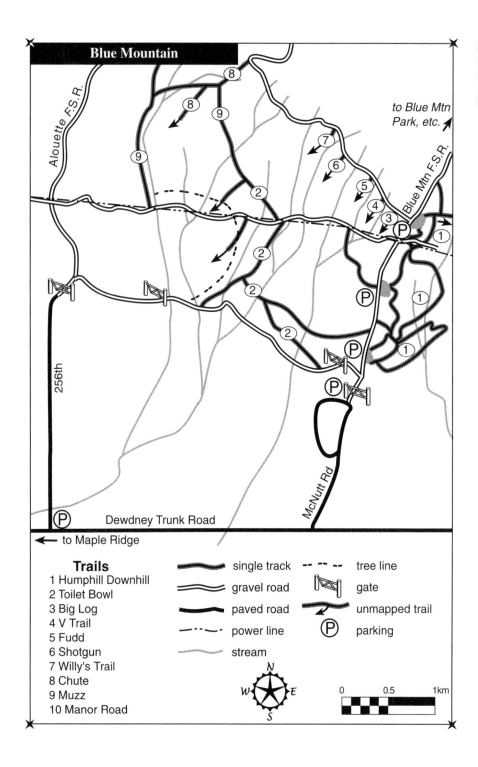

Blue Mountain

Alouette F.S.R.

to Blue Mtn Park, etc.

Blue Mtn F.S.R.

256th

Dewdney Trunk Road

← to Maple Ridge

Trails
1 Humphill Downhill
2 Toilet Bowl
3 Big Log
4 V Trail
5 Fudd
6 Shotgun
7 Willy's Trail
8 Chute
9 Muzz
10 Manor Road

McNutt Rd

single track

gravel road

paved road

power line

stream

tree line

gate

unmapped trail

parking

N
W E
S

0   0.5   1km

Chute and the Muzz trails. After a couple of kilometers the road forks; take the left fork. This is The Chute. It eventually branches. You can keep right and follow the Muzz trails down to the powerline road or keep left down The Chute where you can cross the powerlines and continue down the Toilet Bowl trails. Hitting the Toilet Bowl will give you a much longer singletrack descent back toward McNutt Road.

THE TOILET BOWL TRAILS (INTERMEDIATE)

This is a good singletrack descent, but the conditions of the trails have changed a little due to logging. To access the Toilet Bowl, climb up the main road and go left at the powerlines. Ride past the first trail on the left, and start looking for the Toilet Bowl around the third tower near an intermittent creek. If the trail you choose spits you into a cutblock it's the wrong one. Simply double back and take the next trail into the woods on your right. Once you are flushing your way down, the trail splits up into a couple of different options. Stay left, and take the next right to get the best ride. This trail makes for a fun technical climb as well.

Photo: Steve Dunn

what to expect

Golden Ears Provincial Park, Alouette Lake Area trails, are located north of Maple Ridge, approximately 45 kms east of Vancouver. Follow the road signs once you're in Maple Ridge and they will lead you to the park. The area was once a logging site, and remnants of its operation over 60 years ago are still visible. Today, the park is filled with mature second growth forest and the trails have dense vegetation and a sect coat flavor without the steep gnarl of the North Shore.

Photo: Lyle Knight

Alouette Lake is the primary recreational focus of the park. In regard to trail use, the local horse group has been involved in trail projects throughout the park and mountain bikers may feel as though the park is a trial monument to our four-legged friends. Mountain biking is definitely a more recent addition to the park user list than the horses, however. Today, the efforts of the Golden Ears Trail Preservation and Restoration Committee (GETPARC) are working toward the "enhancement of opportunities for all user groups in the park". Currently, the only trails designated for mountain biking are the ALOUETTE MTN. FIRE RD., the EAST CANYON TRAIL and the ERIC DUNNING TRAIL.

trail descriptions

ALOUETTE MTN. FIRE ROAD (EASY)

This old logging and fire road provides a gentle grade for mountain biker to climb. The trail is an out-and-back ride that can be confidently tackled by all levels of cyclists. The trails that you see starting out from the main

trail are not open to riding. The road stops at a dead end at the top. Mountain bikers may want to combine a hike to the top of Alouette Mtn. and grab a view from the 1371-meter peak. Descend down the road, where you have the option of taking the ERIC DUNNING TRAIL (aka – THE SWITCHBACKS) back to the Mike Lake Road. It's a great alternative to descending the road. It's fun, fast and not technically difficult.

EAST CANYON TRAIL (EASY)

The East Canyon Trail is an out-and-back ride that skirts along the eastern side of Gold Creek. The trail starts as an old logging road and slowly transforms into a singletrack horse trail. The trail has a slight climb up and then down to the creek bank, some sandy sections, and a few technical portions with cabbage-sized boulders. The trail eventually deteriorates about 14 km from the start. Once the trail becomes unrideable, turn around and head for home. This ride quickly takes you into a wilderness valley and riders should plan accordingly. A solitary dip in the creek will quickly adjust your core body temperature on a hot day making the return trip as enjoyable and refreshing as the way out.

Photo: Chris Rollett   *Bean*

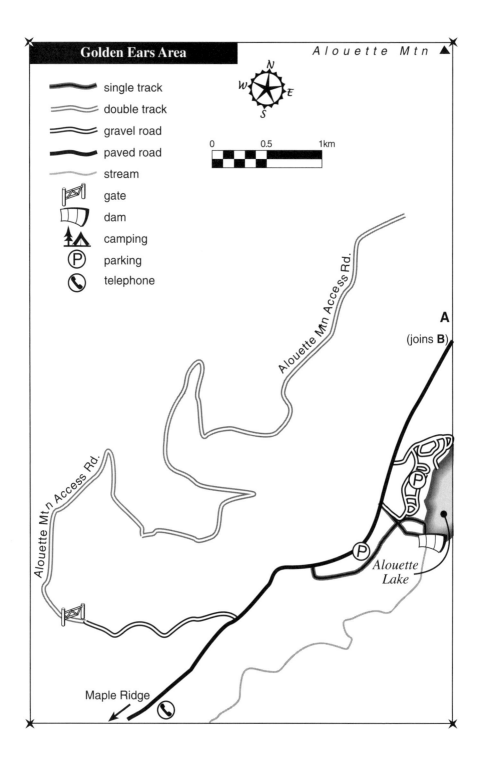

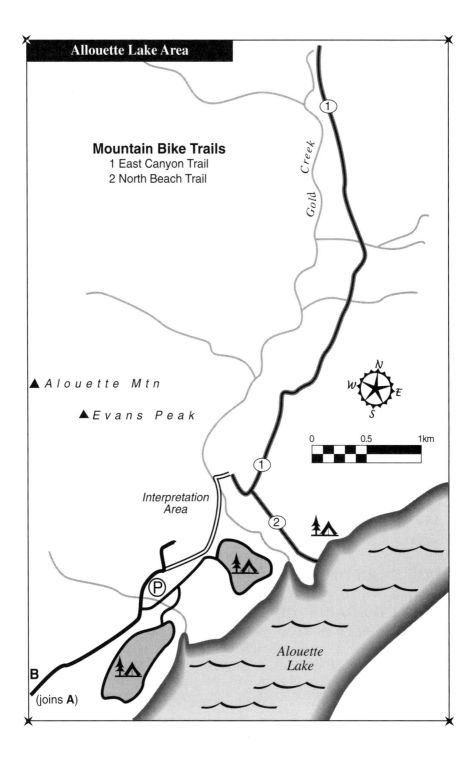

Allouette Lake Area

Mountain Bike Trails
1 East Canyon Trail
2 North Beach Trail

Gold Creek

1

N
W   E
S

0   0.5   1km

▲ *A l o u e t t e   M t n*

▲ *E v a n s   P e a k*

1

Interpretation Area

2

P

Alouette Lake

B

(joins **A**)

what to expect

In the further reaches of the Fraser Valley there are pockets of quiet, verdant forest that have been the playground of riders for years. You may have driven through this area many times on the Trans Canada Highway, never knowing that the surrounding hills were teeming with luscious singletrack from top to bottom. You could be forgiven for not venturing into these mountains astride your bike, in search of singletrack bliss. However, these areas have grown in size and popularity in recent years and each one now has its own distinct flavor and charm so your excuses are getting a little thin.

Fraser Valley rides have tremendous variety. Red & Bear Mountains have old-school downhill's while nearby Vedder Mountain has great long singletrack loops from a bygone era of XC racing. These areas contrast with the North Shore-style rides of McKee Peak/Ledgeview and Big Sumas to make the valley a great riding destination with all areas less then a half hour drive from one another. This region has enough great riding to make you move to the Valley or at least keep you coming back for a long time. So load up the car, head into the valley and start exploring. Who knows, you may just be lucky enough to hook up with some members of the Mediocre Cycling Club; if you do, be sure to thank them for all the great trails. For detailed information on these areas, visit the folks at Wenting Cycle in Mission, 33235 N. Railway Ave., (604) 826-1411 or Life Cycles in Abbotsford, 104-1520 McCallum Rd., (604) 859-2453.

trail descriptions

BEAR MOUNTAIN (INTERMEDIATE - DIFFICULT)

Bear Mountain was the site of the biggest BC Cup event ever held. Hundreds of ravenous singletrack fiends descended upon the mountain in May 2001 to test their skills against BC's best. With challenging and fun terrain, it is a great spot to race or just ride with trails like BIG GUNS, BACKDOOR and THE PLUNGE guaranteed to cement the muddy smile on your face for days.

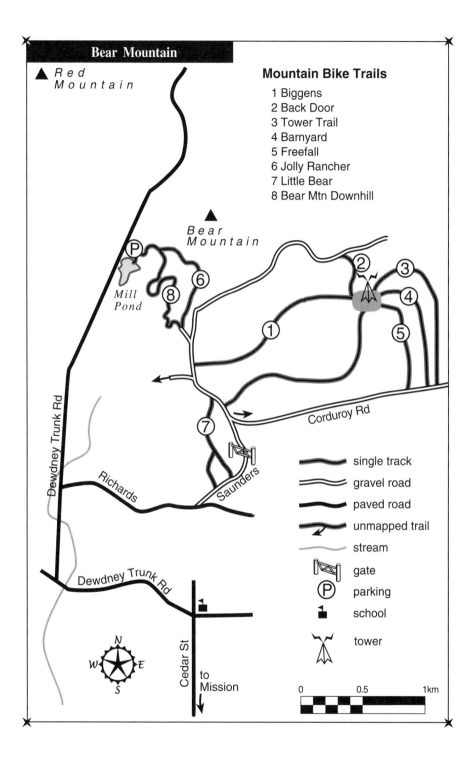

These trails are accessed by heading north on Dewdney Trunk Rd. out of Mission. Turn right on Richards Ave., and then left on Saunders St. about 1.5 kms later. You may want to park at Mill Pond, across from the Rod & Gun Club (makes friends with these folks), which is further up Dewdney Trunk Road. From the gate on Saunders St., climb to the tower by keeping right at the fork. Drop into BIG GUNS and beware, they're loaded. If you keep descending, you'll reach a road and if you go left then take your first right, you'll reach the Bear Mountain Downhill Course. See how you measure up to BC's best.

RED MOUNTAIN

The lower flanks of Red Mtn. have some great technical cross-country singletrack that is used in the Bear Mountain Challenge. RED, BETTER RED and RED RIDER can be linked to make a great challenging loop. To access these trails, follow Dewdney Trunk Rd. north from Mission, passing Keystone Ave. and Richards Avenue. Park at Mill Pond and enter LOWER RED about 100 meters south of the Rod & Gun Club. DO NOT ENTER THE ROD & GUN CLUB. Climb up to the main gravel road and go left, then right to climb a steeper road. Once you're in a clearing at the top, take a left onto another old road, which slowly becomes an overgrown doubletrack called RED. BETTER RED begins on the left, a few hundred meters up this trail. RED leads you to a new singletrack descent called RED RIDER. Another option at this point is to go right at the road and take the old Red Mtn. Race Course.

VEDDER MOUNTAIN

Vedder has long been a classic racing and riding location for southwest BC. The Vedder Classic was virtually a cycling institution in BC, but now it is no more. All things must pass, I suppose. Recent development in the area has caused some changes to the riding flavor. The old steep luge section has been logged. A good trail these days is THE DEN. The loop can be a little confusing, but you'll figure it out quickly.

Vedder Mountain is a BC Demonstration Forest Site with a well maintained gravel road which borders the riding area and serves as an access road to

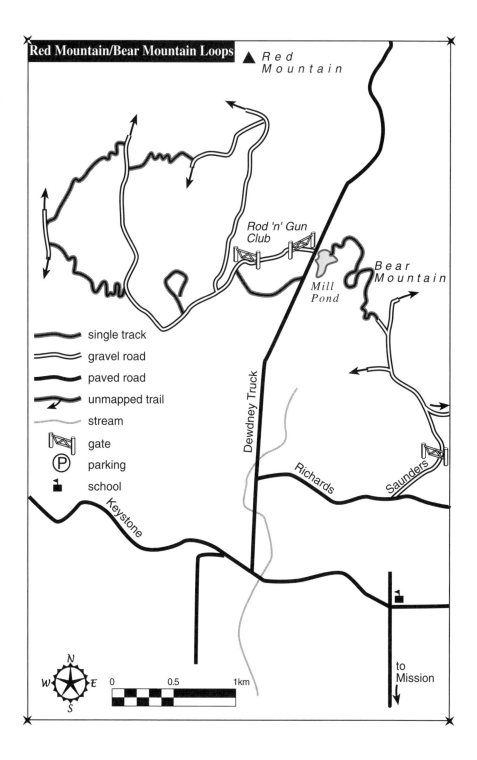

Red Mountain/Bear Mountain Loops

▲ *Red Mountain*

Rod 'n' Gun Club

Bear Mountain

Mill Pond

single track

gravel road

paved road

unmapped trail

stream

gate

ℙ **parking**

school

Dewdney Truck

Richards

Saunders

Keystone

N
W E
S

0   0.5   1km

to Mission

some of the great double and singletrack trails which this area is famous
for. The Vedder Race Loop is still a BC mountain biking classic, although
it's been logged in some places and changed a bit. Combining rolling gravel
roads, steep double and singletrack climbs, and outstanding, hand-numbing,
downhill singletrack, it will seem like it goes on forever.

To access these trails, turn off Hwy. 1 at the Cultus Lake / Yarrow exit.
Follow the road into Yarrow and turn right at the lights up to Cultus Lake.
Turn right again onto Parmenter Rd., and then take the first right fork.
This is the gravel access road, which climbs Vedder Mountain. There is a
labyrinth of old singletrack on the mountain, but because of the small size
of the area, it is tough to get lost. Ride it for awhile and have fun
exploring.

VEDDER RACE LOOP (DIFFICULT)

Although parts of this famous loop have been logged, the trail does
remain. From the parking area, ride up the main gravel road which will
slowly climb. A flatter open area about 15 minutes into the ride is where

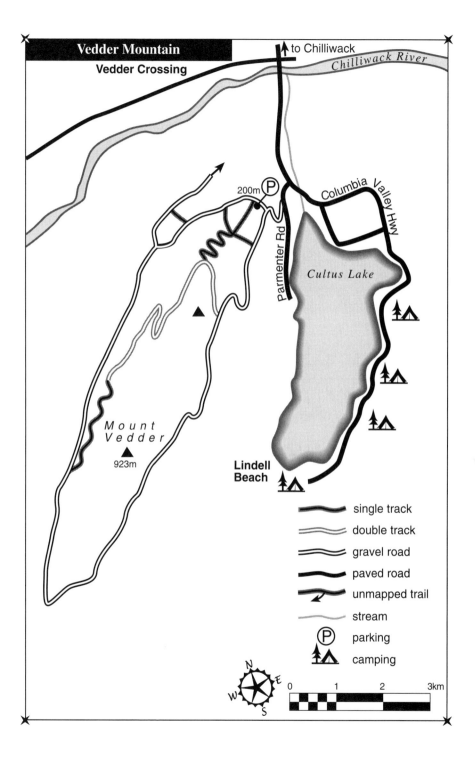

Vedder Mountain

Vedder Crossing

to Chilliwack

Chilliwack River

200m

Columbia Valley Hwy

Parmenter Rd

Cultus Lake

▲

Mount Vedder

▲
923m

Lindell Beach

single track

double track

gravel road

paved road

unmapped trail

stream

Ⓟ parking

camping

N
E
W
S

0   1   2   3km

the start/finish area for the annual race is located. There is a short singletrack on the right, which, if you go left at the bottom, rejoins the main road. Continue along the main road for about 7 km until an abrupt left turn doubles you back westward on a series of steep singletrack climbs and descents. The singletrack continues until a right turn at the bottom of a fast descent. From here the serious climbing begins on a steep doubletrack. You'll switchback once before the grade gets ugly. Yes, people do climb this stuff, although 2 or 3 times in a race humbles the most goat-like of mountain bikers. As you crest the summit, a trail to the left gives you a well deserved break and a great view. The downhill starts out fast on a doubletrack, interrupted by a few more climbing sections before the real descent begins. On the downhill, be sure and go left onto the singletrack where the going gets steep and more technical. This trail splits into two parts, the course on the left, and a slightly longer section on the right. The car should be less than 1 km away if you go right. Pro racers can do one lap of this course in 1 hour at full throttle. A more sociable pace is somewhere under 2 hours.

MCKEE PEAK / LEDGVIEW AREA

The Ledgeview area of McKee Peak offers a lot of fast, turny and fun trails that are great for most intermediate to advanced riders. Recently, this area has been turned into a genuine mountain bike playground. New trails have sprung up and old ones have been buffed. If you haven't ridden here in a few years, you may not recognize it these days. Although it's hard to get lost here, try heading up on a weekend, you're bound to hook up with some local riders who can point you in the right direction. THE SOFT TACO is a fun yet scary little romp with ladders, bridges and teeter-totters that will keep you coming back here to try and ride it clean. You can still find THE BUTTAFUCO up on McKee peak as well as a horde of other newer trails to satisfy your singletrack desires. Take the Sumas Way exit from the Trans Canada Hwy. near Abbotsford.

trail descriptions

THE BUTTAFUCO (DIFFICULT)

This trail is a McKee Peak original. A few steeps, and a handful of rolls; some up, some down. It will drop you out onto the road you climbed. To access this trail, take the Sumas Way exit follow the Old Clayburn Rd. to McKee Road. The old road you will be climbing starts on the right, just past the Ledgeview golf course. Climb this road to the top where you'll see the singletrack heading off to the left.

LITTLE AMY FISHER (INTERMEDIATE)

This is a short trail that acts as a natural finish for THE BUTTAFUCO. When Buttafuco ends at the main gravel road, cross it and continue down Little Amy Fisher.

SPEEDWAY (DIFFICULT)

This is a short but very fun trail that will allow the uninitiated to cut their teeth on dirt jumping. With BMX style jumps of all sizes, you may spend more time in the air than on the ground. Watch out for "the Matterhorn".

THE SOFT TACO (DIFFICULT)

Hungry? How about a Soft Taco? Careful, this one may bite back. With steeps, ramps, ladders and teeter-totters, you'll have your plate full on this ride. It's best ridden in dry weather, so avoid it when wet. To access this trail from Sumas Way, drive until you reach Hwy 11 (which goes to Mission) then take a right at the lights for Clayburn Road. After passing through Clayburn Village, you'll cross a bridge and the road will fork. Keep left and follow Straiton Road. After a few windy kilometers, the road will climb and you'll pass a pullout on the right. Park here and look for the entrance on the right just before the concrete blocks. You'll hit a long log bridge and begin climbing, reaching a small clearing. Take the right fork and from here it's hard to get lost.

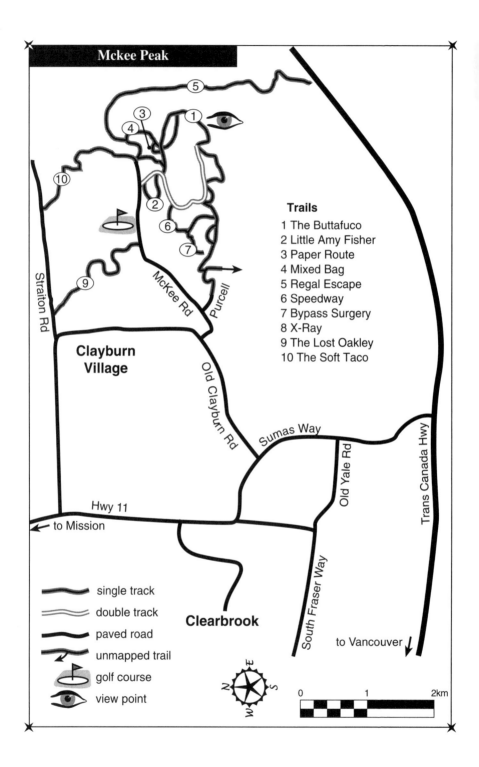

Mckee Peak

Trails

1 The Buttafuco
2 Little Amy Fisher
3 Paper Route
4 Mixed Bag
5 Regal Escape
6 Speedway
7 Bypass Surgery
8 X-Ray
9 The Lost Oakley
10 The Soft Taco

Straiton Rd

McKee Rd

Purcell

Clayburn Village

Old Clayburn Rd

Sumas Way

Old Yale Rd

Trans Canada Hwy

Hwy 11

← to Mission

South Fraser Way

Clearbrook

to Vancouver ↓

single track
double track
paved road
unmapped trail
golf course
view point

0   1   2km

THE WOODLOT

In every sport there are those special places that people just want to keep for themselves. There's no hype, no crowds and only the sound of a few, dedicated people having fun doing what they love to do. For riders in the Fraser Valley, this place is Woodlot 007. It's been developing into a 'destination' riding area over the past few years because of its challenging 'North Shore' style riding. One thing the Woodlot has got that makes it a special place to ride is flow. The trails here flow like water. They are skillfully crafted, well maintained and built with heart. No pesky pick up trucks here, and the only high-speed quads getting you up this mountain are the ones pushing your pedals up the old logging road. It does get steep at times, but it is definitely worth it.

Regrettably, the Woodlot is a victim of its own popularity these days. With the crowds comes controversy. Local trail advocates have been battling to keep the area open to riders but this will be a difficult task as the forest is primarily used for research purposes by BCIT. Rogue trail builders, ignorant of the damage they cause, have done the sport no favors. This is a great riding area that may not be rideable for much longer. It is for this reason and others that no map is included herein. Please drop in to Wenting Cycle in Mission (33235 N. Railway Ave., 604-826-1411) and check the status of the trails before considering riding the Woodlot.

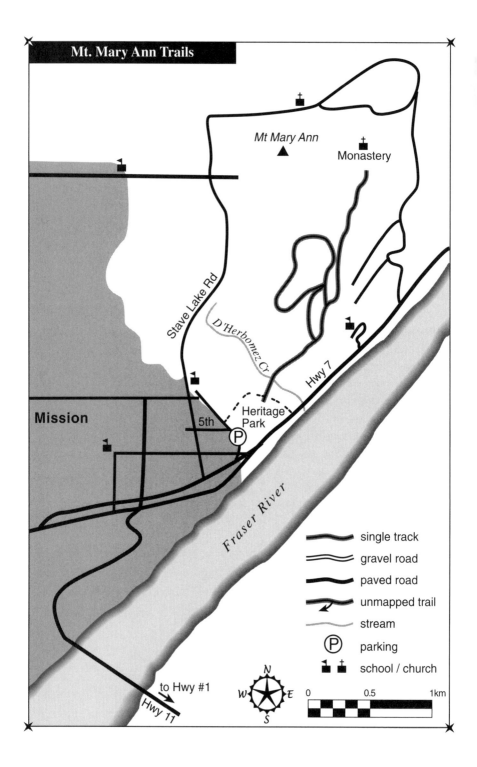

what to expect

The name "Sunshine Coast" conjures up images of long, white sand beaches and palm trees. However, in the Pacific Northwest of Canada "Sunshine Coast" brings to mind tall trees, verdant forests, ocean vistas and long, loamy singletracks. A short ferry ride from the urban craziness of Vancouver lands you in a unique hideaway for adventure seekers. Whether it's an epic day trip or a weekend getaway, a trip with your bike to the land of the "Beachcombers" will put everything back into perspective!

As far as mountain biking goes, the Sunshine Coast is an advanced civilization. The riding community works in almost perfect harmony with governments and industry to ensure the trails will always be outstanding and accessible. The area is home to SPROCKIDS, a mountain bike program for school-age kids that is designed to provide them with opportunities to experience success and build self-esteem through this great sport. It integrates mountain biking into every aspect of the school curriculum to make learning relevant and exciting for the kids. Sprockids is one of the groups that spearhead "Trail Fest" each year. This meeting of trail user-groups comes together to build and upgrade large sections of trail each year in the area and is the largest festival of its kind in North America and possibly the world! Thanks to the hard work of Sprockids, the Ministry of Forests and the other user groups, the trail network on the Sunshine Coast is one of the best in the country.

trail descriptions

SPROCKIDS MOUNTAIN BIKE PARK (EASY – DIFFICULT)

This park was created by the mountain bike visionaries of the Sprockids program. It can be a fun, friendly place to introduce a novice rider to the singletrack experience or a challenging day of fast riding for the intermediate or advanced rider. This map is merely a guide, detailed maps are available on the Sprockids website (http://home.istar.ca/~sprockid/) or on the information boards in the park. To access the park from the Langdale ferry, drive up the Langdale ferry bypass to the top. Turn right on Hauka Rd. then left onto the dirt access road.

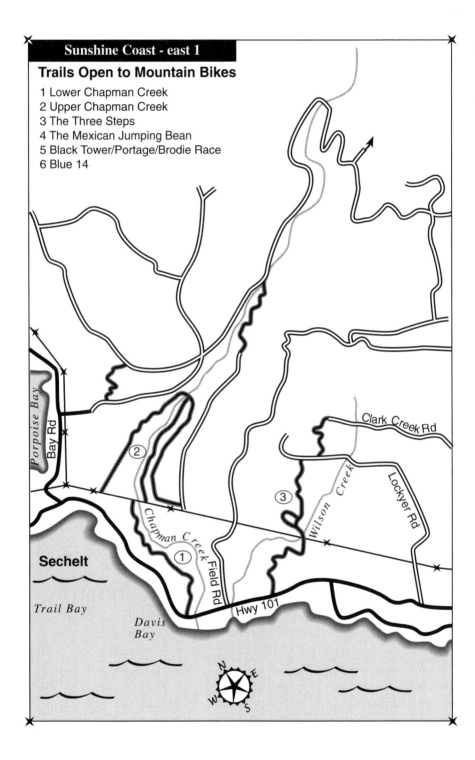

Sunshine Coast - east 1

Trails Open to Mountain Bikes

1 Lower Chapman Creek
2 Upper Chapman Creek
3 The Three Steps
4 The Mexican Jumping Bean
5 Black Tower/Portage/Brodie Race
6 Blue 14

Porpoise Bay

Bay Rd

Clark Creek Rd

②

Wilson Creek

Lockyer Rd

③

Sechelt

①

Chapman Creek Field Rd

Trail Bay

Davis Bay

Hwy 101

N E S W

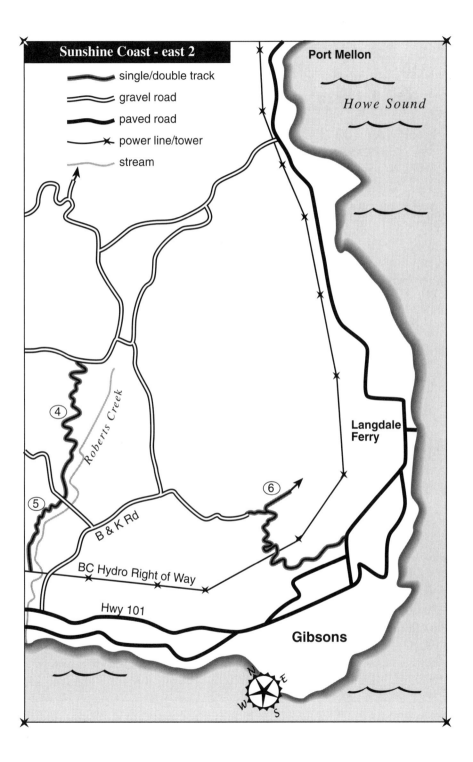

Sunshine Coast - east 2

single/double track
gravel road
paved road
power line/tower
stream

Port Mellon

Howe Sound

④

Roberts Creek

⑤

⑥

B & K Rd

BC Hydro Right of Way

Hwy 101

Langdale Ferry

Gibsons

N E
W S

HIGHWAY 102 (INTERMEDIATE - DIFFICULT)

This is trail is the quintessential Sunshine Coast trail. It's beautiful, well built and serves a greater purpose as a connector for many of the local trails. Thanks in part to this trail, it is now possible to ride from Gibsons to Sechelt on trails only. The Highway 102 trail is rideable in both directions, although the climb is a little tough. This trail features beautiful bridges, some fun log rides and it is usually rideable year round. It is accessed from the Sprockids Mountain Bike Park just west of the Langdale ferry. Go through the park to the SIDEWINDER trail and ride it west to the HIGHWAY 102 trail, which will bring you to the now deactivated B&K FSR (forest service road). Turn right and climb 200 meters to reach the access for the HIGHWAY 103 trail on your left.

HIGHWAY 103 (INTERMEDIATE)

This is another great functional trail that is very fun to ride. It has a mostly level grade, and beautiful bridge crossings that will leave you wondering how the backcountry carpenters do it. Not only is it a great section on a long ride, it serves to connect the Gibsons trails to those in the Roberts Creek area. Access it from the HIGHWAY 102 trail by turning right after reaching the B&K FSR and then climb for about 200 meters or so to reach the trailhead for 103 on the left.

GUY'S GULCH (INTERMEDIATE)

This is a great downhill from the highpoint of your traverse across the mountain. Acts as a natural extension of HWY. 103.

WAGON ROAD (EASY)

This is an old access road that was used by wagons in the early 1900's. It is a fun trail for anybody because of its fast, rolling, and mossy terrain. The Wagon Road is a combination of single and doubletrack that will carry you further across the mountain without dropping much vertical. This can be a busy multi-use trail because it connects with many other roads and trails in the area, so watch out for horses, hikers and motorbikes. To access Wagon Road from GUY'S GULCH, simply keep right when you reach the cross-trail intersection just before you hit the logging road. And then keep right

Hot Rides.
Different flavours.

check out our all new line-up at your
authorized Brodie Dealer or visit us online
@ **www.brodiebikes.com**

brodie

North Shore Born & Bred. Fifteen Years Young & Randy.

ROCKY MOUNTAIN BICYCLES.
DESIGNED TO GET YOU FROM A TO C
AND IF NECESSARY, SURVIVE B.

RIDE THE DIFFERENCE

visit your local Rocky Mountain dealer

1 866 600 1181
CALL TOLL FREE ANYWHERE IN NORTH AMERICA

SIMON'S BIKE SHOP

SALES

SERVICE

RENTALS

THE WORLD'S LARGEST ROCKY MOUNTAIN DEALER

www.simonsbikeshop.com

608 ROBSON STREET   VANCOUVER   BC   V6B 2B9

(604) 602 1181

again on all forks. To access it from Sechelt or Gibsons, take Hwy. 101 to the B&K FSR (at Cliff Gilker Park) and climb it, following all major left forks until you reach the old double and singletrack WAGON ROAD. To reach the FIVE STEPS trails from WAGON ROAD, keep right at the major intersections and forks while traversing across the mountain.

THE FIVE STEPS (EASY - INTERMEDIATE)

This is actually a series of five trails that can be connected together to make one long downhill. They get progressively faster the further down you go. Start at the top with the FIFTH STEP by riding to the west end of WAGON ROAD or by riding up the B&K FSR then going left on the ROBERTS FLUME (aka CLACK CREEK) FSR and proceeding to the very end. This brings you to the bottom of the FOURTH STEP. To reach the top of the Fourth Step, follow the right hand spur road just before the end of the Roberts Flume FSR and take the trailhead on the left hand side near the top. Because all of these trails flow together like one long trail, you're never more than a few pedal strokes away from the next trailhead when you reach an intersecting road. Follow the THIRD, SECOND and FIRST STEPS all the way to Hwy 101, finishing just west of Roberts Creek Provincial Park, which is a great spot to camp while in the area.

WILSON CREEK/ DAKOTA FOREST SERVICE RD (EASY - INTERMEDIATE)

This is a great ride for catching some incredible views of the Straight of Georgia and the surrounding mountains. It's a grunt on the way up, but a scream on the way down. This is an ACTIVE LOGGING ROAD so watch for trucks and ride with caution. Access this ride from Hwy. 101, about 6 KMS south of Sechelt between Field Road and Blower Road.

OLD CANFOR MAINLINE (EASY)

This is a spur road that branches off of the Wilson / Dakota FSR. It features some gentle climbs and superb views. It can provide access to Chapman Creek trails. To access this ride, take the left fork at about the 1 KM mark of the Wilson / Dakota FSR. The top of the road is gated, with trails continuing higher, and crossing Chapman Creek.

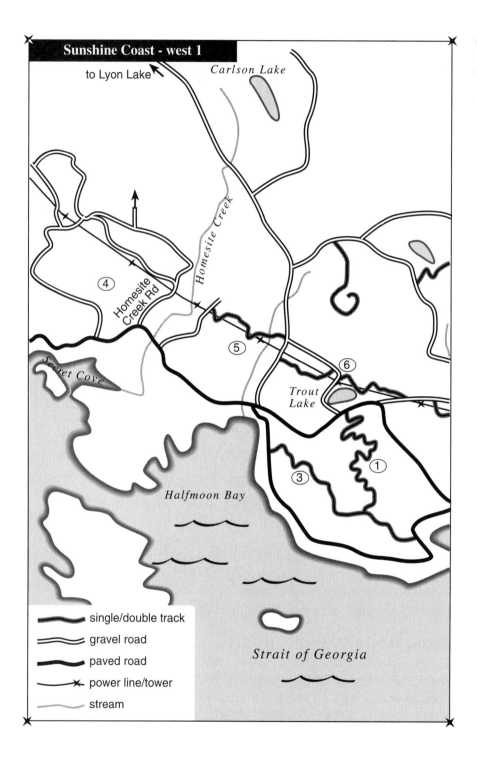

Sunshine Coast - west 1

to Lyon Lake

Carlson Lake

Homesite Creek

④

Homesite Creek Rd

Secret Cove

⑤

⑥

Trout Lake

①

③

Halfmoon Bay

single/double track

gravel road

paved road

power line/tower

stream

Strait of Georgia

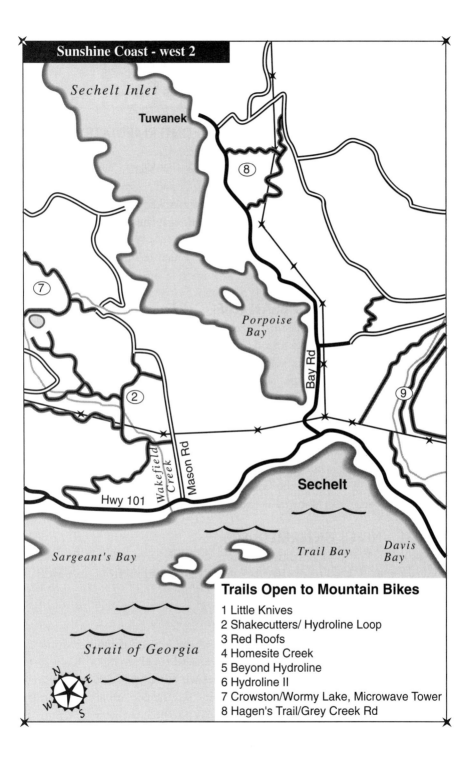

Sunshine Coast - west 2

Sechelt Inlet

Tuwanek

⑧

⑦

Porpoise Bay

Bay Rd

②

⑨

Wakefield Creek

Mason Rd

Sechelt

Hwy 101

Sargeant's Bay

Trail Bay

Davis Bay

Strait of Georgia

Trails Open to Mountain Bikes
1 Little Knives
2 Shakecutters/ Hydroline Loop
3 Red Roofs
4 Homesite Creek
5 Beyond Hydroline
6 Hydroline II
7 Crowston/Wormy Lake, Microwave Tower
8 Hagen's Trail/Grey Creek Rd

UPPER /LOWER CHAPMAN CREEK (INTERMEDIATE)

Fun winding singletrack that parallels Chapman Creek. Access Upper Chapman Ck. Trail by taking Field Rd. just east of Sechelt, which turns into Wilson Creek FSR, then following the left fork and continue past the Sechelt Airport. At the fork just past the airport, keep left and continue to climb the FSR until you reach the old clearcut near the dam on Chapman Creek. The trail starts at the top of the dam just above the falls. Cross the powerlines and continue down to the Lower Chapman Creek trail. This will drop you onto Hwy. 101.

MEXICAN JUMPING BEAN (DIFFICULT)

An old Sunshine Coast classic. It's rough and rocky, but quite a fun ride down to the Clack Creek FSR. Access from Hwy. 101 is via the B&K FSR. Climb the FSR from Hwy. 101 at Roberts Creek until the first major left fork about 1.5 KMS. At the next major fork, about 1 KM later, keep right. The trailhead for the Jumping Bean is on the left about 600 meters past the fork.

BRODIE RACE TRAIL (INTERMEDIATE)

A great ride up or a fun cruise down. Climb the B&K FSR to the Clack Creek FSR and drop into the first trailhead on the left. This drops down to the powerline road. Many trails exist in this area. Explore and enjoy.

LITTLE KNIVES (INTERMEDIATE)

This trail is best ridden from Trout Lake down to Sargeant's Bay Prov. Park. Access the trailhead from Hwy. 101 directly across from Trout Lake west of Sechelt.

SHAKECUTTERS (INTERMEDIATE)

This is an enjoyable loop in either direction with a good climb at the start. To access from Sechelt, drive west to Mason Rd. and turn right. Go left at Norwest Bay Rd. and park by the West Sechelt Store. Continue climbing Mason Rd., taking a right at the yellow gate past the powerlines. Once through the gate, take your first left then keep right at the next fork and continue to climb the Shakecutters trail. This will bring you to an FSR descent. Be sure to watch out for the hairpin left that will bring you on to the Hydroline Trail, which leads back down to Norwest Bay Road.

HOMESITE CREEK (INTERMEDIATE)

This is a great area for intermediate riders to "rip it up" and feel at home. A good climb with lots of riding under the powerlines, and a downhill that will curl your toenails. Head west of Sechelt to Homesite Creek FSR and park. Climb the FSR until it meets the powerline road and then climb it to the top, where it meets Homesite Creek FSR again. Go left, pass under the powerlines again and enjoy a gripping downhill to Hwy. 101.

local knowledge

tasty bites & frosty pints

Molly's Reach, 647 School Rd., Gibsons (this is a Canadian cultural landmark as it was the shooting location of CBC TV's "The Beachcombers" for 19 years!)
Gilligan's Pub Co. Ltd., 5770 Toredo St., Sechelt
Sun Fish Café, 5530 Wharf St., Suite 114, Sechelt
Gibsons Fish, #2-292 Gower Pt. Rd., Gibsons

camping / shelter

Roberts Creek Prov. Park, about 12 KMS west of Gibsons
Wilson Creek Campground, 4314 Highway 101, just east of Sechelt

off the bike on the sunshine coast

Life on the Sunshine Coast revolves around the ocean, so it's no surprise that the area boast such a long list of things to do around the water. Diving, sailing, kayaking, whale watching, fishing and swimming to name a few. The first inhabitants of this area, the Sechelt people have a long, rich history that is worth a closer look. The Tems Swiya Museum in Sechelt (5555 Hwy. 101) tells the great story of the Sechelt Nation. Drop in to Big Pacific Tourism Information (5571 Nickerson, Sechelt) or visit their website at www.bigpacific.com.

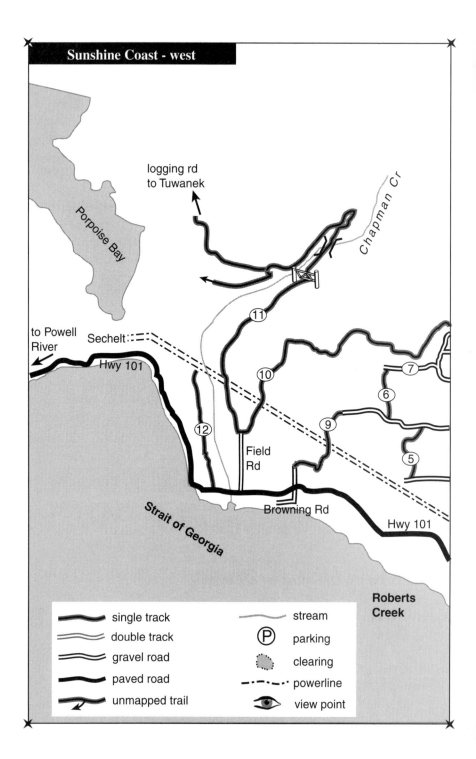

Sunshine Coast - west

Porpoise Bay

logging rd
to Tuwanek

Chapman Cr

to Powell
River

Sechelt

Hwy 101

⑪

⑩

⑦

⑥

⑨

⑫

⑤

Field
Rd

Browning Rd

Hwy 101

Strait of Georgia

Roberts
Creek

	single track		stream
	double track	ⓟ	parking
	gravel road		clearing
	paved road		powerline
	unmapped trail		view point

Trails

1 Highway 102
2 Highway 103
3 Guy's Gulch
4 Wagon Road
5 2nd Step
6 3rd Step
7 4th Step
8 5th Step
9 1st Step
10 Wilson/Dakota Forest Service Rd
11 Old CanFor Mainline
12 Lower Chapman Creek Trail
13 Brodie Race Trails
14 Black Tower Trail

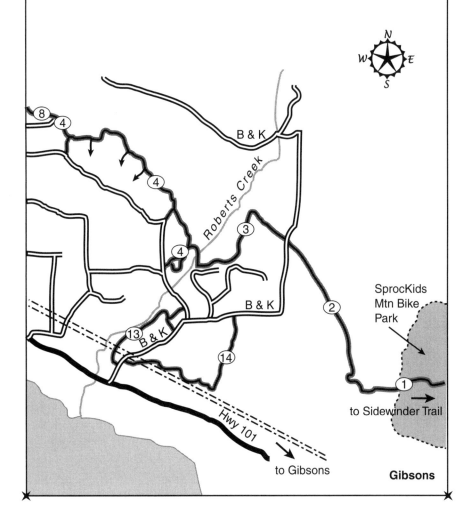

what to expect

The North Sunshine Coast is just two short ferry rides away from Vancouver but it has a soothing west coast island charm, despite being part of the mainland. Much of the riding in this area climbs the coastal mountains on old logging and railway grades. Although some of the climbs can be long, the views of the ocean and islands 4000 feet below are spectacular! Some of the trails in the area use parts of the Sunshine Coast Trail, which stretches 160 km from Saltery Bay in the south almost all the way to Desolation Sound in the north. This trail is a grand undertaking and is a testament to the hard work of the Powell River Parks & Wilderness Society. It is a great complement to the beautiful riding of the area. There are a few new trails in this area. Part of the SUNSHINE COAST TRAIL near Elephant Lakes offers a fun, technical loop for riding. TOASTER is a short, technical loop off of the HAMMIL HILL TRAIL that is worth checking out, as well. If you would like more detailed information on some more of the local trails, drop into see Dean at Taw's Cycle & Sports in Powell River, (604) 485-2555.

trail descriptions

BUNSTER HILLS LOOP (DIFFICULT)

This counter clockwise loop features a 12 km long grind up 750 meters, but the rewards are views of Okeover Inlet and Georgia Straight that make the big push less of a chore. Follow Wilde Rd. north east for 2 km to where the road becomes Theodosia Forest Service Road. Once on this road, the climb begins. Eight km up from Hwy. 101, you will pass the Appleton Creek Trail, but stay on the main road. The Appleton and Marathon Trails cut across the big loop. Once you crest the climb, a 6 km long descent will bring you to an intersection; turn left and follow the road for 3 km to Hwy. 101 and then turn right onto the start of the loop. This loop is on old logging road and is marked with the white mountain bike symbol, or double orange band of paint.

THE INLAND LAKE LOOP (EASY)

This wheelchair accessible loop around Inland Lake is an easy ride for all levels of mountain bikers. The crushed limestone surface has gentle grades and passes by picnic sites and fishing wharfs that beg you to stop and relax. Be aware that this is a busy multi-use trail and respect all other trail users. The Inland Lake area has a trail leading to Powell Lake as well as a trail leading from Inland Lake Rd. to Persen Lake.

MUD LAKE TRAIL SYSTEM (INTERMEDIATE)

Access to the Mud Lake Trail is found by following Hwy. 101, 4 km south of Powell River and then left on Duck Lake Road. Drive or ride 7.5 km to Duck Lake. Turn right at the intersection just before Duck Lake and you'll find a small parking area after 1.5 km. The trail is a circular system at the end of a 2 km access spur.

SWEETWATER CREEK LOOP (INTERMEDIATE)

To access this loop from Duck Lake Rd., turn right just before Duck Lake and left at the first intersection about 2.5 km from the right turn. Take the next left fork and look for the trailhead on the right. The first section of the trail follows an old railroad grade to Sweetwater Creek toward MacGregor Falls. Approximately 1 km up the trail, it crosses a logging road and continues, following along the creek to the summit where Donnelly Falls cascades down the grade. Return down the hill following the same trail but take the branch to the left, and follow the old railway grade back to the main road.

BLUE TRAIL (EASY)

To access this short loop drive or ride 7.5 km up Duck Lake Rd. to the middle of a logged area. You can also access this ride from Fred's Trail in Pleasant Valley. From the recently cut area, backtrack along the road south for 1.5 km. On the right, just before a small quarry you will see a trail leading into the woods, and a short distance later, the old rail bed. Turn right and follow the rail bed 1.5 km past Fred's Trail on the left. Turn right on the marked trail and follow the singletrack 500 meters to a recently logged area. Stay on the trail when it becomes a skid road and descend

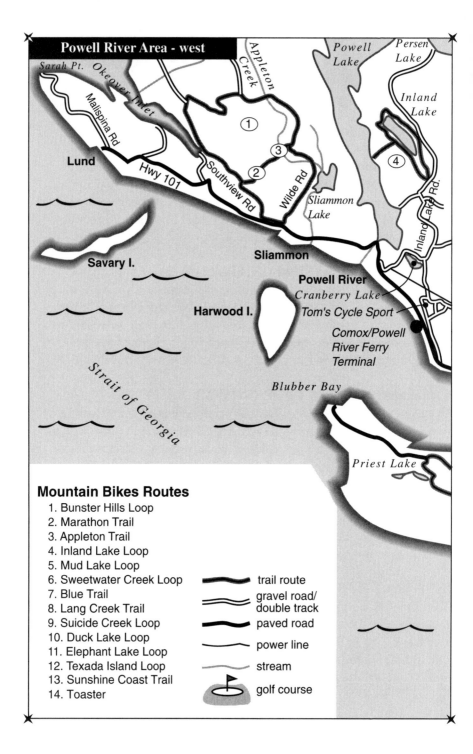

Powell River Area - west

Powell Lake

Persen Lake

Inland Lake

Appleton Creek

Sarah Pt. Okeover Inlet

Malispina Rd

①

③

②

Wilde Rd

Lund

Hwy 101

Southview Rd

Sliammon Lake

④

Inland Lake Rd.

Savary I.

Sliammon

Powell River

Cranberry Lake

Harwood I.

Tom's Cycle Sport

Strait of Georgia

Comox/Powell River Ferry Terminal

Blubber Bay

Priest Lake

Mountain Bikes Routes
   1. Bunster Hills Loop
   2. Marathon Trail
   3. Appleton Trail
   4. Inland Lake Loop
   5. Mud Lake Loop
   6. Sweetwater Creek Loop
   7. Blue Trail
   8. Lang Creek Trail
   9. Suicide Creek Loop
   10. Duck Lake Loop
   11. Elephant Lake Loop
   12. Texada Island Loop
   13. Sunshine Coast Trail
   14. Toaster

～～ trail route

＝＝ gravel road/ double track

━━ paved road

── power line

～ stream

🚩 golf course

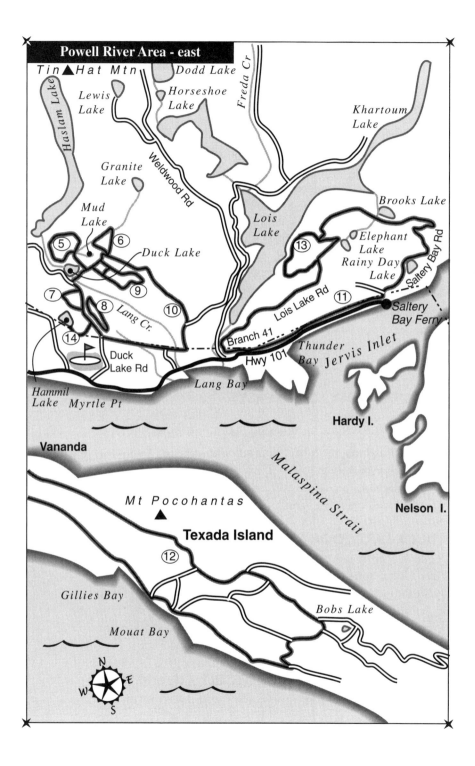

Powell River Area - east

back to the start. Trail markers should lead the way. This trail was built by the Ministry of Forests in conjunction with a federal government employment assistance program. The local Junior Forest Warden Club provided signs along the trail, which relate to the "Powell River Demonstration Forest Blue Tour" brochure.

LANG CREEK LOOP (INTERMEDIATE)
Drive or ride 6 km up Duck Lake Rd. to a trail marker on the right. You can also access this ride from Fred's Trail via the Blue Trail. This ride has some of the best singletrack in the area and has a few steep pitches leading down to the Land Creek Recreation Site. The southern part of the trail features easy, shallow grades on an old rail bed. This loop is marked with a double band of orange paint. Be sure and look for the returning salmon in September and October.

SUICIDE CREEK LOOP (EASY)
To access this trail, turn off at the intersection just before Duck Lake and follow along to a small parking area about 1.5 km further. This route heads in a southeast direction following an old rail grade. Two connector re-routes have been built to avoid two bridges and rough terrain. Two waterfalls and a picnic site will tempt you off your bike. The route is marked with orange squares and the small mountain bike symbol.

DUCK LAKE LOOP (INTERMEDIATE)
This longer loop combines the powerlines with Duck Lake Rd. and makes for a long, non-technical ride where you can explore many of the area's shorter loops. From the powerlines on Duck Lake Rd., ride to the intersection just before the lake. Keep right at the next 3 forks, and left onto the main road 300 meters after the gravel pit. The next turn will be right onto the powerline road and a return to the start.

ELEPHANT LAKE LOOP (DIFFICULT – due to length)
For those mountain bikers who want a long day tour with outstanding views, while riding exclusively on old logging roads, this is your ride.

Access the loop at the Saltry Bay ferry terminal, or at the intersection of Hwy. 101 and the M&B main.

From the ferry terminal, follow the Saltry Bay FSR west for 300 meters until a steep fork goes left. This is the start of an 8 km climb. Keep right at the first fork. Continue past Rainy Day Lake and the steep rocky switchback until the view of Jervis Inlet forces you off the bike. At the bottom of a steep downhill turn, stay left on the main road. Views abound on the long downhill. At the bottom there is a gate; go left onto the M&B mainline. If you go right, it leads to Lois Lake Forest Service Recreation Site. Go left at the mainline and left again onto Hwy. 101 to return to Saltry Bay. If this sounds confusing, follow the bike symbol or a double band of yellow or red paint markers.

TEXADA ISLAND (EASY – INTERMEDIATE)

This all day off road tour of the island is accessible by ferry. It is possible to camp overnight at Bob's Lake or Shingle Beach and make this a two-day tour. It is recommended that you leave your car in Powell River.

Start at the Esso station and ride northeast into Vanada. Leave the town on High Rd. and ride 16 km past Pocahontas Bay intersection and School Road where the road becomes Bell Road. Follow Bell 4 km to an intersection marked "B.C. Hydro Reactor" and follow the right fork for 5 km to another intersection. Take the right fork to a Hydro Sub-station. Bob's Lake Recreation Site is accessible by the left fork. At the sub-station, keep left around the fence and follow for 5 km. This is a steep and sketchy section. At the bottom, the left fork leads to Shingle Beach. To continue the loop, stay on the main road. Finish the loop by following Davie Bay Rd. through Gillies Bay, 21 km to the Esso station.

local knowledge

tasty bites & frosty pints
Rocky Mountain Pizza & Bakery Co., 4471 Marine Ave., (604) 485-9111
Red Lion Pub, 5987 Lund St., (604) 483-9081

camping / shelter
Sea Breeze Cabins & Campsite, (604) 487-9534
Kent's Beach, 2.5 kms north of Saltery Bay, (604) 487-9386

off the bike in powell river
The Powell River area is home to BC's largest marine park, Desolation
Sound Marine Park, which is only an 11 km boat ride away. The park
features a glacier-carved fjord surrounded by 7000 ft. peaks that rise
straight from the ocean. Divers from around the world are attracted to the
clear waters off Powell River for the abundant, colorful marine life as well
as old wrecks. There are about 20 world-class dive sites within a few
kilometers of the town. Contact one of the local dive shops to sample the
briny deeps. (Don's Dive Shop (604) 485-7609)

Sea kayaking is the obvious choice here if you're looking for alternatives to
mountain biking. Powell River Sea Kayak, (604) 483-2410, offers one day
and multi-day tours as well as rentals. This is definitely one of the best
ways to explore this area.

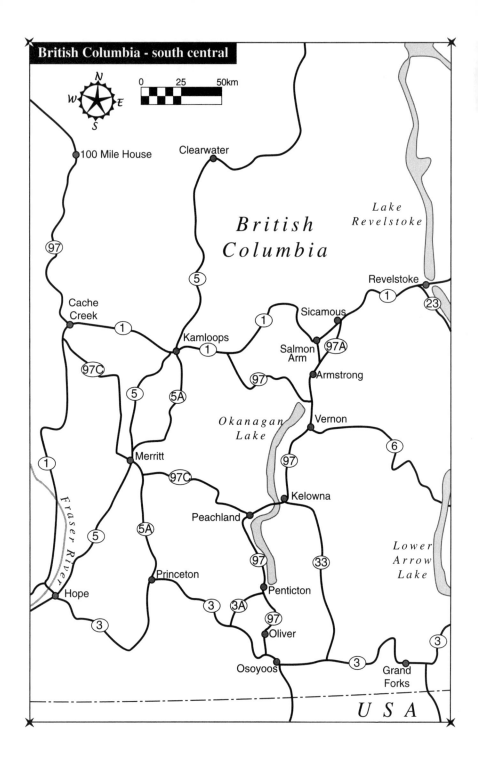

British Columbia - south central

what to expect

This area is home to Canada's only pocket desert and is really very unique in this country. The desert surrounding Oliver and Osoyoos is a continuation of the Sonora Desert that extends all the way to Mexico. It hosts a range of plants and animals found nowhere else in Canada. It should be no surprise then that the riding in this area should be unique as well. The International Bicycling & Hiking Society Trail, (IBHS trail) skirts along the river in Oliver and offers great views and a relaxing spin on a gravel path. Although it's not really a mountain bike sort of trail, it's worth a visit if you're in the area. If nothing else, it's a great leg-stretcher on a road trip. In the Osoyoos area, there are plenty of doubletrack rides through the grasslands above the desert. Desert riding is fantastic and both of these areas serve up a small taste of it and are definitely worth the trip.

trail descriptions

THE I.B.H.S. TRAIL

The International Bicycling & Hiking Society trail is a flat, wide gravel path that doesn't typify the usual mountain bike trail, however it's setting is outstanding and should not be missed if you're in the area. It takes only an hour to ride it out and back. It runs along the river from Osoyoos Lake past Oliver and ends on a road connecting to Hwy. 97. It has several entry/exit points along the way.

OSOYOOS WEST BENCH TRAILS

A great network of beat up old jeep roads and singletrack is located on the east facing slopes overlooking the Osoyoos Golf & Country Club, and the town of Osoyoos. To access the trails, follow the signs toward the golf course, turning left on Fairwinds, and park at the first cattle gate. The trails are generally steep doubletrack that are scattered all over the hillside. The higher you climb, the steeper the trails become. This is the type of area where you just ride and explore. The views of the valley and lake are excellent.

local knowledge

tasty bites & frosty pints
The Ridge Brewing Co, Osoyoos,
(250) 495-7679
Ye Olde Welcome Inn, 39008 97th
St, Oliver, BC

photo: www.freeriders.org

camping / shelter
Haynes Point Provincial Park, 2 km south of Osoyoos off Hwy 97 onto
32nd Avenue. This is a beautiful park located on Osoyoos Lake.

off the bike in the desert
While the desert sun is baking your brain, you may experience temporary
hallucinations. You could hang out and just enjoy them in the sun all day or
you could visit the Pocket Desert Reserve, take a winery tour, see the
Vaseaux Lake Bird Sanctuary, or try an ostrich farm tour, just make sure
you wear a hat and sunscreen, the vultures get hungry 'round here. Talk to
the nice folks at the Osoyoos Travel Info Centre, Box 227, Osoyoos, B.C.,
V0H 1V0, (250) 495-7142.

Photo: Lyle Knight

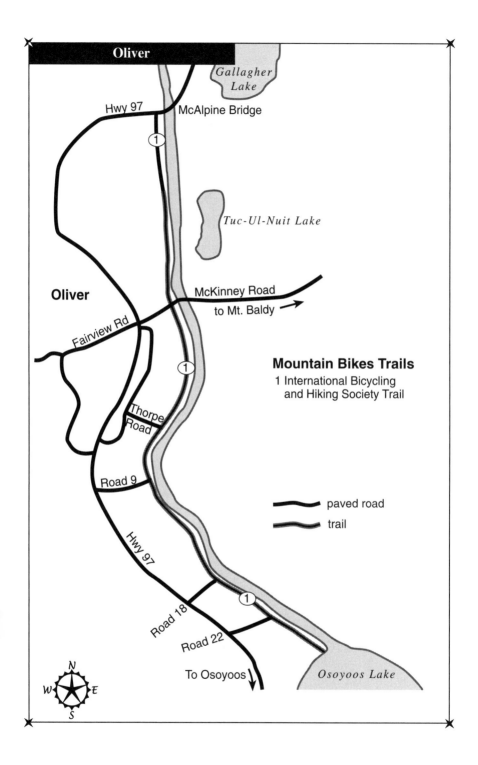

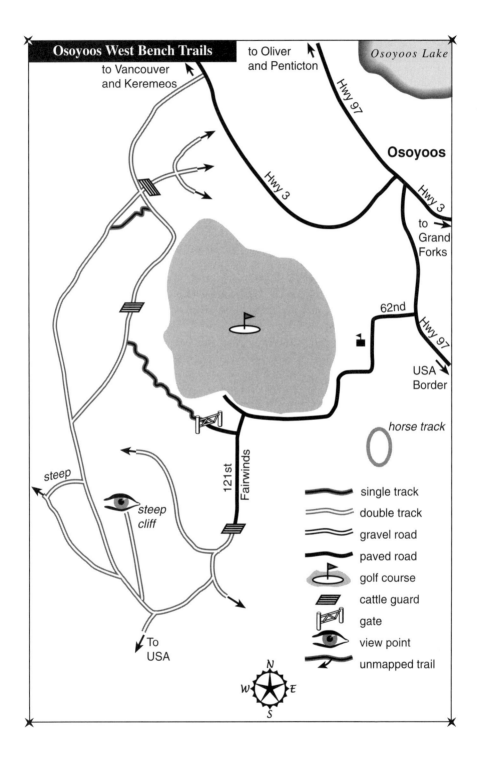

Osoyoos West Bench Trails

to Vancouver
and Keremeos

to Oliver
and Penticton

Osoyoos Lake

Hwy 97

Osoyoos

Hwy 3

Hwy 3

to
Grand
Forks

Hwy 3

62nd

Hwy 97

USA
Border

horse track

121st

Fairwinds

steep

*steep
cliff*

To
USA

single track

double track

gravel road

paved road

golf course

cattle guard

gate

view point

unmapped trail

N

W   E

S

what to expect

Just when you thought there couldn't possibly be anymore five star trails in the Okanagan, you stumble onto Penticton's stellar network of singletracks. In the past, you could have easily driven by this little known riding destination filled up the car with fruit, swerved by a few triathletes weaving down highway 97 and kept on moving. However, today fast, fun & flowing singletrack trails are sprouting here like weeds in a rental-home garden. Typically, the trails here meander through well-spaced pine and fir forests and offer excellent views of Lake Okanagan and Skaha Lake. Rides like PEAT BOG will challenge those looking for vertical adventures and the trails of THREE BLIND MICE are so close to town that they just beg to be explored. Wherever your choices take you, you're bound to open the throttle a little wider on some of the Okanagan's best intermediate singletrack. Drop in to Freedom Bikes, 533 Main St., (250) 493-0686, for more detailed information and to share some trail tales.

trail descriptions

THREE BLIND MICE TRAILS (INTERMEDIATE – DIFFICULT)

"Three blind mice, see how they ride." You could spend all day exploring the fun singletrack loops here with the smell of Ponderosa pines filling the air. Open glades and shady groves typify much of this area. You'll want to stop and drink in the views of the lakes below while exploring these fun trails. Expect to find predominantly cross-country style riding with some testy little rock ridges and chutes to keep you on your toes. Technical climbs abound here, so eat your Wheaties and give them a try. Watch out for rattlesnakes, they love it here too!

To access this area, ride north out of Penticton on Naramata Rd. (see map) for about 5 KMS to Riddle Road on your right. Climb this road, passing the Kettle Valley Railway on your way up. Ride all the way up to the Pearly Gate, (white cattle gate), proceeding through it, but PLEASE REMEMBER TO CLOSE THE GATE. Cattle have been getting loose here and it only jeopardizes the access to these trails. Once through the gate, the trails begin to wind northward. Many side trails and intersections exist here, but they all come back to the start. It's fun and easy exploring this riding area.

SUMMERLAND RACE COURSE (INTERMEDIATE)

This area has some beautiful singletrack. So nice, in fact, that Cycling BC chose it as the venue for the Summerland BC Cup cross country race. The course has over 90% of that classic Okanagan hardpack singletrack with just the right amount of "moondust" on top. The terrain is varied and has a few punchy climbs that'll get you wheezing. Watch out for cattle, they're thicker than you are.

To access these trails, take Hwy. 97 north from Penticton for about 15 KMS to Summerland. Take a left off of the main highway at Rosedale Avenue. As Rosedale bends to the right, it becomes Prairie Valley Road. Follow this to Morrow Ave. and take a right. Go to the end of Morrow Ave. and take a left, following this until you reach a gate. This is the start of the loop. As this a BC Cup cross country racecourse, you have three options for length. Keep right at the first singletrack split and follow all subsequent right-handers until you've reached Prairie Valley Rd. again. This loop is about 20 KMS. For a slightly longer ride of about 26 KMS, avoid

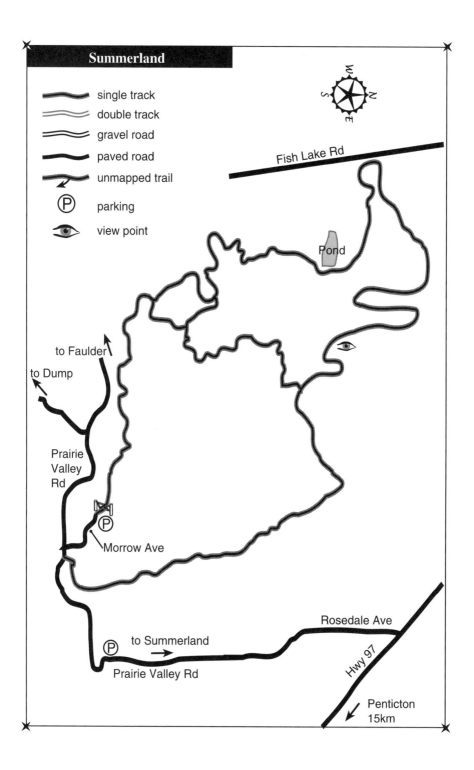

the first right and take the second right fork, then follow the main singletrack route back to Prairie Valley Road. The elite loop of about 40 KMS can be ridden by keeping left at the major singletrack intersections.

ELLIS RIDGE (INTERMEDIATE)

Over 2000 feet above Penticton, winding through the tall Ponderosa pines is a trail that epitomizes what singletrack should be. Ellis Ridge is a fantastic trail that follows a south facing canyon wall and offers amazing views of the lake and valley far below. It's not too long, not too difficult and in the heat of the summer, it's usually nice and cool.

To access this trail, turn off Main St. on to Carmi Avenue at the Dairy Queen. As the road begins to climb higher into the hills, there will be a right hand turn with a sign for the XC ski area. Turn right here and continue past the cattle guard for about 3 KMS to the parking lot at the XC ski area and park your car. The trail takes off from here and a left turn puts you onto the singletrack. You'll probably quickly realize why this is an awesome trail, so take your time and enjoy the impeccable views and brilliant meandering singletrack. After a steep climb, be sure to go left because there is more to enjoy. The ride will finish at the cattle guard that you drove past. This can be ridden from town in one, great 27 KM loop. You should be very proud of yourself if you ride up to enjoy this. The PEAT BOG downhill is up in this area, but you'll need a personal guided tour if you haven't ridden it before. Drop in to see the folks at Freedom Bikes, 533 Main St., (250) 493-0686 for the juicy details.

local knowledge

tasty bites & frosty pints
Hog's Breath Coffee Co., 202 Main St.
Gun Barrell Grill, #205-399 Main St.

camping / shelter
Waterworld, 185 Yorkton, (250) 492-4255
Cedarbrook Campground, 5011 Hwy. 97, Summerland, (250) 494-0911

off the bike in penticton
Penticton boasts one of the best rock climbing destinations in North America. Climbers come from all over Canada and the USA to pull on the beautiful rock at the Skaha climbing area. Skaha has just recently been granted park status, thus protecting the beautiful gneiss bluffs set amid a mature pine forest. There are guides and outfitters in town who offer hourly or daily trips up to the bluffs above Skaha Lake. (Skaha Rock Adventures, 250- 493-1765.) For a real taste of local fun, I highly recommend a trip up to the Stock Car Oval on Carmi Ave. on the weekends. Meet the locals and watch cars drive in circles at insane speeds; you can't beat it, (250 490-0420). With 2 big, beautiful lakes, life on the water is natural and easy in Penticton. Head down to the beach on Skaha Lake for some sun or charter a houseboat for the day, the weekend or the week, (Okanagan Boat Charters, 1-800-524-2212).

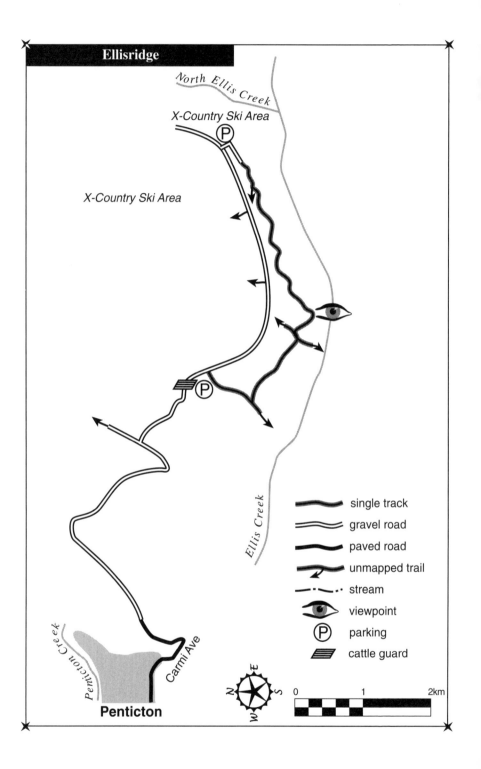

Ellisridge

North Ellis Creek

X-Country Ski Area

X-Country Ski Area

Ellis Creek

Penticton Creek

Carmi Ave

Penticton

single track
gravel road
paved road
unmapped trail
stream
viewpoint
Ⓟ parking
cattle guard

N

0   1   2km

what to expect

Kelowna is a great riding destination in the heart of the Okanagan. It has
five different riding areas within a short distance of the city center as well
as one huge, beautiful lake at its doorstep. I used to think that Kelowna
was the native word for 'strip mall', but then I started riding here and
found out that it may mean "really fun, fast singletrack". (It actually means
'Grizzly Bear') The city really does have a lot of beautiful places to hang
out and relax. Most of these are by the lakeshore. As with many areas in
BC, the riding community in Kelowna is growing fast and along with it,
grows the network of trails. The most prolific building is happening in the
Crawford area, south of town. Kelowna is conveniently located in the
center of the Okanagan, making it a great place to stop and ride on your
tour of the area. For more detailed information drop in to Fresh Air
Experience (2070 Harvey St.) and pick up one of the Kelowna Mtn. Bike
Club's detailed maps.

trail descriptions

OKANAGAN MOUNTAIN PARK (INTERMEDIATE)

This park is a perfect example of Okanagan riding, fast, open and hot
with continuous lake and valley views. The park boasts a full 10,000
hectares of grasslands and spruce-fir forests with winding, hard-pack

Photo: Lyle Knight

singletrack with no motorized access, which means wide-open spaces for the adventurous rider. There are some really amazing loops through this park that offer fantastic views of Lake Okanagan.

To access this park, take Pandosy St. south from Hwy. 97 to Lakeshore Dr. and park about 1 km after the pavement ends. Consult a park map at the entrance for detailed trail information.

BOULDER TRAIL (INTERMEDIATE)

The Boulder Trail is a short, steep loop, which is mostly rocky technical singletrack. The trail features some testy little climbs, heart pounding drops and numerous white-knuckle sections. BOULDER TRAIL is common with the COMMANDO BAY TRAIL until the top of Dead Horse Creek Hill. The Commando Bay Trail goes straight while the Boulder Trail goes left, looping back to where you started. This is a popular hiking trail as well, so please ride with caution.

COMMANDO BAY TRAIL (INTERMEDITATE)

This is a long out-and-back ride that takes you into the heart of Okanagan Mountain Park. The ride is mostly on loose, rocky doubletrack with the last 1.6 kms being technical singletrack. Sections of Wild Horse Canyon can be very hot in the summer and flooded in the spring. Despite the flooding, it is usually possible to make it through.

From the parking lot, ride down the road 1.7 kms and turn where you see a metal gate on the left. This rocky doubletrack is an old pioneering road that was used to connect early valley residents. At Dead Horse Creek, turn right to cross the bridge and climb the long hill. At the top, go straight, or take the singletrack to the right, which loops back to the road. From here, the trail goes through Wild Horse Canyon and is fast, rolling and very fun. At the end of the canyon, go right toward Buchan and Commando Bays. The singletrack to Commando bay is on the left. This trail is steep and rocky down to the beach. Explore the First Nations petroglyphs on the

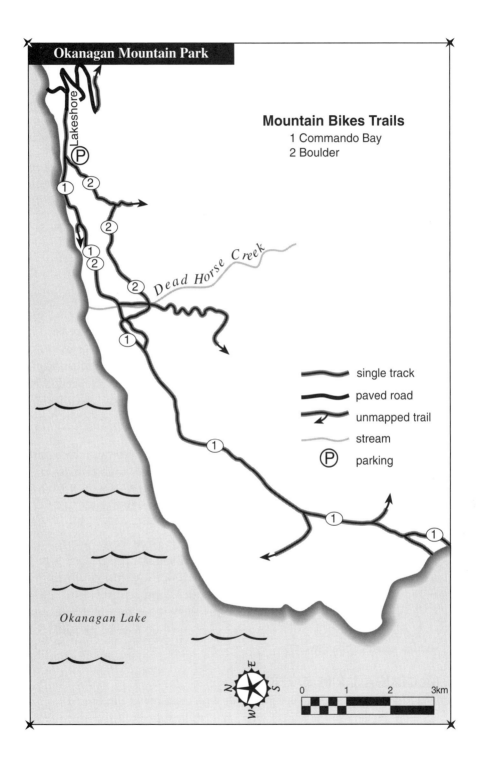

Okanagan Mountain Park

Lakeshore

(P)

Mountain Bikes Trails
1 Commando Bay
2 Boulder

Dead Horse Creek

single track	
paved road	
unmapped trail	
stream	
(P) parking	

Okanagan Lake

N E S W

0   1   2   3km

rocks above the beach. Also, check out the plaque at the end of the beach commemorating the role this area played in W.W.II.

Ride options include staying on the doubletrack down to Buchan Bay. Also, check out the view from the RIM TRAIL, which is on the right about three quarters of the way through Wild Horse Canyon. On the return trip, the Boulder Trail can add some distance and technical challenges to the ride.

KETTLE VALLEY RAILWAY – MYRA CANYON (EASY)

The Kettle Valley Railway (KVR) is an abandoned railway line that runs for 600 kms across south central BC. The rails and ties have long since been removed, leaving a smooth, near constant 3% grade which passes over many trestles and tunnels. Several bike magazines have rated it as among the "top 25 bike tours in the world". The 20 km Myra Canyon section of the route is perhaps the most spectacular, passing over almost 20 trestles,

Photo: Klaus Gattner

some of which are well over 300 feet high.

To access this route from Orchard Park in Kelowna, take Benvoulin Rd. to K.L.O. Rd., then McCollough Rd. to June Springs Road. When the pavement ends, June Springs Rd. becomes Little White FSR. While driving or riding up this road, be sure to veer left 3 km after the pavement has ended, coming to a parking pull out about 1.2 km after this left. The KVR is on your left. Myra Canyon begins about 4 km from the parking area. Since the KVR is at an elevation of about 4000 feet, be prepared for sudden weather changes.

McDOUGALL RIM (DIFFICULT)

The McDougal Rim Trail is a great ride with challenging climbs and winding singletrack that snakes through typically varied Okanagan terrain.

The first half of the ride is steep doubletrack climbing that will test your endurance, but remember: what goes up must have a great time coming down. Snow will linger until late May and possible appear in early October.

To access the trail, take Hwy. 97 south from Kelowna and turn right at Bartly Road. Park at the McDougal Rim trailhead and ride down the road. Turn right on the doubletrack just before the bridge on McDougal Creek. At the 3rd switchback, about 8.5 kms up, take the doubletrack straight ahead. Continue past the first doubletrack to the right which comes in at a 45° angle, and take the second overgrown doubletrack to the right. This doubletrack comes to a junction after 400 meters and changes to a singletrack. At the junction, turn right and continue past the weather recording station on the left and downhill until you reach the next major viewpoint where the trail briefly turns to a doubletrack. Shortly past the mud holes, take the singletrack to the left. This section of the trail will descend to the trailhead and is likely to have hikers on it so please don't hit them as it makes for messy situations.

CRAWFORD AREA TRAILS (INTERMEDIATE – DIFFICULT – EXTREME)

The Crawford area is the most popular riding area around Kelowna. It has seen the most furious fits of trail building over the last few years with many man made structures as well as creative rock drops that will curl your toe nails. Because this area is so intensely infested with singletrack, it proves to be difficult to map and is out of the scope of this book. It is recommended that you drop into Fresh Air Experience, #18-2070 Harvey Ave., to pick up a map and get a more detailed description of this great area.

If you're the adventurous type and would just prefer to head on out there and get lost, you can reach it by following Benvoulin Rd. from Orchard Park Mall to Casorso Road, which becomes Bedford Road. Turn onto Stuart Rd. East and fork near the power station. The Lost Lake Trail veers left into the trees ahead on the uphill side of a clearing. Many other trails will braid off of these trails so good luck and have fun. This may be the best place to "smoke yer noggin' in the Okanagan" so make sure your helmet fits and you or your buddies & buddiesses know first aid.

local knowledge

tasty bites & frosty pints

Bohemian Bagel Café, 363 Bernard Ave.
Doc Willoughby's Downtown Grill, 353 Bernard Ave.

camping / shelter

Kelowna International Hostel, 2343 Pandosy St., (250) 763-6024

off the bike in kelowna

The climate and soil conditions grow some dam fine grapes and other soft and hard fruits. To sample some of natures fruits, I recommend taking a hot afternoon off and taking a wine tour. Try Cedar Creek Estate Winery (5445 Lakeshore Rd., 250-764-8866), which is one of BC's best, offering tours, tastings and great deals on excellent wine. You'll feel like you've been transported back to the old west when you explore the beautiful grasslands in the rolling hills above Lake Okanagan by horseback (Lake Okanagan Resort Stables, 2751 Westside Rd., 1-800-663-3273). How about a birds-eye view of Lake Okanagan? Kelowna Parasail Adventures (1310 Water St., 250-868-4838) will be the expeditor of all your flying dreams and a great help scouting your next riding adventure from high above.

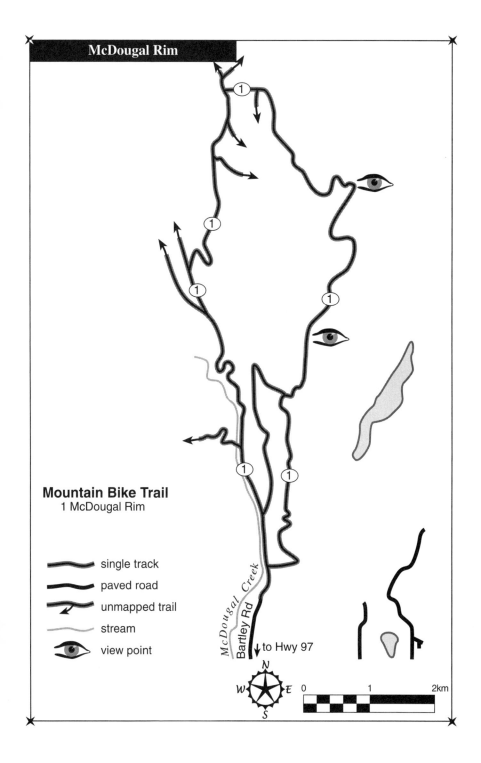

McDougal Rim

① 1

Mountain Bike Trail
1 McDougal Rim

single track
paved road
unmapped trail
stream
view point

McDougal Creek

Bartley Rd

↓ to Hwy 97

N
W ✦ E
S

0   1   2km

vernon

what to expect

You've just finished one of the most beautiful and satisfying rides of your mountain biking life. It was a smooth, fast trail with the

don't mess with the locals

Photo: Tourism Rockies

occasional rock drop for a good scare and postcard perfect grassland vistas at every other corner. You've fought the urge to stop and drink it all in because the desire to keep tearing down the mountain is a strong one. You finish the ride with a short spin to the jade green lake for a refreshing swim… the natural option to cap this ride. Maybe you'll hook up with some friends at one of the charming local coffee shops later on and talk about today's wicked ride and plan tomorrow's. You fall into bed with a grin on your face, anticipating another blue-sky beauty in the morning. Just another day of riding in Vernon.

There are some tough decisions to be made when riding here. Like which 'perfect 10' trail to hit today and which incredible lake to swim in afterwards. It's a rough life here, but you'll do OK if you just read on. For all the juicy details on the great riding spots around Vernon, drop in to see Pete and the folks at Olympia Cycle, 3102-31st Ave., (250) 542-9684.

trail descriptions

COSEN'S BAY TRAILS (INTERMEDIATE - DIFFICULT)

Cosen's Bay has seen the most prolific bout of trail building in recent years in the Vernon area. The trails tend toward the North Shore style with man made stunts such as trestle bridges and ramps; however, these trails connect with the rider on a different level because of their amazing flow. Expect great, loamy singletrack with fun drops and some incredible views of Kalamalka Lake and surrounding hills. Kal Lake has been called "one of the most beautiful lakes in the world", when you come here to ride, you'll see why. The riding area is adjacent to Kalamalka Lake Provincial Park, which has some amazing riding of its own. This area is a great
destination for a full day of
riding and swimming.
To access these trails, from
downtown Vernon, drive south
on 32nd St. or 27th St. until you
reach Hwy. 6 (to Lumby). Turn
left (east) and then left at the gas
station on Kalamalka Lake Road.
Follow Kal Lake Rd. past the
beach, keeping left when the road

Photo: www.freeriders.org

forks at the lake. Follow the blue and white BC Prov. Parks signs to Kalamalka Lake Prov. Park, turning right on Coldstream Creek Road. After Coldstream Creek Rd. makes a right hand turn and passes a wooded creek, make a sharp left onto Cosens Bay Rd. and continue to the park gate.

From the Cosens Bay gate, enjoy a short pleasant spin through the grasslands of the Cosens Valley following the gravel road. After dropping down toward the lake, the road will curve left and begin to climb. Shortly thereafter, a smaller doubletrack veers off to the left and begins climbing again. This doubletrack provides access to most of the trails in this area and trailheads can be seen dropping off of it, as well as depositing onto it. For the best longer rides, climb this road for a few kilometers, until it becomes narrower and you see three trailheads in close proximity, two on the right and one on the left. The first one reached on the left is PURPLE HAZE (difficult), followed by TWISTA (difficult) and 36 DOUBLE D (very difficult), both on the right. All of these trails drop back down to the doubletrack road you climbed. Many options exist once you hit the road. 36 DOUBLE D has great flow, amazing trestles and some fun log rides. TWISTA and PURPLE HAZE have similar flavors. PURPLE HAZE links up perfectly with SPOOKY and EGG SHELLS which bring you further back into Bear Valley and makes for a superb longer ride of up to 3 hours or more. From the end of 36 DOUBLE D, keep right at the pond and climb out of the creek to the doubletrack road, turn right and then left at the first trailhead to access CROSS TOWN TRAFFIC (intermediate), a wickedly fun, fast and turny little romp back down to Cosens Valley and the grassy fields that lead you back to the Cosens Bay gate.

Photo: www.freeriders.org

KALAMALKA LAKE PROVINCIAL PARK (INTERMEDIATE)

Riding in Kalamalka Lake Park in the spring is close to mountain biking Nirvana. There are many kilometers of singletrack that weave through the park. Some are steep climbs; others are flowing, rolling beauties. If you hit this park in the spring, the Black-Eyed Susans are out in full bloom and the weather is usually perfect. Cruising along on immaculate singletrack through flower-filled grasslands above a warm, jade green lake is hard to forget. Bring your camera anyway.

To access these trails from Vernon, head south on 27th St. to Hwy 6. Go left on Hwy. 6 and then take the first right on Kalamalka Lake Rd. Kal Lake Rd. comes to a T intersection at the lake. Go left and following the blue and white Provincial Park signs for Kalamalka Lake. There are two entrances to the park, Kidston Rd. on the west side and Cosen's Bay Rd. on the east side. Cosen's Bay Rd. is off of Coldstream Creek Rd. and is the entrance is the access point for the COSEN'S BAY TRAILS.

off the bike in vernon

How about a swim in a warm, jade green, un-crowded lake near town? Check out Kalamalka Lake Provincial Park (see directions⁻

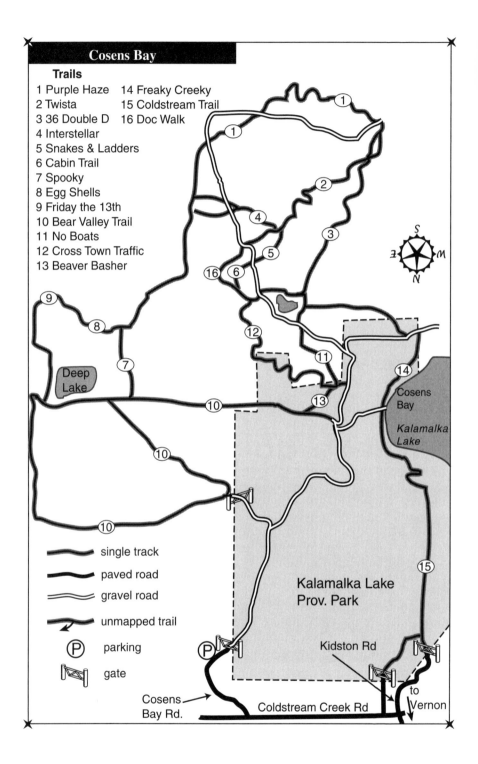

Cosens Bay

Trails

1 Purple Haze
2 Twista
3 36 Double D
4 Interstellar
5 Snakes & Ladders
6 Cabin Trail
7 Spooky
8 Egg Shells
9 Friday the 13th
10 Bear Valley Trail
11 No Boats
12 Cross Town Traffic
13 Beaver Basher
14 Freaky Creeky
15 Coldstream Trail
16 Doc Walk

Deep
Lake

Cosens
Bay

*Kalamalka
Lake*

Kalamalka Lake
Prov. Park

~~~~~~~ single track

▬▬▬▬ paved road

═══════ gravel road

~~~~➤ unmapped trail

Ⓟ parking

⊠ gate

Cosens
Bay Rd.

Kidston Rd

Coldstream Creek Rd

to
Vernon

above) for an idyllic, colorful lake with warm, inviting waters. Aerial tours of the Okanagan are cheap and a great way to suss-out your next riding destination. Okanagan Aviation (1-877-356-6528) offers several different tours at a variety of affordable prices. Innerspace Dive & Kayak (1-877-549-2040) offer kayak rentals and scuba lessons or rentals; two great ways to explore some of the Okanagan's most beautiful lakes. For a more relaxing day, sample some of the stuff that makes the Okanagan Valley famous: wine. Bella Vista Vineyards (1-250-558-0770) offers tours of this beautiful vineyard.

local knowledge

tasty bites & frosty pints
The Italian Kitchen – 2916 30th Ave., (250) 558-7899
The Bean Scene – 2923 30th Ave., (250) 558-1817
Alexander's Beach Pub – 12408 Kalamalka Lake Rd., (250) 545-3131

camping / shelter
Ellison Prov. Park, 16 km from Vernon on Okanagan Lake

SILVER STAR MOUNTAIN

Silver Star is an old haunt of Darrin and myself and has now become a favorite riding destination. The trails around Silver Star Mountain are first rate and will only continue to get better. The mountain now has its own professional trail building crew to create new trails and buff up existing ones.

At over one mile above sea level (6280 ft. at the summit), it's a perfect destination when the summer sun is cooking the valley below. There is a fantastic network of trails up here, which are the legacy of the 1994 Grundig World Cup as well as the hard work and dedication of such fine folks as Dag Abbey (a legend in his own right and worthy of his own book), Peter Dorey, Robin Baycroft, Jaime Morrison, Matt Pinto and a cast of dozens. There's a spot for all of them in mountain bike heaven.

One of the most remarkable trails in this book begins at Silver Star. SPANKY'S can be ridden on its own in a single, superb 13 km downhill extravaganza, or linked up with some of the summit trails on Silver Star Mountain (highly recommended). Ride from the village, to the summit, drink in the view and then ride the gravity train to the valley far below. Take ABERDEEN, DAGAMAL, STITCH and then right across the road into the legendary SPANKY'S and then down, down, down. I guarantee it will be a ride you won't soon forget. This is steep and unrelenting technical singletrack, so mind your noggin'. This is just one of the many things that make Silver Star a fantastic mountain biking destination.

trail descriptions

THE FULL MOUNTAIN TOUR

A recommended route for a great tour of Silver Star Mountain is to start in the village and climb the PARADISE TRAIL to the summit. This trail is a wide, gently graded path that begins right in the village and wraps its way around the back side, eventually winding up on the summit at 6280 feet giving you a 360 degree view of the Thompson Plateau and the Monashee

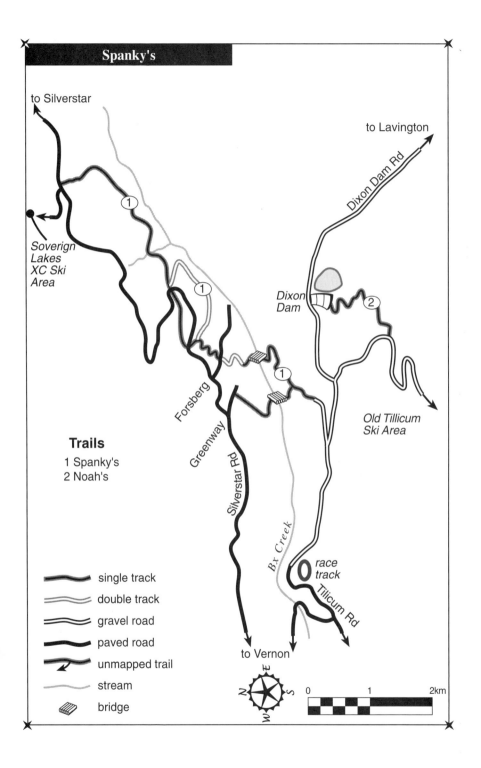

Mountains to the east. You have many options from this point to get you back down to the village. Ride one of Silver Star's famous downhill race courses for a fast, technical drop to the village or continue further west from the summit towards the Attridge trails. This wind-scoured ridge offers incredible views of the village as well as Okanagan and Swan Lakes, over 3000 feet below. From here, continue west, off the backside of Attridge and follow ABERDEEN, which loops around and eventually brings you back to the front side of the mountain via DAGAMAL and GOLD MOUNTAIN and right back into the village. Pick up a detailed map and get more information, from the friendly folks in the kiosk in the center of the village.

SPANKY'S (DIFFICULT)

"The most fun you'll ever have going down." was one of the better descriptions I've heard of this classic BC downhill. It was built by some friends of mine in the early '90's and continues to "spank" even the most skilled riders today. Spanky's drops almost 3000 feet over a twisting, technical 13 km. Much of it is beautiful singletrack, which links old sections of doubletrack. It starts directly across from the Sovereign Lakes XC ski area turn-off of Silver Star Road. Once you ride through the grassy area, the singletrack begins immediately. The trail follows an old powerline for a while and is generally a well-worn path. This section drops you down to the first switchback of Silver Star Road, at which point, you must cross the road, climb up for 100 meters or so and drop into the steep re-entry on the left in the pull-out. This section will parallel Silver Star Rd. for 1 km or so before crossing it and dropping back into the forest. This section will drop you onto Forsberg Road. Cross it and you'll find the doubletrack beginning on the other side immediately. This fast section will take you over BX Creek and up a short, steep climb onto an even faster wooded, double track downhill. Follow the main double track up to a clearing in an old cut block, keep right and follow out the main road as it joins up with Dixon Dam Road. This is the finish rip for Spanky's.

NOAH'S (INTERMEDIATE)

Noah's is a great option to have at the end of SPANKY'S because sometimes 13 kms is just not enough. A bit of climbing will get you to the top of this tight, fun singletrack. On the way down the finishing double track of Spanky's, take the first hard left at a fork in the road and begin climbing. After about 1 km, the road will fork, stay right and look for the entrance to Noah's on the left at the top of a short, steep climb. This trail dumps you out onto the retaining wall of Dixon Dam on Dixon Dam road, which can be ridden back down to Tilicum Rd. and down into Vernon.

local knowledge

tasty bites & frosty pints

Bugaboos –(In the village) great coffee and even better desserts.
The Aberdeen Deli Co. –(In the village) a deli to die for.
The Saloon –(In the village) the obvious choice for pints & pool.

camping / shelter

Silver Star boast the world's first custom built ski in/ski out hostel (Same Sun International) in the village, which is an excellent option for the budget road trip. As of printing, the cost per night is $15 ($19 non members) for a dormitory bed and $35 ($42 non members) for double occupancy private rooms. (250) 545-8933.

off the bike in silver star

Technically you're still on your bike on chair lift runs, but it's a good rest day option, and a viable alternative to pedaling up the 1000 ft of vertical to the summit. Hiking opportunities abound as well as ATV adventures. They even have an indoor rock climbing gym at the National Altitude Training Centre. Consult the friendly, helpful Silver Star-ians who live inside that little round kiosk in the center of the village for heaps of adventure ideas on the mountain. Contact the mountain for reservations or information at 1-800-663-4431 or on the web at: www.silverstarmtn.com.

salmon**arm**

what to expect

"I didn't know they had arms." That was my response when I first heard of this charming little town in BC's North Okanagan. Now I know better. Salmon may not have arms but Salmon Arm has superb mountain biking. The riding scene here is virtually unknown outside of local circles. However, word is spreading. If you've driven by the town a hundred times with your bike on your roof on your way to the Rockies or some other destination, A quick glance at the trails in the area will have you out of the car in a hurry. You'll be reaping the rewards of discovering a new area.

Salmon Arm is located on the shores of Shuswap Lake, which has got to be the houseboat capital of the world. In the summer, people flock to the lake, inhabiting their floating RV's for weeks at a time, just floating the summer away under the towering mountains that teem with superb singletrack…. sounds like the making of a road / float trip to me.

Make sure you drop in to see Jim and the kind folks at Skookum Cycle in Salmon Arm, 416- 4th Street, (250) 832-7368, and thank them for the work they do for the trails in this area.

trail descriptions

RUBBERHEAD (INTERMEDIATE)

To access the Rubberhead, head northeast of Salmon Arm on Hwy. 1 to the Co-op Lumber Mill parking lot. The trail starts climbing between the two lots. You'll reach the FSR (Forest Svc. Rd.) and climb for around 7.5km. When you get to the top of the Rubberhead, you will see two rock cairns on the side of the road on each side of the trailhead. When the road takes a definite switchback to the west and then back east, you're there. The trail goes up for about 500m then begins to hurl you back to earth. It's a super fun trail with stunts and switchbacks and it flows the way a real trail should, like a roller coaster.

PRUDENTIAL (INTERMEDIATE)

To access this trail, drive up 10th avenue and park at the bottom of the Larch Hills Canoe Creek Forest Service Road. The best tour of the area requires you to ride up the main road 1.5 km until a right turn, where a convergence of old roads has a single track going off to the left. This is a very nice trail that reaches a gully about 2 km later. From the gully, a couple of options can make some nice loops; read on.

KATIE / COLIN MEMORIAL TRAIL (DIFFICULT)

Continue climbing the FSR up to about 4 kms and hang a left. About 2 km down it veers left and the fun begins. This trail comes at you with stunts and drops you back onto the FSR where you can easily hook back into the Prudential, Paranoia or Malibu.

At about the 2 km marker on the FSR you'll see a trail dropping in. In about 50m Paranoia branches to the left and goes up past another drop in that comes in from higher up the FSR. It's all downhill form here. Paranoia eventually hooks up with the Prudential making for an alternate start. Well worth the look, it has a 50-foot log ride that will get you puckered.

WHITE LAKE DOWNHILL (INTERMEDIATE - ADVANCED)

This downhill is a wickedly fun, twisty, turny speed-fest. It has a bit of a steep climb to access it, but it is worth every drop of sweat and every swear word uttered on the climb.

To access this trail, take Hwy 1 west from Salmon arm to White Lake Road and turn right. Follow this road until you get to the lake, which you will see on your right. At the intersection, turn right, and follow the road for 200m, where you will see a parking area on your right, across from the church. You can either park here and ride up or shuttle from here. Go back towards the intersection and look to your right, where you will see a fire road (Little White Lake FSR). Follow this road up to the 2.7 km mark, where you will have the option to go straight or right. Go right, and follow the road for 1.1km, where you will see an old fire road going up to

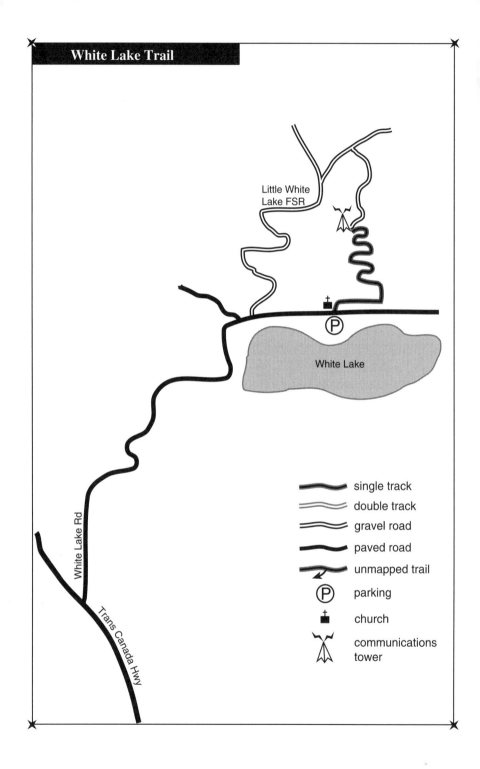

White Lake Trail

Little White
Lake FSR

White Lake

White Lake Rd

Trans Canada Hwy

single track
double track
gravel road
paved road
unmapped trail

Ⓟ parking

✝ church

communications
tower

your right. Take this road to the top (1.2km) to the radio tower. The climb is steep, so take your time. At the tower, if you look over to the left you will see a trail dropping down. This is the trailhead. Follow it all the way down to the church parking lot. There are only a couple turn options near the bottom. Go left and then right, or follow the most used trail. This trail has some steep sections, with a few gnarly rock sections. All in all, a moderate downhill that is mostly tight singletrack at the top, opening to double track near the bottom.

local knowledge

tasty bites & frosty pints

Success Café, 240 Shuswap St. (250) 832-0106
Kelly O'Brien's, 20 Shuswap St. (250) 832-8855

camping / shelter

Shuswap Lake Prov. Park, located on the north shore of the main arm of Shuswap Lake. Exit Hwy #1 at Squilax, and drive 19 km on paved roads.

Glen Echo Resorts, 8 km west of Salmon Arm, cottages & campsites on the lake in a beautiful setting, (250) 832-6268

off the bike in salmon arm

House boating is probably the town's biggest attraction. Shuswap Lake is a deceptively enormous lake with countless bays, coves and several long inlets called "arms", hence the town's name. Combine that geography with a very warm lake, warm summers and great weather and it's easy to see why it is an annual ritual for many. I have partaken in the annual rite of the houseboat trip a number of times and can say that it is one incredible way to relax and enjoy the water. There are several houseboat rental companies in town. Each one takes care of everything but the food and booze. The boats are extremely comfortable and can sleep up to 12. When in town, head down to the lakeshore and check them out.

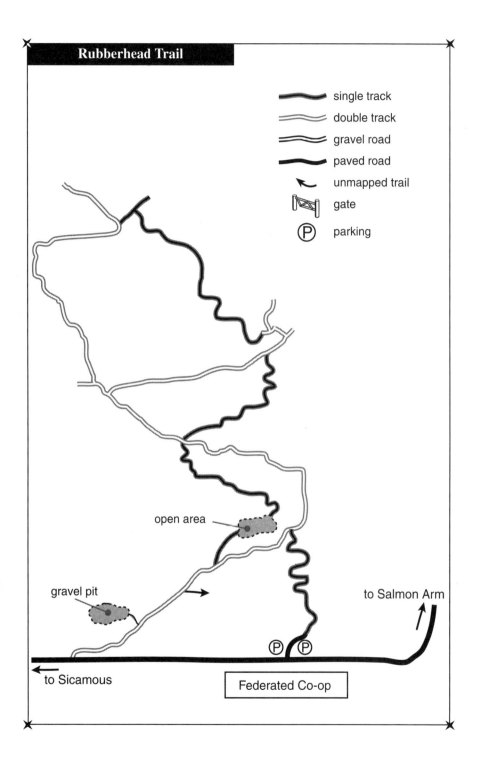

Rubberhead Trail

single track
double track
gravel road
paved road
unmapped trail
gate
ⓟ parking

open area

gravel pit

to Salmon Arm

to Sicamous

ⓟ ⓟ

Federated Co-op

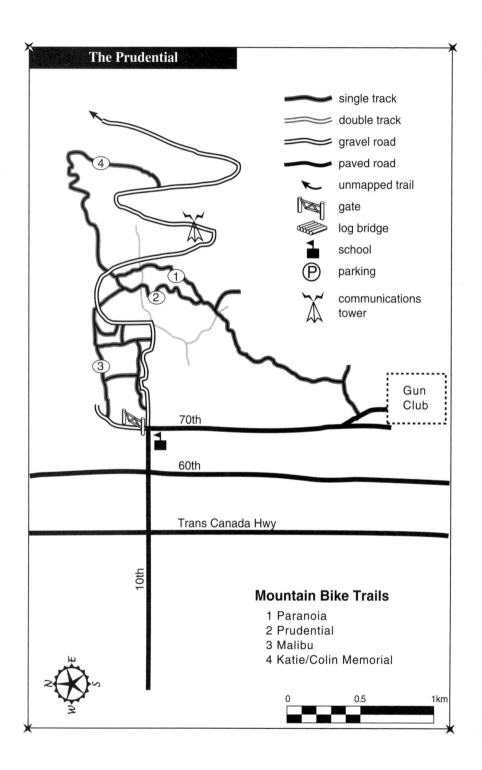

The Prudential

single track
double track
gravel road
paved road
unmapped trail
gate
log bridge
school
parking
communications tower

4
1
2
3

70th

60th

Trans Canada Hwy

10th

Gun Club

Mountain Bike Trails

1 Paranoia
2 Prudential
3 Malibu
4 Katie/Colin Memorial

N E S W

0   0.5   1km

what to expect

If you've never ridden in Kamloops, it is something you'll never forget, like the first time you aired your bike off that curb when you were a kid.

Kamloops has become an international riding destination through the exposure its been receiving in films liked '*Kranked*' and the ample coverage in *BIKE* magazine. I thought I'd seen fast and steep until I came to Kamloops, where a good 'rage in the sage' is only a short ride away. The terrain here is responsible for developing the whole concept of 'off piste' riding or freeriding and honed the skills of riders like Wade Simmons and Richey Schley. These guys shred 'the 'Loops' in the best postcard I've seen yet for Kamloops: the '*Kranked*' series of mountain bike films.

Because Kamloops sits in the middle of a desert-like valley, the summers tend to be smoking hot here making water a must on all rides. However, this is more than compensated for by the abundance of extraordinary dry, fast and rolling singletrack. There are short loops near town within riding distance of your friendly neighborhood coffee shop as well as epic long tours through the brush and grasslands and everything in between. There are just so many extraordinary rides here that the thought packing up the dog and moving to Kamloops may become the master plan once you've had a taste of it.

trail descriptions

MT. DUFFERIN

Mt. Dufferin is the most popular mountain biking area in Kamloops because of its easy access and satisfying terrain. Recently, the area has been declared parkland and is now officially known as Kenna Cartwright Park. The riding is still the same fun romp in the bush, just watch out for hikers and stay on the trails. Parched, semi-arid land, with thinly spaced trees and scrub brush on an old network of double track roads and ultra buffed singletrack is what riders can expect. The riding on the southern exposed slopes and valley bottoms is very desert-like, contrasting sharply with higher elevation rides and slopes with hidden northern exposures. The riding here is fast, and the climbing is steep although usually short. Novice riders have plenty of room to explore the lower trails and take the gentle main climb up to the radio tower at the top.

photo: www.freeriders.org

To access the Mt. Dufferin trails, head west on Hwy. 1 and take exit 366 to Kenna Cartwright Park and Hillside Drive. Go left on Hillside Dr. and park on the right at the base of the gravel road that climbs to the tower. It's just before you reach the Kamloops Regional Correctional Centre (i.e.- The jail). The 2 km climb up the main road is a gentle grade, and you'll be rewarded with some fine singletrack riding.

At the top, go past the tower and look for a right turn downhill shortly after. This will spit you out on one of the best sections of fast, twisty singletrack you can imagine. If you go left, the trail snakes its way through sparse trees, and lets you go fast but checks your speed with quick, sharp turns. Once onto the double track veer left at the intersections, ride past the jail and up a gradual climb back to the main climb. Scamper to the top and push the reset button for another session.

ROSE HILL DOWNHILL

This is the quintessential Kamloops downhill. It's been featured in several movies for its fast, fun, playful singletrack so I highly recommend you head on up and make your cameo appearance on Rose Hill. Everyone can feel like a "sports porn" film star on this trail. It is a 45-minute downhill extravaganza featuring thrills, chills and is guaranteed to leave a perma-grin on your dirty face.

To access this trail, go east out of Kamloops on Victoria St., which turns into Battle St. and eventually into Valleyview Drive. Just after passing under the Trans Canada Highway on Valleyview Dr., Rose Hill Rd. starts on your right. Park in the gravel pull-out behind the fire station and ride up the approx. 3 km long road to the large, wooden water tower on your left. There you will see the singletrack trailhead for the Rose Hill Downhill. Although this trail is predominantly a fast, flowing singletrack, it has some steep rock and clay drops that will get the adrenaline flowing. It crosses several old dirt roads on its plunge back down to Valleyview Dr., keep left at every road and you'll find the trailhead again immediately. After crossing the first road, there are two options for re-entry into the singletrack: to the left is the steep & gnarly, on the right, just beside it in the bushes is the slightly tamer version which hooks up below the gnarl. When you make it back down to the houses, it's a short spin back to the fire station parking lot where the car is.

RAZORBACK RIDGE (DIFFICULT)

Most riders visiting Kamloops probably don't know the name of this amazing trail. However, they've probably seen some of the world's best riders tearing down its 10-inch wide path that teeters on the razor-thin ridge above Kamloops in the movie *Kranked*. This is a beautiful, challenging trail with an airy perch, indeed.

To access this trail, take Hwy 1 to Highland Road. If you're coming from the west it is the second set of lights after The Brick furniture store, which is visible from the highway. Head south up Highland Rd. to Valleyview Drive where you'll see the exit for Razorback on the left, behind the houses. Continue up Highland Rd. to the end until you connect to Qu'appelle Blvd., which goes east-west in Juniper Ridge. Go left and continue on this road until you reach Juniper Elementary School. Ride up one block east beside the school on Nechako Dr. and look left/north for the first road that goes to Nechako Village. At the end of Nechako Drive is Nechako Village. Ride through the parking lot and the trail begins to the north/left at the end. From the four-way singletrack intersection, take the only one that heads down. A great rolling cross-country romp at first, it soon drops out of the trees and winds through the sage down the ridge to Valleyview Drive. If you like narrow singletrack with a bit of exposure on one side, you'll love Razorback.

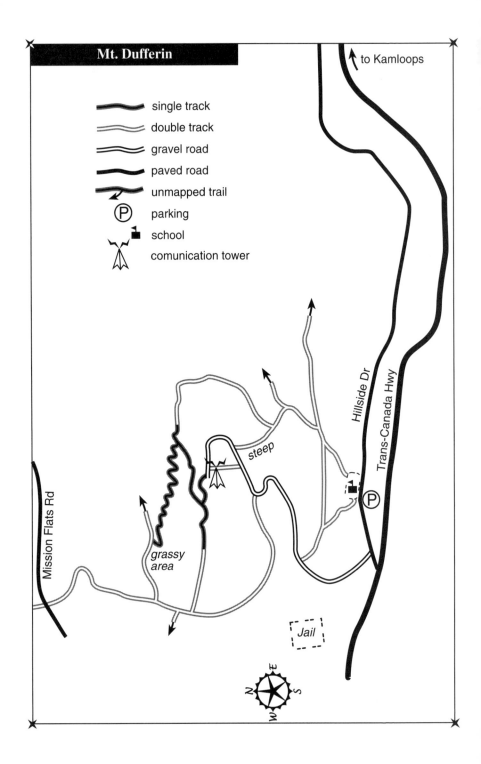

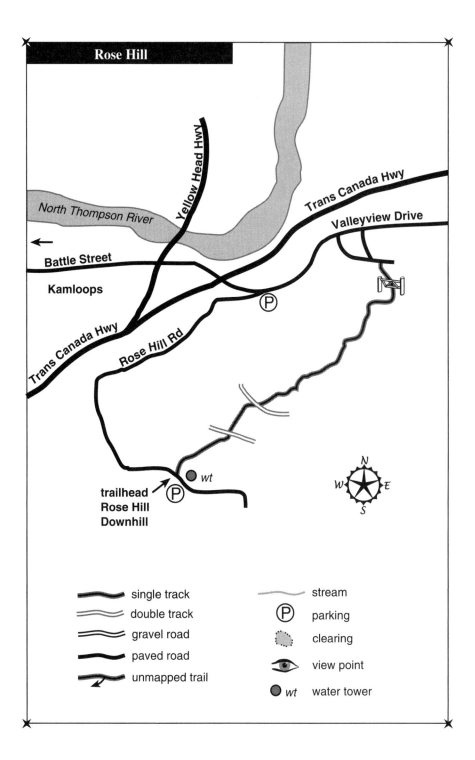

Rose Hill

North Thompson River

Yellow Head Hwy

Trans Canada Hwy

Valleyview Drive

Battle Street

Kamloops

Trans Canada Hwy

Rose Hill Rd

trailhead
Rose Hill
Downhill

wt

N
W E
S

single track
double track
gravel road
paved road
unmapped trail

stream
parking
clearing
view point
water tower

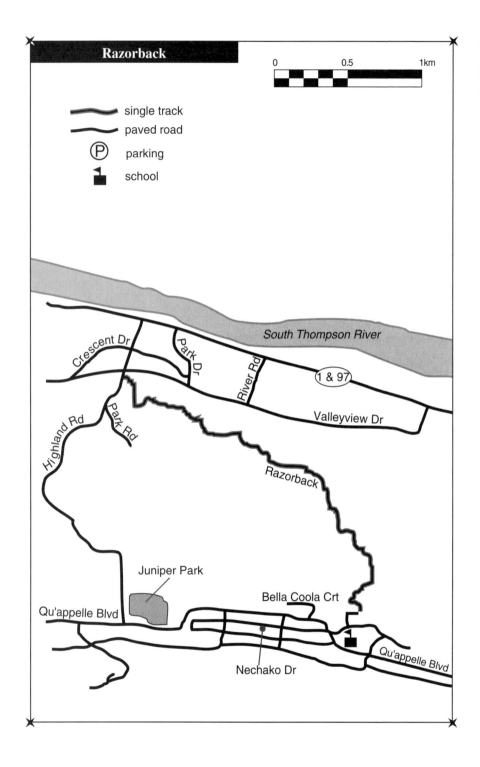

GREENSTONE MTN. POWERLINE (DIFFICULT)

Greenstone is considered by many to be the birthplace of gnarl in Kamloops. Both the climb and the descent are epic. A heroic 4000 foot climb over 23 kms is all it takes to get you to the top, where you'll need your tire irons to pry your lung back into place for the blood-curdling downhill that awaits. This 'old school' riding area has claimed many a frame and many pounds of flesh. It's humbled the great ones, but it's also exalted those willing to try. It is steep, rocky, and fast and it will bite you if you're not in the 'Greenstone Zone' on that day.

In 1998, a forest fire ripped through the area forever changing its face. The riding has slowly regained a toehold here and is beginning to flourish again. It's just a reminder that your favorite riding area, wherever it is, may not be there forever, so work to protect it.

To access this wizened old beauty, head west of Kamloops on Hwy. 1 for 22 kms. Take a left at the old gas station and park. Ride up the Dominic Lake forest service road, staying left at the first intersection. There are a number of forks heading off to the left all along the rest of the road, make sure you keep right at these to enjoy the rest of the climb. Nearing the top, you'll keep right at the last fork to reach the tower. The trail follows the powerline cut straight down.

It starts out like a lullaby and then breaks into a few bars of "Crazy Train". About 500m after the trail comes out under the powerlines, you'll reach a fork. Keep left through the little meadow and the trail will return to the powerlines. Below this point, keep right and hold on tight. You'll get spit out on Duffy Lake Rd., (no not in Pemberton, shake your head) go right and it's a short spin back to the parking lot.

VEGETATION TUNNEL (DIFFICULT)

A trailhead on the left at the 15.5 km mark is Vegetation Tunnel. A nice combo of single and doubletrack that drops you back down onto the Greenstone Rd. at KM eight.

THE REVENGE (DIFFICULT)

Just before you reach the tower at the top, there's a trailhead on the right called 'The Revenge'. This is a serious bit of singletrack that will rattle a few screws loose. A few hundred meters down the trail you'll keep right at the fork. After some sweet riding through the trees, you're back onto a logging road for just over 5 km. Spot the flagging for the singletrack climbing up left before you reach the main road. Some more singletrack and then it's back to a short logging road section, take a left and you'll reach the powerlines soon. You can now hook up with the bottom part of the Greenstone Powerline descent.

local knowledge

tasty bites & frosty pints

Java Cycle (Bike Shop & Coffee House), 1ˢᵗ and Seymour, (250) 314-JAVA
McCracken Station Pub, (250) 878-7100, 1676 Valleyview Dr.

camping / shelter

Paul Lake Prov. Park, 15 mins. from Kamloops on Paul Lk. Road
Lac Le Jeune Prov. Park, 37 kms. southeast of Kamloops on Hwy. 5

off the bike in kamloops

Even though you're probably not going to get off your bike while you're here, I'll give you some rest day options. Chairlift runs up at Sun Peaks are a good bet for the truly addicted. Jet boat tours on the Thompson or Fraser rivers are a cool way to see the Wild West landscape of the area. If you want a

super relaxing day with nothing else to do but hang out and sun bake, then I suggest you head up to Paul Lake, (from Hwy #5, five km north of Kamloops, take the paved Pinantan Road for 19 km to the campground, located on the north side of Paul Lake). A great spot to swim and camp; and there's even some wicked riding up on Harper Mountain that spits you out into your campground. How convenient.

Photo: Trails Kamloops

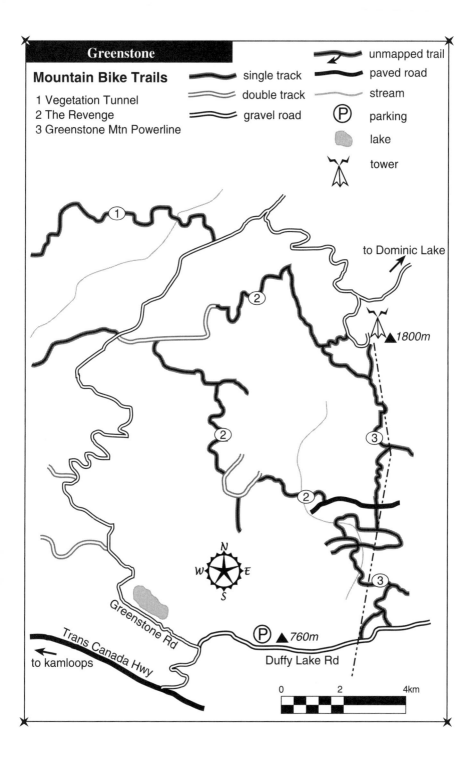

Greenstone

Mountain Bike Trails

1 Vegetation Tunnel
2 The Revenge
3 Greenstone Mtn Powerline

- unmapped trail
- single track
- paved road
- double track
- stream
- gravel road
- ⓟ parking
- lake
- tower

to Dominic Lake

▲1800m

to kamloops

Trans Canada Hwy

Greenstone Rd

ⓟ ▲760m

Duffy Lake Rd

N
W · E
S

0   2   4km

revelstoke

what to expect

Revelstoke, or simply 'the 'Stoke' to some, has been luring mountain bikers off the Trans Canada Highway for years, but the riding there has been keeping the locals happy for a lot longer. Revelstoke is a great little town full of history. Like many of the mountain towns in BC, it got its start in the late 1800's thanks in part to the railway. Because it's in between two mountain ranges, the Monashees and the Selkirks, fantastic alpine rides are close and accessible. The Keystone/Standard Basin Trail is an unforgettable alpine ride through the meadows above Revelstoke. It is unique in this guide for it's alpine splendor and quality singletrack. For those with less inclination (or lung capacity) yet still wanting great riding near town, there are plenty of trails that snake along the banks of the Columbia River and Upper Arrow Lake.

trail descriptions

KEYSTONE / STANDARD BASIN TRAIL (DIFFICULT)

High alpine singletrack is a rare species in the mountain biker's lexicon of riding. This trail exists in the dreams of most mountain bikers, but it's for real here in Revelstoke. To access this trail, drive 50 km north of Revelstoke on Hwy. 23, passing the Revelstoke Dam, all the while following the edge of Lake Revelstoke. At the 50 km mark a large sign will direct you to go right, and up a logging road 15 km to the trailhead. Each intersection on the logging road is marked to direct you to the correct parking spot. The Forest Service provides a registration box at the trailhead to sign on and leave comments.

The ride is an out-and-back experience with a cabin at the main turn around point. The beginning of the trail is a technical climb that will have you wondering if you can do this for 22 km. Don't despair, after about 2.5 km of climbing the trail flattens out and rolls through stunning alpine meadows, across rocky scree slopes, through cold creeks, and possible over summer snow fields, all the while begging you to slow down and drink in the view. The trail itself is a narrow track, and at one point dissipates into an open grassy meadow. By following the rock cairns, you will pick up the trail down the meadow as it continues to skirt along the contours of Standard Basin.

After 11 km of near perfect singletrack, you're confronted with the welcoming sight of Standard Cabin, which is located at the foot of an idyllic, un-named lake. The true hard cores can continue past the cabin to Standard Peak. The cabin is always open and visitors can leave their impressions of the area in a guest book. For the majority of us mortals, the cabin means rest, something to eat, and the beginning of the return voyage.

The way back can be a little tiring, but all of the climbing you did on the way there means plenty of downhill on the way back. High alpine rides can be risky ventures for the unprepared; consequently, several common sense things must be kept in mind to ensure a safe outing. First, this ride is only possible in August and September; any earlier and it will be a mud and snow-choked

Photo: www.freeriders.org

nightmare. Any later, and the weather could turn your ride into a made-for-TV movie. Second, the trail averages about 6000 feet in elevation. This means that 22 km of singletrack could be a personal death-march to an unfit, sea level creature. Third, the trail is always exposed, and in some sections, very exposed. Please walk your bike if you're uncertain about your balance on steep, exposed terrain. Simply put, this trail will challenge your body and delight your soul.

BEGBIE CREEK TRAILS (INTERMEDIATE)

The Begbie Creek Trails are located south of Revelstoke on the western shores of Upper Arrow Lake. The trails are maintained by the Revelstoke Forest District, and are the result of an integrated resource plan, which balances the needs of harvesting and recreation. The area has about 5 km of trails, which were completed in 1994. The trails are generally a

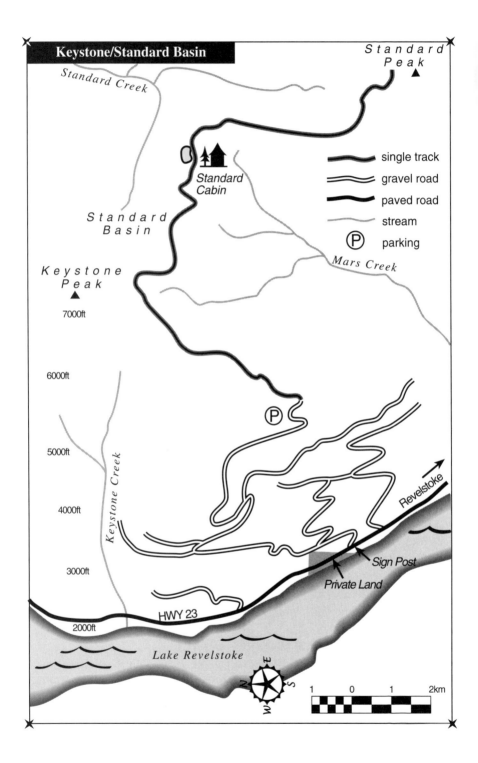

Keystone/Standard Basin

Standard Peak ▲

Standard Creek

Standard Cabin

Standard Basin

Keystone Peak ▲

7000ft

Mars Creek

— single track
— gravel road
— paved road
— stream
Ⓟ parking

6000ft

Keystone Creek

Ⓟ

5000ft

Revelstoke

4000ft

Sign Post

3000ft

Private Land

HWY 23

2000ft

Lake Revelstoke

1   0   1   2km

moderate type of singletrack, which are used by mountain bikers, as well as horses and climbers, hiking into the rock bluffs. Please keep this in mind when riding in this area.

To access the trails, ride or drive sought on Hwy. 23 and turn left on Mt. Begbie Rd., or further down on Cl9ugh Road. Both of these roads will bring you to the main Begbie Falls Road. Another trailhead is located about 1 km past the Mt. MacPherson XC Ski Trails.

The best way to explore these trails is to ride down the main Begbie Falls Rd. to the end. Be sure to walk down to the falls for a look. Next, ride up the singletrack, which gradually climbs up a few meters from the falls parking area. Be sure not to take the old road but the singletrack. This trail will bring you to an intersection in about 1 km. To bail out here, go left to Hwy. 23, or for a great twisty downhill, go right past some climbing areas and down a perfect, bomb-proof singletrack downhill that has plenty of fast switchbacks to test your bike handling skills. For those who drive to the area, park on Begbie Falls Rd., where the road starts to narrow, and if you follow the trail it will come out near your car.

local knowledge

tasty bites & frosty pints
Three Bears' Bistro, in Grizzly Plaza, 112 MacKenzie Ave., (250) 837-9575
Kountry Kwencher Pub, 2108 Big Eddy, (250) 837-6300

camping / shelter
Glacier National Park, Loop Brook Campground, 5km west of Rogers Pass summit
Glacier National Park, Illecillewaet Campground, 3km west of Rogers Pass summit, 60 drive-in sites

off the bike in revelstoke
If you're planning on riding the Keystone/Standard Basin trail, here is some crucial information you'll need to know: the location of the nearest hot springs for the post-ride soak. Canyon Hot Springs, located just 35 km

east of Revelstoke on the Trans Canada Highway has everything you'll need: a large hot springs pool, swimming pool, and secluded campsites. Set up base camp and start exploring from there. You're smack in the middle of two national parks: Mt. Revelstoke National Park and Glacier National Park, making the hiking and camping opportunities beautiful and endless. Contact the local Tourist Info. Office on Hwy. 1 at (250) 837-3522. Also, make sure you check out the abundant history that this area has to offer, in particu lar, the railway history. Stop at the Rogers Pass railway exhibit and learn how the tunnels were built, and how the railway built most of western Canada.

Photo: Steve Dunn   *Capilano River*

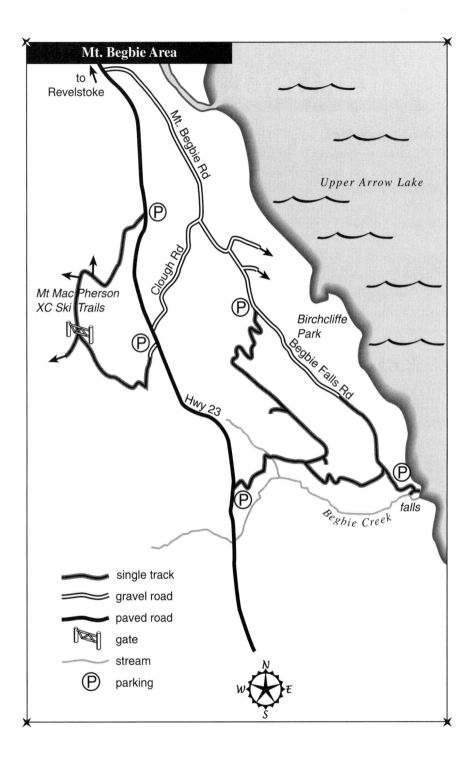

Mt. Begbie Area

to
Revelstoke

Mt. Begbie Rd

Upper Arrow Lake

Clough Rd

Mt Mac Pherson
XC Ski Trails

Birchcliffe
Park

Begbie Falls Rd

Hwy 23

Begbie Creek

falls

single track
gravel road
paved road
gate
stream
parking

N
W   E
S

what to expect

Aside from the jaw-dropping scenery around Nakusp, one of the best reasons for coming here is for the long, relaxing, soul-cleansing, post-ride soak in the natural hot springs nearby. Apart from the developed pools, there are a number of rustic pools in the area. Drop by the info booth for directions to these magic little soakers.

Riding the 'Kuskanax Creek Trail' right to the hot springs, then soaking up all 104 degrees of the healing water is pretty close to the perfect post ride chill out session you can get. Words don't do it justice so I won't try, just come and find out for yourself. Because of its location, and all it offers, Nakusp is a "must-hit" on any Kootenay road trip.

trail descriptions

KUSKNAX HOT SPRINGS TRAILS

The Kuskanax Hot Springs Trail is a point-to-point singletrack that hugs the steep valley leading to the developed hot springs. The trail bed was built in the early 1900's as a horse route to the pools. Today, there is a sweet singletrack that gradually climbs up the valley taking the path of least resistance. The trail is quite exposed in some sections, but despite this potential danger the route is not too technical. One tight set of switchbacks provides the technically inspired with an outlet to vent.

To access the trail, ride east on Hwy. 6 for 1.5 km to Carson's Corner Store. Turn left onto Alexander Road. Proceed north 1.5 km past the Glenbank graveyard, then look for the old road uphill and on your right. You now should be off-road and will see the trailhead sign. Ride 2 km up this old road through a large logged area keeping to the well-worn path. This road terminates in an open area where you can see the trail entering the forest about 300 m ahead. The occasional orange trail marker on the trees will assist you at this point.

You could ride this trail a number of ways; it's all up to you. Ride up the road to the Hot Springs and singletrack it down, or vice versa. Or you could do an out-and-back on the singletrack. Either way, you can't go wrong with a soak in the springs in the middle of your ride.

local knowledge

tasty bites & frosty pints
The Garden Harvest, 212 Broadway, (250) 265-0010
Brew Crew, 206 Broadway, (250) 265-4784
camping / shelter
McDonald Creek Provincial Park, on the shores of Upper Arrow Lake, 10 Km south of Nakusp
Three Islands Resort, Hwy. 6, (250) 265-3023

off the bike in nakusp
Your obvious choice for post-ride or rest day (in)activity in Nakusp is the hot springs, and why wouldn't it be, it's gorgeous. But did you ever consider sea kayaking on Arrow Lake? It offers some truly inspirational scenery and magic little secluded beaches with mountain views. (Columbia Kayaking 1-888-529-2510)
It's no secret that there's great hiking on just about all of those mountains you can see around Nakusp as well. For trail maps and information, phone the Nakusp Travel Information Centre at (250) 265-4234.

Photo: Steve Dunn

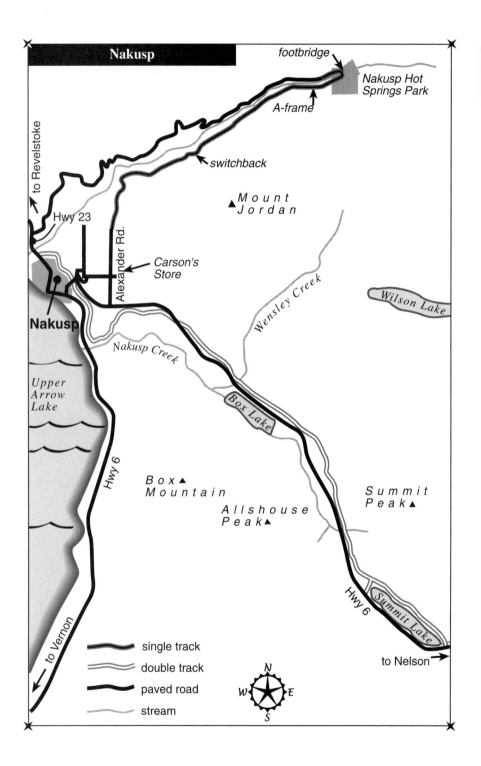

Nakusp

footbridge

Nakusp Hot
Springs Park

A-frame

switchback

to Revelstoke

Hwy 23

Alexander Rd.

Carson's
Store

▲Mount
Jordan

Wensley Creek

Wilson Lake

Nakusp

Nakusp Creek

Box Lake

Upper
Arrow
Lake

Hwy 6

Box▲
Mountain

Allshouse
Peak▲

Summit
Peak▲

Hwy 6

Summit Lake

to Nelson

to Vernon

single track

double track

paved road

stream

N
W   E
S

what to expect

The Doukhobours, a pacifist religious group from Russia that migrated to western Canada in 1899, were among the earliest Europeans to settle here. On your visit, be sure to explore the local history between rides. With the warmest lake in the province, a beautiful setting and great riding, you can't go wrong here. This mountain playground is home to such mountain bike 'old boys' as Matt Pinto, and Dave Swetland, who can be seen laying down some of the most serious freeride lines ever in 'Kranked'. There are many epic rides here, encompassing all levels of ability. Some roll along the lake through huge cedar trees, like the Deer Point trail, and some rip down from the mountaintops in a screaming blur, like the Vertical sMile. For a special treat, ask around for a sampling of "The Mayor's Own".

trail descriptions

VERTICAL sMILE (DIFFICULT)

One vertical mile of downhill fun is what you'll find on this trail. This fantastic singletrack downhill drops you through rolling, flower filled meadows, gnarly rock drops and wicked high-speed corners. It's been the site of a few downhill races in the past.

Follow Hwy 3 north 31 km to Bonanza Creek Rd. on the right. After 2 km take a left, then it's another 1 km to the next junction. Turn right and proceed until you reach the barricade and park. You can ride almost to the summit (short hike-a-bike unless you've mastered molecule disassociation or teleporting) Follow flagging from the radio tower south until you reach the old logging road passing through several beautiful meadows. From here there's nowhere to go but down, down, down to Christina Lake. I highly recommend a dip in the lake after this one, you'll need it!

DEER POINT (INTERMEDIATE)

Deer Point is a great singletrack ride. It's a beautiful trail that takes you out to the head of the lake to a sandy beach and giant cedars. It starts with a bit of a climb, but becomes a great little roller coaster ride above the lake with amazing views.

Drive east on Hwy. 3 past Christina Lake and take the East Lake Rd. to Texas Point. Park in the lot just before Texas Point campground. The trail starts here. From here, you have two ride choices: 1.) 6km to Deer Point - 2hr return. 2.) 10 km to Troy Creek - 3.5hr return. Both are very worthy destinations.

SPOONER TRAIL (INTERMEDIATE)

Spooner is a highlight of any trip to Christina Lake. Spooner's outstanding singletrack plunge goes from loamy cedar forest to more open and fast riding below. This fun, serpentine downhill is sandwiched between Stewart Creek forest Service Rd. and West Lake Drive on the west side of Christina Lake.

From the bridge at Christina Lake, go west on Hwy. 3 for 3 km. Turn right on Stewart Creek road. Look for trailhead on right at about 9 km. Drop in and hold on.

THIMBLE MOUNTAIN (INTERMEDIATE)

It's been called one of the Kootenays best kept secrets, but it's not really a secret, it's just not ridden that often. I find that hard to imagine because it has exceptional cross-country singletrack and offers superb views of the Granby River and the North Fork Valley.

You can reach this trail by heading 21 km west of Grand Forks on Hwy. 3. Park at the pullout. Go through the gate and ride about 150 meters to where a road comes out on the left. Go left for about 500 meters and you'll see the trailhead sign in a box. A total of about 2000 feet of climbing begins as you pop out on the top of an old clear cut where the trail traverses, then hooks onto an old road. Follow this road for about 500 meters to a singletrack on the right marked with diamond-shaped orange thingys. This singletrack rolls till you see a right on the road and then a left 300 meters later at the next intersection. This old road turns into a singletrack. Follow for about 3 km until a crows-foot type opening. Go through the gate and follow the trail until you hit a road. Go right and look for a trail immediately on your left. You're nearing the top of Thimble Mountain. Stay left at the next intersection and soon you will be in a bluff overlooking the Granby River Valley. After the necessary refueling pit stop, return back the same way or turn left on the road that gradually turned into a

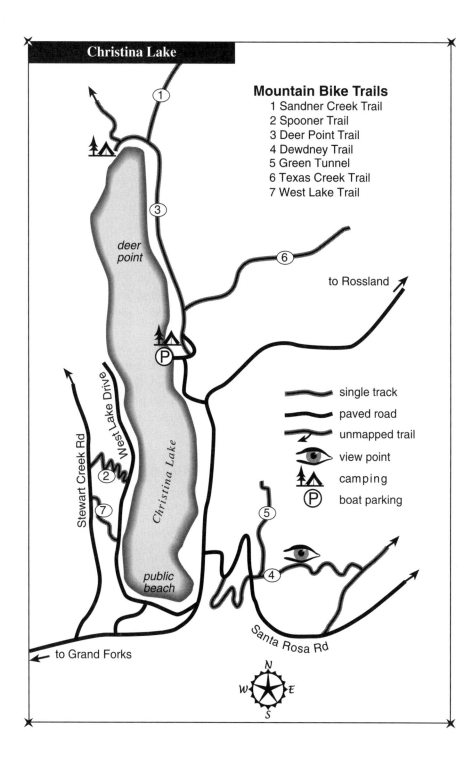

Christina Lake

Mountain Bike Trails
1 Sandner Creek Trail
2 Spooner Trail
3 Deer Point Trail
4 Dewdney Trail
5 Green Tunnel
6 Texas Creek Trail
7 West Lake Trail

deer point

to Rossland

single track
paved road
unmapped trail
view point
camping
boat parking

West Lake Drive

Stewart Creek Rd

Christina Lake

public beach

Santa Rosa Rd

to Grand Forks

N
W E
S

singletrack. The trail is faint in some places, so keep you eyes open until you eventually get to the fence line again, turn left and ride the fantastic downhill.

DEWDNEY TRAIL

Edgar Dewdney first opened this trail in 1865. It was the main route through this area until its replacement in the 1920's by the Cascade Highway (Santa Rosa Road). The Boundary Forest District maintains about 15 kms of the trail, after that it continues another 24km to near Rossland. Look for white and green Dewdney trail signs, as well as reflective orange diamonds. This trail crosses several areas of private land. Please ensure continued use of these lands by staying on marked trails and not littering.

Starting from Christina Lake, head east on Hwy 3, cross the bridge and turn right on Santa Rosa Road. This long steady climb gradually turns into a gravel road. After climbing for about 7 km you go around a corner and turn left on a road. Next, you cross under power lines and climb for about 2 km where you'll see the Dewdney Trail come in on your right and descend to the left. Go left and soak up some great views of Christina Lake to the west overlooking the Kettle Valley, and the south into the States. The ride down is major, screaming fast, downhill fun. You will cross over the road you climbed at one point, but just drop over the other side and keep ripping own. You come out at the first switchback, and from here it's a race to the lake for a swim.

WESTLAKE (DIFFICULT)

This trail has some of the steeper and more technical singletrack overlooking Christina Lake. It's a very fun rip down the mountain.

From the bridge in Christina Lake, go west on Hwy 3 for 3 km, turn right on Stewart Creek Road. The trailhead for Westlake is on the right at around 6.8 kms. Westlake Trail meanders across the hillside and comes out on Chase Rd.

local knowledge

tasty bites & frosty pints

Moon Beans Internet Café, (250) 447-9591, 9A Johnson Rd., Christina Lake

camping / shelter

Texas Point Campground – on the east shores of Christina Lake. Take Hwy. 3 east, then left on East Lake Drive. The campground is at the end.

Xenia Lake Campground- (wilderness) From the bridge at the East End of Grand Forks, follow the Granby Road 21km and turn right onto Miller Creek Road. At 2.5km turn left onto rough, 4X4 road.

off the bike in the boundary area

There are superb kayaking and canoeing opportunities on Christina Lake, with tranquil warm water and numerous sandy beach sites on the north end, part of Gladstone Provincial Park. Paddle up to see the 8' diameter cedar trees or explore the native petroglyphs along the shore. There are also some amazingly beautiful rivers that offer some excellent opportunities for kayaking & canoeing surrounding Christina Lake. Check out Wildways Kayaking in Christina Lk., (250) 447-6561).

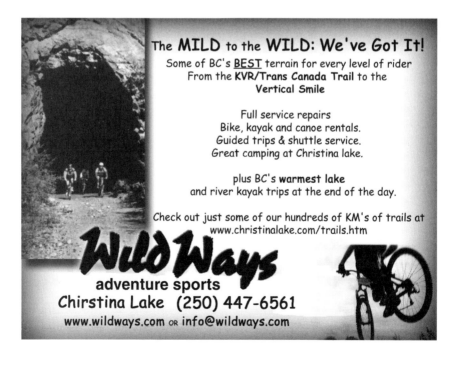

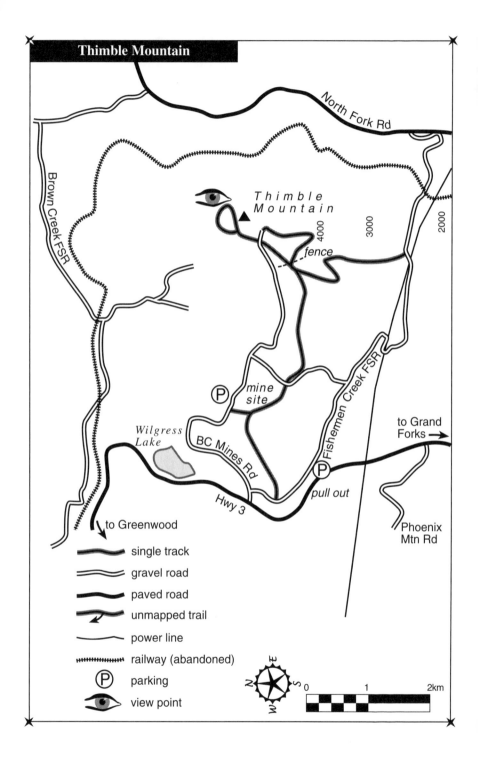

Thimble Mountain

North Fork Rd

Brown Creek FSR

Thimble Mountain

fence

4000

3000

2000

mine site

Wilgress Lake

BC Mines Rd

Fishemen Creek FSR

to Grand Forks →

pull out

Hwy 3

to Greenwood

Phoenix Mtn Rd

single track

gravel road

paved road

unmapped trail

power line

railway (abandoned)

Ⓟ parking

view point

N E S W

0   1   2km

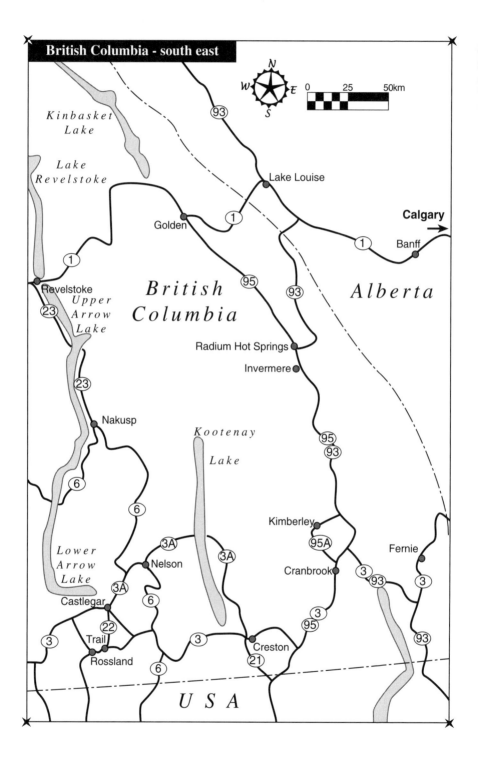

trail descriptions

OTTERTAIL FIRE ROAD TRAIL (INTERMEDIATE)

The trailhead for the Ottertail Fire Road Trail is located about 35 minutes east of Golden, B.C., or approximately 8 km west of Field. If you are driving from Golden, the trailhead will be on your right, shortly after the bridge over Ottertail River. The trail is located in Yoho National Park, with the start located at the old site of the District Warden's Headquarters. At the trailhead, there is a signboard with information updating recent trail conditions, bear sightings, et cetera.

The trail is an old fire road out-and-back to the Macarthur Creek Warden Cabin, which unfortunately is closed to the public. Enroute, you'll cross Float Creek where the trail switchbacks, but eventually levels out as you go through an old burn site that has naturally regenerated itself. Further up the trail, you will ride past the McArthur Creek Trail, which is a closed grizzly bear habitat. All of the trails that shoot off the Ottertail Fire Road are closed to mountain bikers.

photo: Tourism BC

Expect the trail to be accessible from mid June to October, with the best riding conditions in late summer and autumn. The ride is generally smooth and not too technical, with the steeper grades developing within the first few kms of the start. A spectacular view of the north faces of Goodsir Towers is your reward for a long day in the saddle. A nice hiking trail extends beyond the cabin, but it's closed to mountain biking. Please respect Yoho National Park and stay on the main trail.

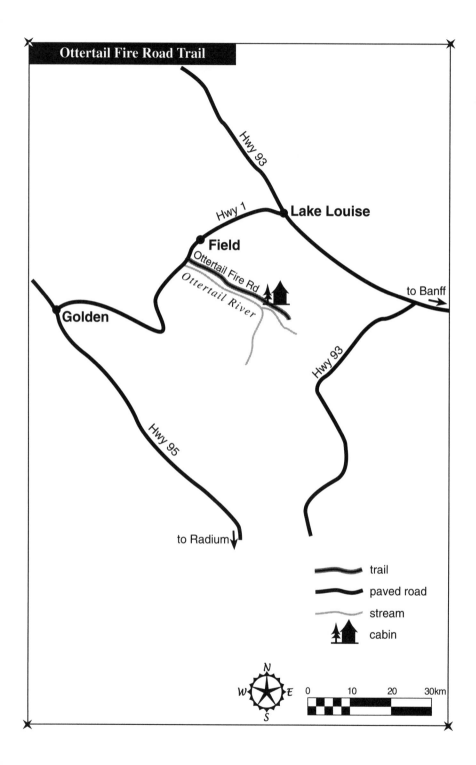

Ottertail Fire Road Trail

Hwy 93

Hwy 1

Lake Louise

Field

Ottertail Fire Rd

Ottertail River

to Banff

Golden

Hwy 93

Hwy 95

to Radium

trail
paved road
stream
cabin

N
W E
S

0   10   20   30km

what to expect

Golden got its name when an old railway survey crew, who were camped at Golden, decided that they wanted to one-up another local crew that named their camp "Silver City". With such an effort given to names years ago it makes you wonder about those who named the killer trails like B12 on Mount 7. That one was named for the shot of vitamins needed after the climb to the top.

Golden is a town we all drive through as it sits off the Trans Canada Highway and is home to a new ski hill development that rivals big, bad Whistler for terrain and size. The biking opportunities at Kicking Horse Resort will continue to grow along with the resort. It's also home to Canada's highest restaurant at 7700 feet. All of this will breathe some fresh recreational life into this pristine mountain town. Pictures and words do no justice to the Rocky Mountain experience despite a billion rolls of Kodak, and a few hundred books like this telling you how awesome it is...just see and experience it for yourself!

For a tranquil spin through the forests of this Rocky Mountain paradise, try the Dawn Mountain Nordic Ski Trails.

trail descriptions

CANYON CREEK LOOP (INTERMEDIATE)

If you can only do one ride while visiting Golden, make it the Canyon Creek Loop. To access the ride, follow the signs to the ski hill, taking a left at the firs T intersection about 7 km from town. Continue another 2 km to a three way intersection, and take the right fork. Climb about 2 km to the first clear cut and take the center road across the cut block. You go back into the forest and pop out in a second cut block. Go left, and down into the cleared area, and take the last climb out of the cut block on the more traveled path. You should pass a swampy area, and nearby, the trailhead should be signed.

Soon you'll spot the canyon. Stop, drink in the view, and get psyched for about a 3 km descent. At the bottom of the canyon, you'll hit a logged area, back up and take the singletrack on your right to get the most out of the downhill. Once at the bottom of the gravel pit, go left on the gravel road. Be sure NOT to take the skidder trail but stay on the main gravel road that climbs

gently. The steady climb will bring you past a wire gate and eventually up to the
Cedar Lake Forest Service Wilderness Campsite. You can start this ride from town
or from Cedar Lake.

MOONRAKER TRAILS (INTERMEDIATE)

On the descent portion of the Canyon Creek Trail, you should eventually see a half-
pipe sort of feature. Once you are near this, look for a trail entrance on the left.
This is the trail leading into the Moonraker trail system. These trails are slow and
technical, but generally rideable in both directions. Use the radio tower as your main
point of reference, because this area is quite confusing, and getting lost is a
possibility. About a 1 km service road leads you from the radio tower back to the
main road just before a gate.

WEST BENCH LOWER ROAD (EASY)

From town, take the left fork just after the bridge over the Columbia River. The left turn
is about 50 meters past the right turn to the golf course. This gentle ride rolls up and
down offering continuous views of the Columbia River Valley. It also passes by a great
example of the Columbia Valley wetlands and should provide great wildlife viewing
opportunities. The trail surface is a novice-friendly gravel road. The ride ends up in the
Nicholson subdivision where you can retrace your steps, ride home on the road, or
continue up the five switchbacks to Cedar Lake. This trail passes through private
property, but the landowner supports cyclists using the road.

POWERLINE DESCENT (INTERMEDIATE)

You could do a lot better as far as trail go around here. It is included for those
who like boulder fields, bone-rattling descents and electromagnetic therapy

GORMAN LAKE CONNECTOR (INTERMEDITATE)

The connector continues past the turn off for the powerline descent. This ride is on
old doubletrack and is a long, moderate tour of the West Bench area. Be sure to
miss the XC ski area because it is a bog in the summer, and if the mud doesn't get
you, the mosquitos will.

MOUNT SEVEN TRAILS (INTERMEDIATE - DIFFICULT)

Generally, when you're starting your bike ride right next someone launching a hang
glider, you know you're in for a great downhill. Such is the case on Mount 7.

Dropping 4200 ft. back down to Golden on some great trails with great views makes Mt. 7 one of the best places to ride in the Golden area. This is the site of the annual "Mount 7 Psychosis Downhill Race" held in June.

The climb to the top of the Mt. 7 FSR (forest service road) is a long one, but very rewarding. Hop on your bike and enjoy the journey, you'll be proud when you reach the top. The road snakes up the side of Mt. 7 for approximately 12 kms to the glider launch where the views will leave you breathless, if the climb didn't already take care of that. There are several options for shorter climbs and shorter rides off of most of the right hand switchbacks on the way up. These 3K, 5K and 10K will all connect on to each other and will all lead down to Spruce Drive.

From the glider launch, the ride back down has several options. DEAD DOG is a short, steep start to the downhill, which links up with the main SUMMIT TRAIL after just a few hundred meters. It begins right at the glider launch. Another option to start with, which also begins at the launch, is the SUMMIT TRAIL, which is a moderately technical trail with some steep, off-camber traverses. It will bring you back down onto the 6.5 km mark of the Mt. 7 FSR. From there, go right and climb for a minute or so and look for the trailhead for B12 on the left. On the SUMMIT TRAIL, you have the option to turn right about halfway down, onto ERICH'S TRAIL. This is a fast one that will take you to the 5K TRAIL. This is a well-worn Golden classic that offers fantastic ridge-top views of the Columbia Valley. This will lead directly to TRUE VALUE. Aptly named, for its fast double and singletrack, finishing with the luge run called Snake Hill.

B12 is 5 kms of steep, technical, downhill fun. It is not for the timid. See if you can spot the rafters or the kayakers in the Kicking Horse River below. B12 will drop you into the Golden Municipal Campground at the end of 9th street, and from there, it's a short spin over to Summit Cycle to thank the kind folks that have built this trail. There are plenty of other options for descending Mt. 7. It is recommended that you drop into Summit Cycle to get all the details on this area, and to buy them all a beer for their hard work.

Golden

Trails
1 Erich's Trail
2 Moonshine
3 Dead Dog
4 Summit Trail
5 True Value
6 The Bars
7 B12
8 Mt 7 FSR

launch site

single track
double track
gravel road
paved road
unmapped trail
stream
Ⓟ parking
clearing
view point

9 St S
10th St
14 Ave S

Kicking Horse River

Rodeo Grounds

Spruce Dr

Hwy 95

Hwy 95

Golden

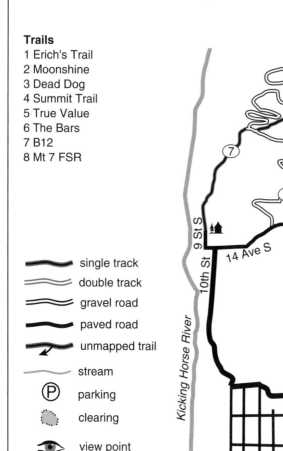
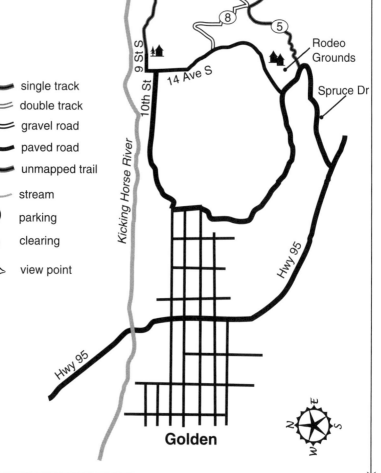

local knowledge

tasty bites & frosty pints

The Mad Trapper Neighborhood Pub, 1203-9th St., (just up from the lights)

camping / shelter

Golden Municipal Campground, (250) 344-5412
Sander Lake Campground, 12 kms (250) 344-6517

off the bike in golden

Golden is endowed with amazingly majestic mountains all around it. Luckily, there are dozens of guiding and outfitting companies in town to help you take advantage of all that beauty. Try Golden Mountain Adventures (1-800-433-9533) for ideas on anything from whitewater rafting to paragliding. For more information on activities or accommodation in the Golden area, phone the Golden Tourist Info. Line at 1-800-622-GOLD.

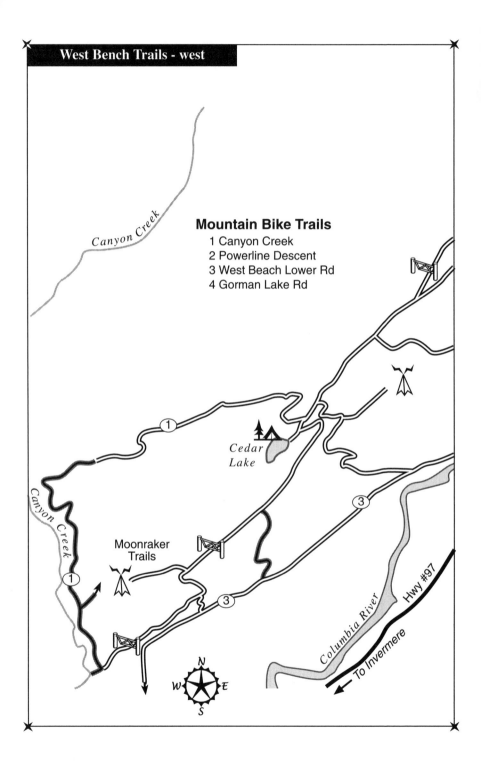

Mountain Bike Trails
1 Canyon Creek
2 Powerline Descent
3 West Beach Lower Rd
4 Gorman Lake Rd

Canyon Creek

Canyon Creek

Cedar Lake

Moonraker Trails

Columbia River

Hwy #97

To Invermere

N
W E
S

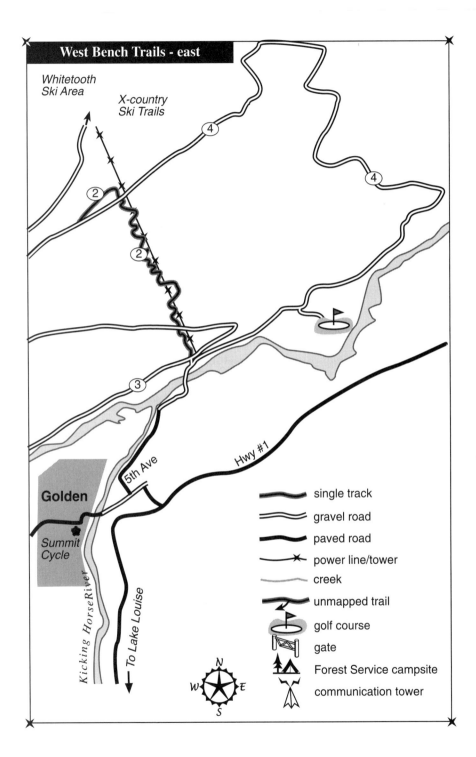

West Bench Trails - east

Whitetooth
Ski Area

X-country
Ski Trails

④

④

②

②

golf course

③

5th Ave

Hwy #1

Golden

Summit
Cycle

Kicking Horse River

To Lake Louise

	single track
	gravel road
	paved road
	power line/tower
	creek
	unmapped trail
	golf course
	gate
	Forest Service campsite
	communication tower

N
W · E
S

what to expect

Millions of years ago a massive river of ice, miles wide creaked and groaned it's way out of the heights of the Canadian Rocky Mountains. This colossal glacier carved out a ditch so deep that it became known as the Rocky Mountain Trench. The Trench forms the headwaters of the mighty Columbia River system, known for pumping hydroelectric power to the American North West, and power hungry California. This ice age event also left us a valley of unprecedented beauty and variety of terrain. Mountain Bike Rides in this region are characterized by rolling rangelands, interspersed with Spruce and Pine groves, crystal clear lakes and streams, with Douglas fir and Larch at higher elevations.

The valley is bordered by the B.C. Rockies to the East and the towering Purcell Mountains to the West. The Columbia Valley is already a well-established tourist destination area, with natural hot springs at both Radium and Fairmont Hot Springs. The surrounding mountain ranges are best recognized as the birthplace of Heliskiing, where Hans Gmoser first lifted skiers into the towering Bugaboos to ski the legendary Purcell Powder. For detailed maps and directions drop into Nipika Lodge, 9200 Settlers Rd (14 kms off Hwy 93 between Radium 32 kms and Banff 114 kms)

trail descriptions

NATURAL BRIDGE / NIPIKA LODGE (INTERMEDIATE)

Nipika Touring center is on the banks of the wild & scenic Kootenay River and the Kootenay National Park. The riding in this area is usually on cross country ski trails and old horse-logged skidder roads at elevations between 3600 and 5000 feet. There is spectacular singletrack riding here from early May to the end of October. Nipika Touring Center has 40 kms. of developed trails and numerous other forestry fire roads. It is adjacent to Kootenay National Park, which has 40 more kilometers of trails connected to this system. You can expect gently undulating XC ski trails along the Kootenay River valley, very beautiful mountain scenery, and some technical singletrack sections.

To access this trail from Radium Hot Springs, travel Hwy. 93 north towards Banff for 20 kms. to Settlers Road. Head south on Settlers Rd.

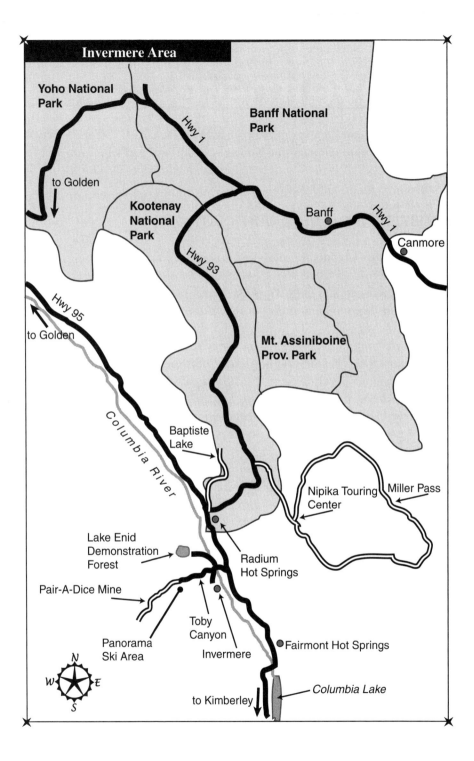

for 12 kms. until you leave the Kootenay Natn. Park, then take the left fork in the road. You will cross the Kootenay River Bridge at km.13, travel 1 more km. to the Nipika Touring Center parking lot (left side) at the junction of the Cross River Rd. and Settlers Rd.

TOBY CANYON TRAIL (DIFFICULT)

This is one of the better singletrack trails in the area. It leads you to some spectacular viewpoints over the deep canyon, and has wickedly fun riding. Most of the ride is single and doubletrack trail, very little road, and all it's options are loop rides right out of Invermere, so no car shuttle. This ride starts right from Invermere, follows the cliffs on the South banks of Toby Creek, into the rolling benchlands and ranches in the hills above Invermere. There are numerous viewpoints and some very challenging sections of singletrack trail. There are many optional loops and shortcuts to this area, so just continue to stay close to the cliffs to pick up the main trail. After 10-12 kms you will come to a hydro line, follow the service road south until you connect with any of the roads which will deliver you back down into Invermere, or double back on the canyon trail itself for the trip back to town.

To access this trail from Invermere, take 14th St. past J.A. Laird School, and continue out of town. The road turns to gravel and climbs a long hill. At the top of the hill turn right and ride about 1 km until you pass over a cattleguard, then leave the road at the Hoodoos lookout on the right. The singletrack trail starts on the left side of the lookout and heads West along the cliffs overlooking a spectacular deep canyon.

LAKE ENID DEMO FOREST (EASY - INTERMEDIATE)

This BC Forest Service Demonstration Forest has an incredible cross section of different elements from recent forest fire regeneration, to upland grassy meadows, to wetlands. One can view the spectacular Horsethief Canyons from sections of singletrack trail; plunge into beautiful Lake Enid after their ride, or picnic on the bluffs overlooking the wetlands watching eagles and osprey soar. The area is rich with mule and whitetail deer, bear, coyotes, lynx, occasional elk and an abundance of small wildlife. This area is a maze of trail options with about 100 kms of trail to choose from. Most of the trails are grassy double tracked cart trails and old dirt roads. There are no sustained climbs, but the total vertical gain & loss in riding this area is considerable. The system can be accessed from a number of locations, the village of Wilmer, the Lake Enid Recreation Site, and from two trailheads on the Westside Rd. north of Wilmer. Loops vary from a 15 minute ride around Lake Enid, to 2 or 3 hr. rides. A good way to finish your ride in the Lake Enid Demo. Forest is to take a short side trip down to the Columbia Valley Wetlands and Wilmer Slough to view the fantastic bird life.

To access these trails from Invermere, follow the Panorama Rd. across the lower Toby Cr. Bridge, then immediately turn right to Wilmer (2 kms). At Wilmer you can chose to park and ride from there. Turn left and follow the Munn Lake Rd. for 7 or 8 kms to the Lake Enid Recreation Site, or continue north on the Westside Rd. for 1 km or 5 kms to the two trailheads (watch for Lake Enid Demo Forest signs).

PAIR-A-DICE MINES / WILMER (DIFFICULT –DUE TO LENGTH)

The Pair-a-Dice Mine is a turn of the century gold mine above Panorama Resort at an elevation of 7500 feet. The ride up is on a rough gravel road for 15 kms with barely a level spot on the whole climb. At the mine take the right junction to continue uphill to the pass, then check your tires and brakes for the classic descent into Invermere via the hamlet of Wilmer 35 kms. below. This ride can be done as a full circle if you don't mind the 15 km ride back to the trailhead on the Panorama road.

This ride is NOT for the lily-livered or faint-hearted! The climb to the pass is relentless, with numerous creek crossings for water. Take the time for the short hike to the 100' waterfall just off the road 2/3 of the way up. It's a great way to cool off. The mine is at treeline and the rest of the climb provides some really amazing alpine views of the Rockies to the east as well as Mount Nelson in the Purcell Range. The mine makes a perfect lunch stop. The descent starts steep and fast on a shale slope with countless turns and fun switchbacks. As you reach the valley the trail flattens out and the ride into Wilmer is a high-speed cruise on backroads. Some vehicle traffic uses these roads so keep to your own side on the curves. After Wilmer it's another high-speed drop down the road until you are just outside of Invermere, then if you are riding the whole circle, head back up the Panorama Road. Due to its elevation, this trail is usually open from late June to late September. Riding times are long and can vary from 5-6 hours for a one-way trip and up to 7-9 hours for a round trip. Wear comfy shorts.

From Invermere take the Panorama Road. If you are leaving a shuttle vehicle for pickup, leave it at the bridge just before the Wilmer Junction. There is a parking spot beside the bridge. Continue towards Panorama, but about 1 km before you reach the resort you will notice a large rust colored parking area on the right. There is a gravel road entering this field. This is the Pair-a-Dice road. Park your vehicle, follow the road, and remember to start slow because it's a long ride.

RADIUM HOT SPRINGS / BAPTISTE LK. (EASY – INTERMEDIATE)

Most of the riding in this area is on grassy cart trails through rolling hills with great views of the Columbia River. The area has been used for many years to produce Christmas trees, so you will notice many pruned trees along the way. All forms of wildlife indigenous to the area are found here in abundance. As with most of the riding areas in the near here, there are options galore: from basic beginner routes to intermediate rides. Some of the trails are shared with horses, so courtesy is essential towards horseback riders. Elevations range from 2800' to 3500' of rolling hills with many vistas of the Columbia River valley. Much of this territory consists of large private properties, so please respect private property and leave gates the way you found them.

The most popular trailhead is right in Radium Hot Springs, 1 km North of the Hwy 93/ 95 Jct. on Hwy 95. Head up the trails at the Riding Stables. Other roads between Radium Hot Springs and Edgewater lead east into

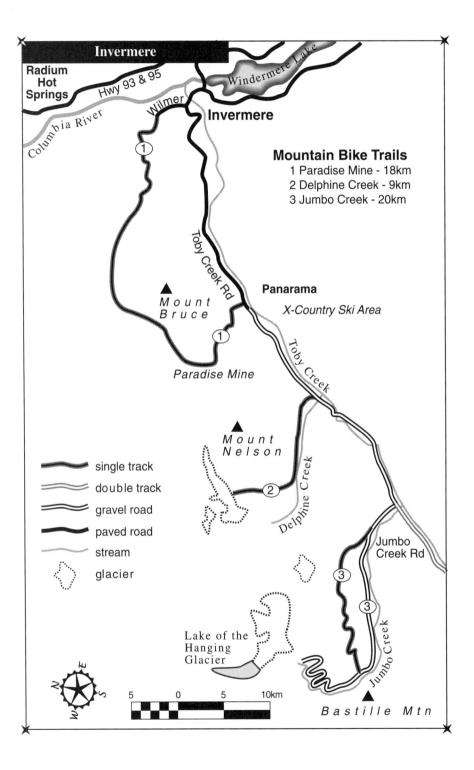

Invermere

Radium Hot Springs

Hwy 93 & 95

Wilmer

Columbia River

Windermere Lake

Invermere

Mountain Bike Trails
1 Paradise Mine - 18km
2 Delphine Creek - 9km
3 Jumbo Creek - 20km

①

Toby Creek Rd

▲ *M o u n t
B r u c e*

①

Paradise Mine

Panarama

X-Country Ski Area

Toby Creek

▲ *M o u n t
N e l s o n*

②

Delphine Creek

Jumbo
Creek Rd

③

③

Jumbo Creek

*Lake of the
Hanging
Glacier*

single track

double track

gravel road

paved road

stream

glacier

N
E
S
W

5   0   5   10km

B a s t i l l e   M t n ▲

the system from numerous points along the highway. From the north end of the area at Edgewater, drive east on Hewett Rd. 2 kms to a small parking lot on the right side of the road. Ride south into the trail network from this trailhead.

ALBERT RIVER / MILLER PASS (DIFFICULT - DUE TO LENGTH)

This is a remote ride, so go prepared, you are in the Height of the Rockies Wilderness Area, and it's pure wilderness. The ride starts from the Albert River Rd. (km. 35) and heads uphill until you reach treeline, and get bird's eye views of Mount Assiniboine, the Matterhorn of the Rockies. The wildlife in this country includes all of the species known to the Rocky Mountains. Once over the top follow the trail downhill into the Cross River valley and eventually down the Cross River Rd. to Nipika Touring Center, where you should leave a shuttle vehicle on your way in to the trailhead.

This ride is through extreme country, starting with a gut-busting climb from the Albert River Rd. drop off point, to the summit of Miller Pass. Once at the pass the ride levels out for a short time, then starts it's long cruising descent into the Cross River Valley. The descent is on old deserted skid roads with numerous washouts, slides, and surprises along the way. The trail eventually feeds into the upper reaches of the Cross River Rd. Keep to the left at intersections until you are out on the well-traveled road, which you follow for about 20 kms. mostly downhill back to Nipika Touring Center, where you should leave a vehicle. During midweek rides **WATCH FOR ORE & LOGGING TRUCKS** on this section of the ride. I suggest that when you do the drop-off on the Albert River side that you conscript a driver to return the shuttle vehicle to Nipika and meet you there, or you will face a long drive after this ride to retrieve your drop-off vehicle. The total riding distance is around 45 kms, or 5-6 hours, if you do the pick-up at Nipika Touring Center, at the Cross River Rd., and Palliser River Rd. intersection.

To access this trail, take Settlers Rd. from Hwy 93 in Kootenay National Park, 20 kms. north of Radium Hot Springs. Follow Settlers Rd. to Nipika

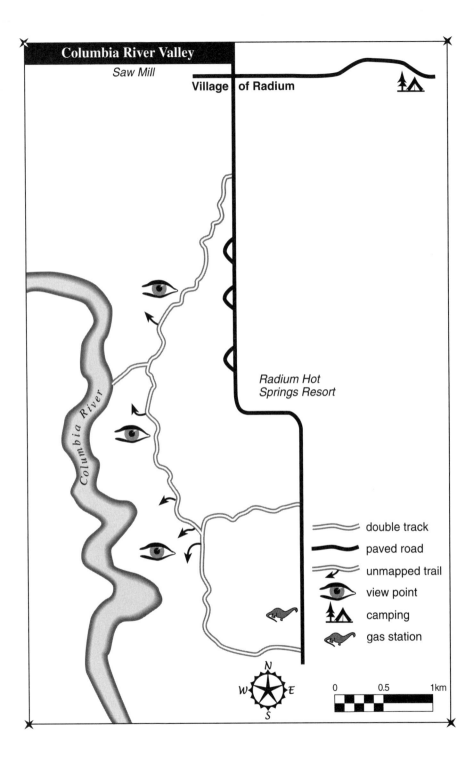

Columbia River Valley

Saw Mill

Village of Radium

Radium Hot
Springs Resort

Columbia River

double track
paved road
unmapped trail
view point
camping
gas station

N
W E
S

0   0.5   1km

Touring Center, where you should leave one vehicle, then continue South (right turn at Nipika) on to the Palliser Rd. (approx. 25 kms) to the Albert River Rd. then left up the Albert River Rd. for about 10 kms until you reach a beautiful old growth stand of giant Western Red Cedar (this stand of trees is so unique the B.C. Forest Service is preserving the whole area). As you travel through the Cedars, keep your eyes peeled for a brushed over road on the left hand side. This is the trailhead, start uphill on this road, and you will soon be out of the brush and heading for Miller Pass.

local knowledge

tasty bites & frosty pints

Blue Dog Café, 1213 Seventh Ave., Invermere, (250) 342-3814
Station Neighborhood Pub, 1701 Sixth Ave., Invermere, (250) 342-8346

camping / shelter

Cross River Cabins, near Invermere, (403) 271-3296
Nipika Lodge, 9200 Settlers Rd., 14 kms off Hwy. 93

off the bike in invermere

Adventures abound in the Columbia Valley. Whether you're paddling a voyageur canoe through some of the 150 kms of river wetlands (Columbia River Outfitters, 250-342-7397) or experiencing the lofty winds in a glider plane (Invermere Soaring Center, 250-342-7228) you will be amazed by the beauty of the valley and surrounding mountains. Columbia Rafting Adventures (1-877-706-RAFT) will show you the goods on Toby Creek, Class II and III + whitewater that will curl your toenails for under $50 a day. Check out www.adventurevalley.com for a great wealth of recreation ideas in the Columbia Valley.

what to expect

Cranbrook is another one of BC's mountain gems. At an elevation of just over 3000 ft., and sitting between Nelson and Fernie on Hwy 3, it is perfectly situated for a visit on a tour of southeastern BC. Drop in to Gerick Sports Experts, 907 Baker St., and they should be able to let you in on some of the areas tastier singletrack secrets.

trail descriptions

FORESTRY HILL BYPASS TRAIL / YELLOW LOOP (EASY – INTERMEDIATE)

The Forestry Hill Bypass Trail is an after work classic for those who need to do a little deep breathing at the end of the day. This trail is conveniently located just east of the city and consists primarily of singletrack. The highlight of this ridE is the final third, which is a fast, downhill singletrack. When bombing down this last part of the loop, be cautious of two-way traffic and hikers.

To access the trailhead from the College Parking lot, ride back on College Way towards the city center, turn left on 24th Ave., then left on 2nd St. S. Follow this route uphill as it changes to a gravel road and leaves the residential areas of town. About 1.5 km past the last houses, at the start of an S bend, you'll see a fence on the left and a small parking area. The trail begins just through the gate on the right. Look for the yellow circles and orange ribbons on the trees.

BIG HILL TRAIL (INTERMEDIATE – DIFFICULT)

This trail shares the trailhead with the Yellow Loop Bypass Trail. This long loop has two demanding climbs of about 200 meters each where excellent views of Cranbrook and the Rocky Mountain Trench reward your efforts. From the Big Hill Viewpoint, the downhill is steep, loose and rutted by the motorized folks. Once you are on the main road, follow it past the big puddle and down a long, gradual hill for about 400 meters until you reach a small clearing on the left. Look for white circles here, marking the start of a singletrack section. Once you finish this section at Kettle Lake you will join the Yellow loop for the remainder of the ride.

ISIDORE CANYON TRAIL (EASY)

This is a great out-and-back ride that is perfect for all levels of riders. The route is built upon an old rail bed that heads east from Cranbrook through a narrow canyon eventually opening up to a great view of the Rockies. The trail passes through ponds and marshes, offering good wildlife viewing opportunities. Bring a camera!

local knowledge

tasty bites & frosty pints

Swing Street Coffee House, 16-11th Ave. S

camping / shelter

Regency Park Campground, 2370 Cranbrook St. N.
Moyie Lake Prov. Park, south of Cranbrook on Hwy 95

Photo: www.freeriders.org   *A good rage in the sage*

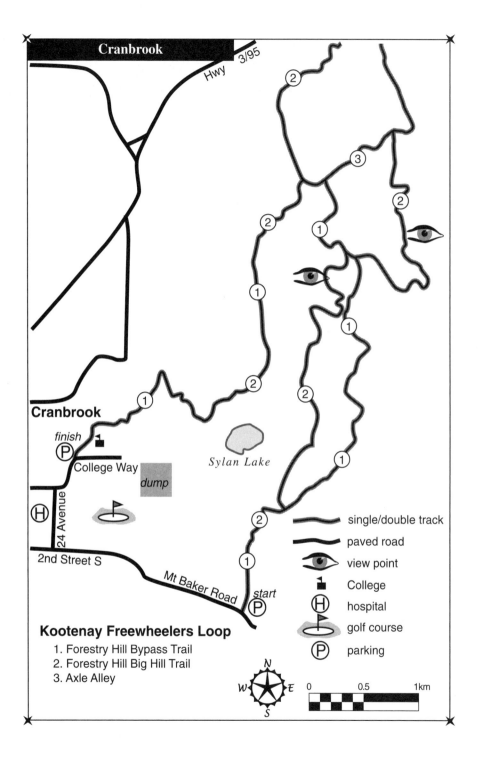

Cranbrook

Hwy 3/95

Cranbrook

finish
Ⓟ

College Way

dump

⊞ College

Ⓗ

24 Avenue

2nd Street S

Mt Baker Road

start
Ⓟ

Sylan Lake

— single/double track

— paved road

👁 view point

⊞ College

Ⓗ hospital

⛳ golf course

Ⓟ parking

Kootenay Freewheelers Loop

1. Forestry Hill Bypass Trail
2. Forestry Hill Big Hill Trail
3. Axle Alley

N
W ✦ E
S

0   0.5   1km

fernie

what to expect

Once you've been to Fernie, the locals ask that you keep it a secret. This is because it's BC's secret mountain hideaway. They don't want everyone packing up the dog and moving here. Once you've been to Fernie, you'll know what I'm talking about. It is incredibly beautiful with a warm, small town charm that welcomes everyone.

Fernie is the focal point of recreational activities in the East Kootenay. The famous powder stories from Snow Valley are now equaled by stories of stellar singletrack. The infrastructure of Fernie's history as a coal mining center is prominent on many of the rides. The old roads and railbeds leading into coal seams played a part in the trail network. The Coal Creek Trail and the Fernie Classic Trail are the two "best of" rides detailed here, as well as some brief information and map containing most of Fernie's singletrack, which emanates from the city center. Drop into the Ski Base, 432 2nd Ave., and they'll get you going on some of Fernie's best singletrack. Read on, and ride on in the East Kootenay.

trail descriptions

COAL CREEK TRAIL (EASY)

This ride is not included on the map, but is user friendly and signed. Expect moderated grades, utilizing an overgrown road and railbed from downtown Fernie to the old Coal Creek Townsite. The trail begins on 2nd Ave., across from the Ski Base. Signage and trail maps provide the directions and historical information on the former town of Coal Creek. Intended as a lazy afternoon ride, the scenic views of the forested valley should calm the most frantic, highway-frazzled urbanite.

If you feel adventurous, a strenuous ride or hike along a skidder trail will bring you to the closed mine tunnels that tell a story of this area's origin and purpose. You can coast all the way back as an alternative on Coal Creek Rd., although dust may deter you. If not, return the same way you came, back to the start.

THE FERNIE CLASSIC (DIFFICULT)

The Fernie Classic is the mountain biking equivalent of a 'best of' CD box set that you cherish. Several of the best trails in the valley are incorporated into this ride: ROOTS, HYPER EXTENSION, ERIC'S TRAIL, and DEADFALL. Deadfall is a mean, masochistic challenge that will have you wondering if you're up for the challenge.

Begin your journey at the nature trails off Coal Creek Rd., which is 2 minutes by bike from town. The trails loop and twist drunkenly upon themselves, but if navigated properly, will deposit you at the powerlines. From here, climb the powerline road. At the top, River Rd. almost intersects this road. A short climb to the 'window' provides an exceptional view south to Mt. Broadwood. The root, for which ROOTS is named, lies here; ride over it clean and call yourself lucky.

Next begins a twisting, singletrack downhill rip with country charm. Enjoy the log bridge over the creek. Turn right and welcome yourself to Roots Extension, where some hared climbing on loose sidehills will eventually bring you to HYPER EXTENSION, which is marked by a rock cairn. This trail demands granny-gear climbing and a slalom ride down. Retrace your original route, or pick a new one. Once at the bottom of HYPER EXTENSION, turn right and continue on the singletrack until it exits onto River Road. Ride down River Rd., cross Coal Creek and head up Ridgemont Rd. behind the city dump. These are logging roads, so watch out for trucks. As you ride up Ridgemont Rd., watch on the uphill bank for a worn path, this is ERIC'S TRAIL. ERIC'S is a hill climbing suffer-fest that the true endurance masochist will enjoy. Ignore the level areas as they are just teasers. About one third of the way up, there is a bailout for those who need to go home and cry. If you continue, you will pass the remnants of a cabin and then, undoubtedly on into enlightenment. Eventually, a short downhill brings you to a clearcut and onto Ridgemont Road. Look up the road to where it forks at the treeline. At the apex of the fork, is the trailhead for DEADFALL. Beware of moose. This is the original mountain bike trail in the valley. It is fun, scary, challenging, narrow, rooted, rutted and steep that dishes up the smiles in spades. At the end of

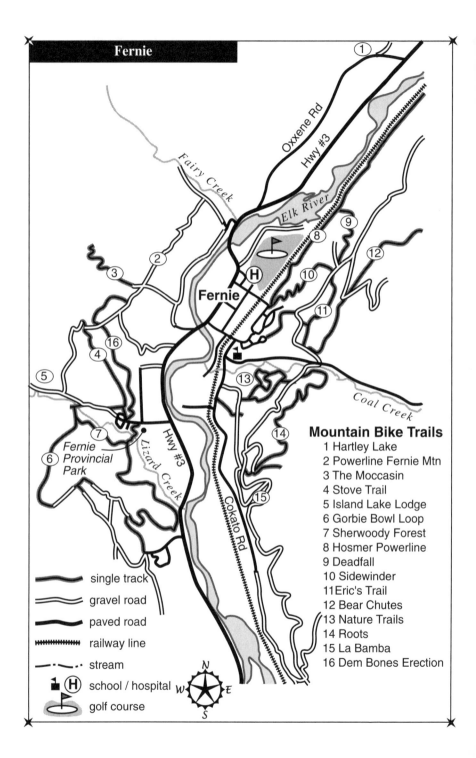

Fernie

Mountain Bike Trails

1 Hartley Lake
2 Powerline Fernie Mtn
3 The Moccasin
4 Stove Trail
5 Island Lake Lodge
6 Gorbie Bowl Loop
7 Sherwoody Forest
8 Hosmer Powerline
9 Deadfall
10 Sidewinder
11 Eric's Trail
12 Bear Chutes
13 Nature Trails
14 Roots
15 La Bamba
16 Dem Bones Erection

single track
gravel road
paved road
railway line
stream
school / hospital
golf course

DEADFALL is the powerline road. Turn left and head back to town. Please close cattle gates, and don't chase the cows. Grab a burger in town instead.

OTHER FERNIE TRAILS

Other Fernie Trails to explore include the 10 km grind up to Hartly Lake on a smooth, generally easy road. The MOCCASIN TRAIL is a brutal 4x4 road, which leads to a hiking trail to the peak of Fernie Mountain. The STOWE TRAIL is a granny-gear climb and is quite technical; return down the same route. The long, winding, dirt-packed road to Island Lake Lodge will surround riders with some of the BC interior's largest cedar trees. The GORBY BOWL LOOP uses old skidder trails and singletrack. This is a fun, strenuous loop that can be ridden in both directions. Stick with the climbing to get the reward of great views. SHERWOODY FOREST has plenty of great flowing, technically challenging trails. Cross the creek at the corral on Island Lake Lodge Road. The HOSMER POWERLINE will give you about 10 km of trail on a grassy, hard-packed surface. SIDEWINDER is a tough one to find but has some fun, sweeping downhill turns. This trail can be ridden in both directions. THE BEAR CHUTES are extreme technical challenges. They're rough and unforgiving. LA BAMBA is a short little trip up to River Road fro Cokato Road. This trail is believed to the resting place of Ritchie Valens. DEM BONES is the home of the sacred skeletal meadow. It is a long, hard climb and part of the FERNIE CLASSIC described above.

local knowledge

tasty bites & frosty pints

Edge of the World Diner, (250) 423-9292
Jamocha's Coffee House & Bagel Co., 851 7th Ave. 423-6977

camping / shelter

Same Sun International Hostel, Hwy. 3 & 9th St. (1-877-56-CARVE)
Mt. Fernie Prov. Park, 3 km south of Fernie on Hwy. 3

off the bike in fernie

Being the quintessential mountain town that it is, Fernie is blessed with incredible terrain and a population that knows how to make the most of it. No matter what your recreational desire, you can quench it here. Hiking in the Lizard Range, Paddling on the great local rivers, rock climbing on secluded crags and peaks, the list is endless.

The kayaking in the Fernie area is among the best in BC. There are several excellent rivers around with varying degrees of skill levels required. Paddling guides and river outfitters abound in Fernie as well. Check out www.paddlefernie.com for a complete list of guides and river information. Head on up to Fernie Alpine Resort for some above-treeline fun. Hiking in alpine meadows, horseback rides or just plain relaxing in the wildflowers is all worth checking out. Contact the resort at (250) 423-4655 or go to www.skifernie.com.

Photo: www.freeriders.org

what to expect

Muslims orient themselves to Mecca, in the east, when they pray. Mountain bikers in BC do the same because to mountain bikers, the small town of Nelson in southeastern BC *is* Mecca.

British Columbia has the best riding in the world; the Kootenays have perhaps the best riding in BC and Nelson arguably the best riding in the Kootenays. It shouldn't surprise you to figure out that Nelson is one of the ultimate riding destinations there is. There are tons of incredibly challenging singletracks that will make you bleed, laugh, cry and fly all in one ride. There is such an incredible sense of community among the riders here that it just feels like home. Someone will always be there to point you in the right direction or help you fix a flat or even fix your body.

There are also several excellent intermediate trails in the Nelson area. Riders of all levels of ability will find Nelson to be an unforgettable experience. Your best bet is to drop in to see the nice folks at The Sacred Ride downtown, 213 Baker St., and they will point you in the right direction. The STANLEY LOOP is recommended for those who wish to keep the rubber side down and on the ground. For those in the other camp, try just about any other trail that Nelson has to offer. You will not be disappointed, I guarantee it. In fact I'll eat this book if you are. (Guarantee valid until Jan. 1, 1985).

trail descriptions

THE STANLEY LOOP (EASY-INTERMEDIATE)

This loop is fun to ride in either direction. To access the trail from town, ride up Stanley St. to the top. Follow the trail until it ends. There is a trail to your left that follows a barbed wire fence up to abandoned rail tracks. Follow the tracks left, cross two main trestles, and find the trail on your left after the second trestle. Climb until you hit a logging road. Turn right and ride until you hit the active sand pit. Cross through the pit to the road on the far side. From Hwy. 6 go right for about 100 meters and left onto Giveout Creek FSR. At the 3 way road junction, look for the trail down

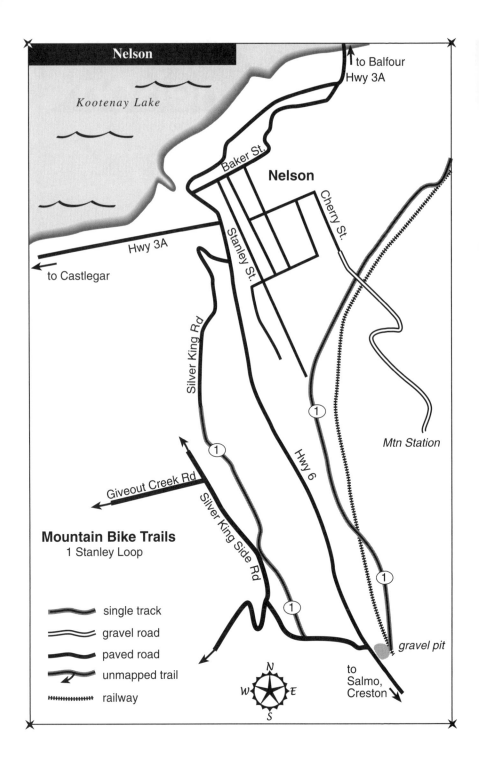

the Silver King Side Rd. to your right. After the glorious descent, you pop out on Silver King Road. Follow this road back to town.

PLACENTA DESCENTA (INTERMEDIATE – DIFFICULT)

This is one of the first mountain bike downhills in Nelson. It's a fast, fun and steep trail with some great rock drops. It works well to combine this trail with WAKE 'N BAKE then finish with PULMONARY. This will drop you back down to Hwy. 3 on the lakeshore. To access this trail, head to South Nelson or the Rosemont area and get on Vancouver Street. Ride south on Vancouver St. and it will eventually turn into Silver King Road. Silver King Rd. will bring you to the 2K mark of the Giveout Creek FSR (Forest Svc. Rd.). Climb the FSR to the 9K mark and you'll see the trailhead on the right for Placenta Descenta. If driving, head west of Nelson on Hwy. 3 to the Giveout Creek FSR and turn left.

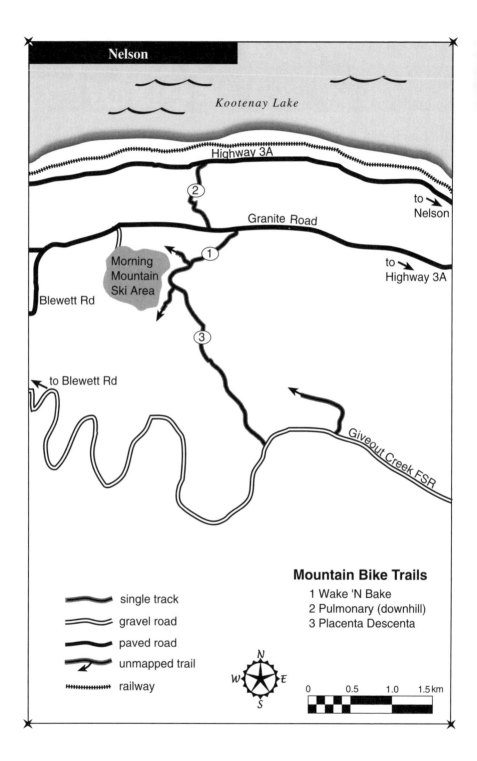

WAKE 'N BAKE (DIFFICULT)

This is a natural extension of PLACENTA DESCENTA. It's quick and it's steep. When Placenta Descenta drops you to the Morning Mtn. Ski Area, keep right at all the forks. Soon you'll be down at Granite Road. From here, turn left and ride for about 300 meters to the trailhead for PULMONARY.

PULMONARY (DIFFICULT)

This is what fun riding is all about. Lots of steep rock faces with some bridges and great singletrack. Body armor is a must. To access this trail either ride up Granite Road for 5 kms to the trailhead on the right or just continue on from the bottom of WAKE 'N BAKE. It finishes on Hwy. 3, with a short spin back to Nelson.

local knowledge

tasty bites & frosty pints

Mike's Place, in the Heritage Inn, 422 Vernon St. at Ward
The Lakeside Coffee Cup, waterfront pathway at the Prestige Inn

camping / shelter

Kokanee Creek Prov. Park, Hwy. 3A, 19 km east of Nelson, 800-689-9025
Nelson City Campground, High St., (250) 352-6075

off the bike in nelson

Nelson may just be the prettiest town in Canada. It has over 350 beautifully preserved heritage buildings dating from the turn of the century era. Just walking around the town and drinking in the history is a great way to spend a rest day for many. Other options include hiking in the old growth forest near Kokanee Creek, on the north shore of the lake. If you would rather be on the water, the Kootenay Kayak Co., (579 Baker St., 1-877-229-4959) can outfit and guide you for a day trip on the lake or a 3 day excursion. Drop in to The Sacred Ride or the Nelson Tourist Bureau for all kinds of other ideas.

what to expect

Castlegar is a charming little Kootenay mountain town with a slow pace and good riding. If you're on a road trip through the Kootenays, you're bound to pass through it, as it's at the junction of Highway 3, 3A and 22. There is some great slickrock riding up on the Beaver Trails as well as some more serious downhill fun nearby. Your best bet is to talk to the folks at Castlegar Bicycle & Sport Shop, (250) 365-5044, and they could point you to some other great trails in the area.

trail descriptions

THE BEAVER TRAILS (INTERMEDIATE)

The Beaver Trails are located on the lower east facing slopes of the Robson Range. The trails range in elevation from about 1600 ft. to a maximum of about 2300 feet. The generally low elevation of this ride makes it hot in the summer. To access the trails take Woodland Dr. up from Columbia Ave. and turn onto Chickadee Lane. When the

Photo: www.freeriders.org

pavement ends, turn left on a loose, sandy doubletrack on your left. This is a mostly rolling trail with a slight climb to an old cabin. Once past the cabin, a fast downhill cranks you quickly down to Merry Creek. This is a fun section but riders have to slow down for the creek crossing to avoid trouble. After the creek, a 5 to 10 minute climb switches back and brings you to the top of a slickrock section. This slickrock is truly reminiscent of Moab, Utah as riders experience the fast, pure-traction feel of the beloved rock. Follow the painted arrows and ride between the rock piles that indicate trail direction. The trail eventually turns into

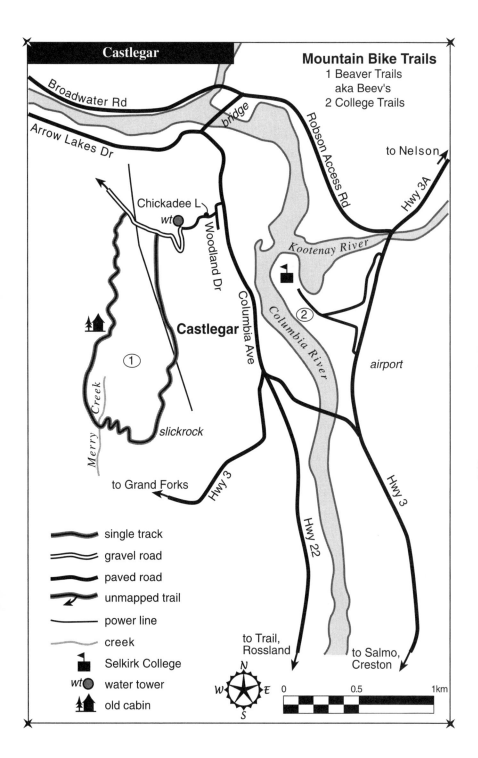

a fast singletrack downhill and shoots you onto a doubletrack. Follow this trail left, back to the road you climbed earlier. Avoid the singletrack on your right. If you want to do it again, simply go left and repeat the process.

local knowledge

tasty bites & frosty pints
Banjo's Pub, 1800 8th Ave, (250) 365-6933

camping / shelter
Pass Creek Regional Park, (250) 365-9535

off the bike in castlegar
A visit to the Doukhobor Village is a must even if you're just passing through. The Doukhobors left Russia in the late 1800's fearing persecution for religious beliefs, settling on the plains of Saskatchewan and then moving once again to the fertile valleys of southeast BC. Their history is rich, and their stories are many. Their colorful culture comes alive at the Doukhobor Village Museum. It is located across from the airport near the junction of Crowsnest, Hwy. 3 & 3A, open 10-6 daily.

what to expect

Imagine a place where your mountain bike dreams can come true: endless singletrack, years worth of exploring and riding and all of this surrounding a true alpine town with friendly folks, loads of history and a local culture that lives the mountain lifestyle. There is such a place. It's called Rossland.

Trails sprawl out of Rossland like a spilled bowl of singletrack spaghetti with trails to suit all different riders' appetites. A little peckish for some doubletrack? Starving for some downhill singletrack? It's easy to satisfy the pallet of any rider in Rossland. After any ride, a cruise through downtown will tempt you to relax on a patio and soak up the vibe of this Kootenay mountain paradise. Due to its higher elevation, the riding season in Rossland tends to be a little shorter than other areas in the Kootenays, usually form May to October. Drop in to see the folks at the Sacred Ride, 2123 Columbia, (250) 362-568, for more detailed information about these trails.

trail descriptions

OLD CASCADE HIGHWAY & DEWDNEY TRAIL (INTERMEDIATE)

One of the longer rides that a visitor to Rossland ought to experience is the Dewdney Trail, part of the original Trans Canada Highway. To access the trail, head out of town to the west on Columbia Ave. until you get to the Mining Museum, then turn left and pedal down the highway for abut 300 meters and turn right onto the Old Cascade Highway. You should see a sign about 60 meters down the road on the right that reads, "There is no dump along this road." If you miss this, double back. If you're looking for a spot to throw that old couch, you can get a life. About 13 km and 100 vertical feet later, you reach a distinct plateau where the powerlines should be seen above you. At this point, there is a dirt road on your left where you turn into, and about 10 meters later on your left is the 2300 ft. descent. Point it down and enjoy the ride!

This trail is well marked except at two points but the best description is never as good as the simple local advice to follow tire tracks and chain ring marks over logs. Riders pop out on Hwy. 22, which is a good grunt away from town. Turn left, and about 8 km later, Rossland awaits. The Bryden sawmill marks about the halfway point on the journey home. Although this ride is rated as intermediate, its length alone is enough to make it difficult for most riders. Expect a 3-5 hour ride, so bring food, and tools.

RAILGRADE (INTERMEDIATE)

The railgrade was used to transport people from the towns of Trail and Warfield. To access this easy, smooth descending old rail grade from Main Street, head into lower Rossland via Spokane Street. This road turns to the left and becomes Le Roi Avenue. Go down this road for about 150 meters and turn left on Davis Street. Ride along Davis until you see Victoria St. at the bottom of a big hill. Turn left and then right up a short street, and then left on Union Avenue. Travel along Union Ave. until you see the RAILGRADE TRAIL on the left about 60 meters from the top of a little hill.

MIDNIGHT LOOP (INTERMEDIATE)

This is a nice trail for those who want a steady workout without the hazards of a fully difficult trail. To access this trail ride out the OLD CASCADE HIGHWAY for about 200 meters until you see a road on the left. Follow this road until you see a yellow bridge. Turn left, and follow the road until you see the Bryden Mill. You can retrace your steps or ride back to town along the highway.

DOUKHABOUR DRAW (INTERMEDIATE)

To access this trail, use the same route as the RAILGRADE, except you turn right on Spokane St. from Union Avenue. Spokane turns into Southbelt Rd. where you ride out until you get to the end and you should spot the trailhead.

SMUGGLERS LOOP (DIFFICULT)

To access this trail, use the same route as DOUKHABOUR DRAW, except you turn left at Gelesz St. onto a gravel road. Ride down for about 1 km and you will pass a road on the left called Maldy Creek Forest Service Road. The next road on the left is the SMUGGLERS LOOP. This is a demanding climb for about 30 to 45 minutes, then rolls around and takes you to the RUBBERHEAD or 007.

007 (DIFFICULT)

Access this trail from the RAILGRADE. Ride down the RAILGRADE for about 2 km and take the fires road up to the right. You will see a carved sign about 20 feet up the road on a tree that says 007 / RUBBERHEAD. You will come to a fork in the road; stay right for 007 or left for RUBBERHEAD and RABBID SLUG.

RABID SLUG (DIFFICULT)

To access this sick & twisted beauty of a trail, follow the instructions for 007. At the fork in the road, go left and follow the RUBBERHEAD until you come under the powerlines and then go back into the forest about 30 ft., where you should see the trailhead on your right. This challenging, balancey, "courage-required" trail will drop you onto the RUBBERHEAD loop. Go left to get back to town.

RUBBERHEAD (INTERMEDIATE)

A Rossland classic. To access this trail, ride up RAILGRADE from Union St. in lower Rossland, just below Spokane. Follow the signs to stay on the rail grade. When you've passed the intersection where 007 reaches RAILGRADE, on the right, begin looking for a sharp gravel turn on your left. This is RUBBERHEAD.

CROWN POINT (DIFFICULT)

You access this trail from 007. After climbing, the road starts to gently descend and then there is a big sweeping left with a stream crossing down the bank on the right. At this point, there is a road to the left; this is the trailhead. This trail has plenty of logs, wet rocky sections and some short, steep sections. Good cheap thrills.

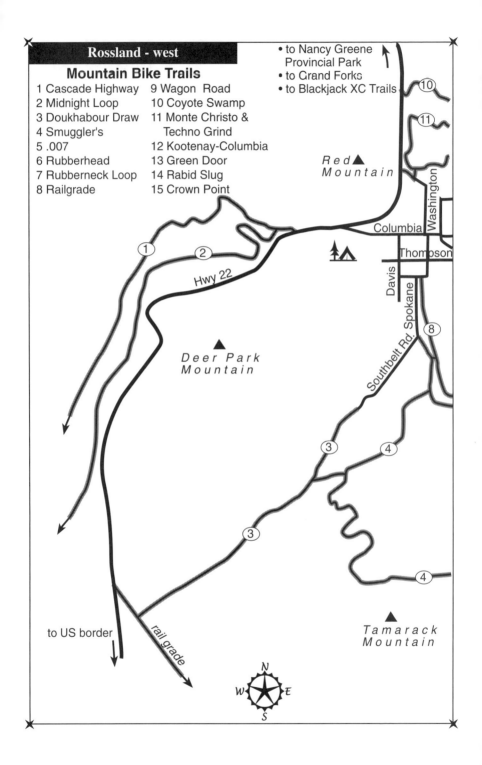

Rossland - west

Mountain Bike Trails

1 Cascade Highway
2 Midnight Loop
3 Doukhabour Draw
4 Smuggler's
5 .007
6 Rubberhead
7 Rubberneck Loop
8 Railgrade
9 Wagon Road
10 Coyote Swamp
11 Monte Christo & Techno Grind
12 Kootenay-Columbia
13 Green Door
14 Rabid Slug
15 Crown Point

• to Nancy Greene Provincial Park
• to Grand Forks
• to Blackjack XC Trails

Red ▲
Mountain

Washington

Columbia

Thompson

Davis

Southbelt Rd. Spokane

Hwy 22

Deer Park Mountain ▲

Tamarack Mountain ▲

to US border

rail grade

N
W · E
S

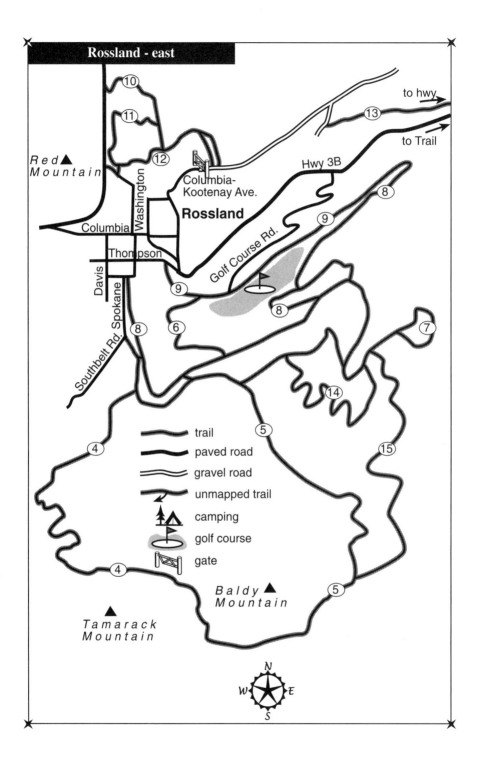

Rossland - east

Red▲
Mountain

Washington

Columbia-
Kootenay Ave.

Rossland

Hwy 3B

Columbia

Thompson

Golf Course Rd.

Davis

Southbelt Rd. Spokane

to hwy

to Trail

⑩
⑪
⑫
⑬
⑧
⑨
⑨
⑧
⑥
⑧
⑦
⑧
⑭
⑤
⑮
④
⑤
④
⑤

trail
paved road
gravel road
unmapped trail
camping
golf course
gate

Baldy ▲
Mountain

▲
Tamarack
Mountain

N
W E
S

GREEN DOOR (INTERMEDIATE)

To access the GREEN DOOR, ride up Main St. to the east until you get to Park St., which is the last street on the left. Here you turn left and follow this road staying to the left as it will turn into Crescent Ave., then onto Georgia Street. Next, turn off Georgia onto Columbia Kootenay Avenue. Ride down, pass through a gate and be very respectful because you are on private land. Continue along until you see a road going sharply off to the right. Follow this road about 80 meters until you see a road going sharply off to the right. Follow this road about 80 meters until you see a trail that goes over a little bank on the left. This trail has a couple of creek crossings, some steep descents and a steep little climb.

This trail will take you to the sand pit corner of the highway where you cross the highway at its apex. Ride uphill and watch for a trail on the left, down into a field. This will lead to the WAGON ROAD and into Rossland. If you are a little hungry or thirsty, stop by the golf course and fill your tanks. If you just want to get back to town peddle over the golf course road to the old graveyard and onto Thompson Avenue. Turn left and head up to the four way stop and turn right onto Davis St. then left on Le Roi Ave., following this up to Main Street.

TECHNO GRIND & KOOTENAY COLUMBIA (INTERMEDIATE)

To access this trail, ride up Washington St. to the top of town. At the junction of Kirkup Ave. and McLeod Ave. there is a road that goes up to the top of Monte Christo Mountain; follow this up the hill. The first fork on the left will take you to the top of Kootenay-Columbia Mountain by following the orange markers marked KC. To access TECHNO GRIND, keep going to the top of the road until you're almost at the top where you turn left. After 20 meters, you'll see a trail on the left. This is the one you're looking for. This eventually reaches a doubletrack; turn right here, and keep looking for the singletrack after a few hundred meters on the right. TECHNO GRIND does its name proud with a great combination of gnarly and fun.

rossland

WAGON ROAD (INTERMEDIATE)

To access this trail, go down Spokane St., which turns to the right onto Le Roi Avenue. Go down to Davis St. and turn left. At the 4-way stop, Thompson Ave., turn left again and ride down along the flats and as the road climbs Esling Dr. is on the right, this road takes you to the trail.

local knowledge

tasty bites & frosty pints

Alpine Grind Coffee House, 2207 Columbia Ave.
Mountain Gypsy Café, 2167 Washington St.

camping / shelter

Mountain Shadow Hostel, 2125 Columbia Ave., (250) 362-7160

off the bike in rossland

You name it, and Rossland has got it. Kayaking (some of the top 'park & play' waves in Canada), golf (two courses nearby), as well as fishing in local lakes and rivers. In addition to the great recreation opportunities in the Rossland area, are the historical side trips. Rossland was founded by gold-hungry miners who stumbled upon the Le Roi mine in 1890. Soon after that, the gold rush started and Rossland boomed. At the Rossland Museum (1-888-48-7444) you can tour the underground Le Roi mine that started it all and find out what it was like to live in the gold rush times of the late 1800's. For more information on the town, check out www.rossland.com.

Photo: Lyle Knight   *Spruce Lake Area*

Photo: Janice Strong/Tourism Rockies

what to expect

You will not find a riding area in all of Canada, let alone North America, quite like Williams Lake. Steep, burly scree chutes, wide-open pine and fir forests with fast, rolling singletrack lines that never end are the standard in these parts. It is fast becoming a popular destination for many riders because of this.

Walking around the back streets of the town, it feels like it was on the short list for 'Bonanza'. Where else would you find the 'BC Cowboy Hall of Fame'? (I highly recommend a trip to see all of your favorite cowboys and their stuffed steeds.) Known to some locals as Bill's Pond, it's been a well-kept secret, up until now, that is. The cat's outta the bag, thanks in part to the *Kranked* trilogy of mountain bike films. Trails like the super steep and fast 'Sweet Pete' or the classic cross-country, enduro-fest 'Southside Trail' are what Williams Lake riding is all about. In the hot, dry summer, you'll finish some rides looking like a soot-faced coal miner. Picking the dirt out of your teeth, having smiled all the way back down to the valley bottom. Finish picking and head on out for another rip.

Photo: Chris Rollett Photo   *yours truly*

williamslake

trail descriptions

FOX MTN LOOP (INTERMEDIATE)

This loop starts just up the hill, north of the lights on Hwy. 97. Turn uphill past the car wash to the end of the road. Turn uphill again and left on the powerline access road and stay on this road until it goes through a gully. At the top of this gully look for the single track climbing off on your right. The moderate climb has a number of switchbacks, some tight turns and gets you to the top of Fox Mountain.

At the top, when the trail levels off, you'll come to another wide trail. Turn left onto a road, another left to paved Mt. Fox Rd., or stay on a short parallel double track to a gravel road. If you stay on the double track the trail opening is straight across up the bank. The trail now twists beside the gravel road for a short section till you hit a wider trail. Ignore the left and right trails at this intersection. The downhill now skirts along the cliff edge. Note the two trails on your right, they are the entrance and exit to a short technical section you can add on if you wish.

At the cliff stay left and check out the sweet view from high above Williams Lake. The ridge across the valley has another stellar ride to check out. The trail basically follows the ridge, with two short detours into the forest. The trail to the left is a bailout to Fox Mountain Rd. After you have left the cliffside and climbed slightly, the trail will turn to the right and start down.

NO LEFT TURN (INTERMEDIATE)

This trail starts at about the 3 km point of the Fox Trail. Just before the viewpoint, hang a right and follow the singletrack down along the cliff face toward Williams Lake. Some wild views and tight twisty sections will take you right back down to where you started at the car wash.

Drop in and see the folks at Red Shreds for some advice on other sweet spots to ride nearby, (250) 398-7873.

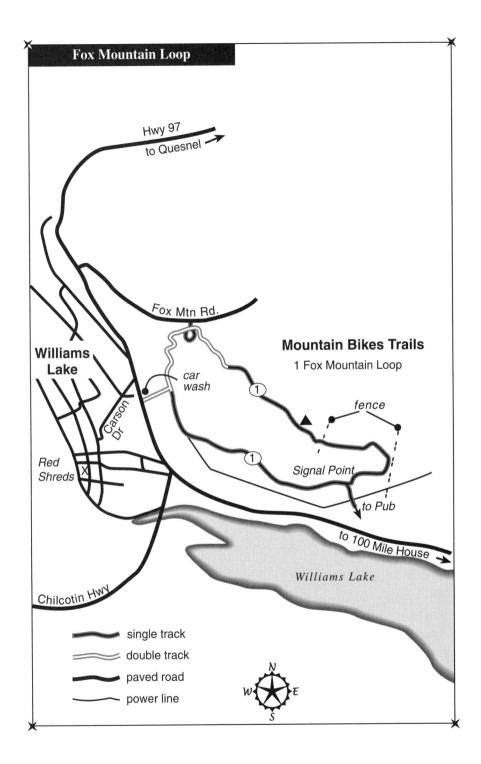

Fox Mountain Loop

Hwy 97
to Quesnel →

Fox Mtn Rd.

Williams Lake

car wash

Mountain Bikes Trails

1 Fox Mountain Loop

①

fence

▲

①

Carson Dr

Red Shreds

X

Signal Point

to Pub

to 100 Mile House →

Williams Lake

Chilcotin Hwy

〰〰 single track

〰〰 double track

〰〰 paved road

— power line

N
W · E
S

williams**lake**

local knowledge

tasty bites & frosty pints
Laughing Loon Neighborhood Pub - 1730 S. Broadway, 398-5666

campsites
Farwell Canyon - 45 minutes west of town on Hwy. 20.
This has got to be one of the coolest places to camp in the whole Cariboo region. No charge, wicked riding on the slopes above camp and the cold, clear Chilcotin River singing you to sleep at night. Directions: take Hwy. 20 west for 47km to Riske Cr., turn S. on Farwell Canyon Rd., for 10-20 mins. until you're in the canyon, then camp where ye may. WARNING: leave no trace! Pack out what you pack in and don't set the world on fire.

off the bike in williams lake
If the weather has crapped out or if you're just plain tuckered, here's your opportunity to live out your boyhood (or girlhood) fantasies to be a cowboy (or cowgirl). Every Canada Day weekend [July 1] the Williams Lake Stampede brings the cowpokes out of the woodwork for BC's largest and oldest rodeo.

Some pretty wicked whitewater rivers crisscross the Cariboo-Chilcotin region so stuff your kayak into the traveling toy box if you've got one, otherwise it's easy enough to rent some 'tupperware tubs' from some local shops.

If cragging is your bag, there are a number of decent climbing crags in the area as well. Drop by Red Shred's and they'll set you up with all your riding, climbing and paddling information. (250) 398-7873, otherwise contact the visitor info. center at (250) 392-5025.

what to expect

You've been driving for what seems like days. You'd kill for even one new CD in your car and the floor is only a memory, covered now by a six inch carpet of beef jerky wrappers, coffee cups and Spitz bags. You're half expecting the "Welcome to the Arctic Circle" sign when SHAZAM! Like a sprawling northern oasis rising out of the forest, Prince George appears around a bend. Unfolding yourself from your bug-plastered vehicle, and feeling every bit the road warrior, your mind gears down to handle the basic necessities of food, shelter and riding. Herein lie the goods.

There are three main riding areas in and around PG, two of which are linked by a beautiful 25 KM glide through the forest called the Cranbrook Hill Greenway. This multi-use trail links the network of trails at UNBC (Univ. of Northern BC) with the Otway Nordic Ski Centre. The other is across the river. It's called the Love Trail and it's a fun rip along the cut banks above the mighty Fraser River.

trail descriptions

OTTWAY NORDIC TRAILS (EASY)

An excellent collection of fast, ripping singletrack, even faster gravel paths and some sweet steep stuff all tucked away in a beatiful wilderness setting just outside town. Take 5th ave. west to Ospika Blvd. north, and continue until you pass over two railway crossings. The cabin and parking area are on the left. Your best bet is to ride out from town and have a blast ripping around for the day.

THE LOVE TRAIL (EASY)

This old classic singletrack, built by the Prince George Cycling Club, is a great ride that meanders along the cutbanks above the Fraser River. Offering fantastic views of PG and some pleasant riding, it is a worthy spin across the bridge and can be easily reached from town by bike. Although it can be ridden in either direction, it is best enjoyed fron north to south. The

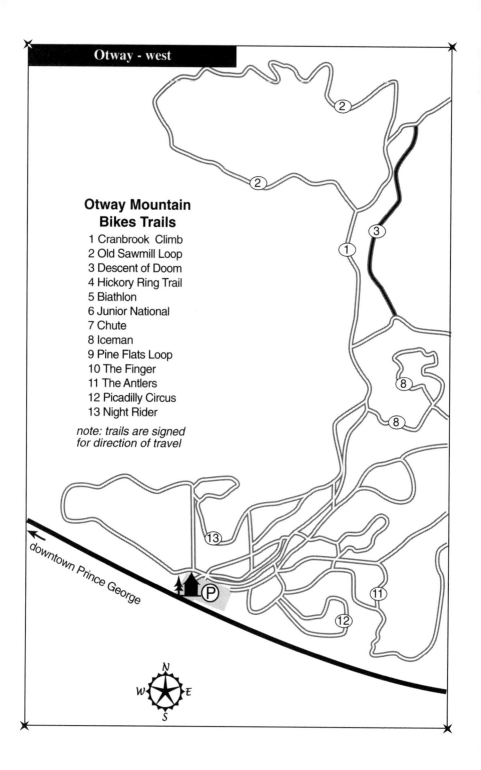

Otway - west

**Otway Mountain
Bikes Trails**

1 Cranbrook Climb
2 Old Sawmill Loop
3 Descent of Doom
4 Hickory Ring Trail
5 Biathlon
6 Junior National
7 Chute
8 Iceman
9 Pine Flats Loop
10 The Finger
11 The Antlers
12 Picadilly Circus
13 Night Rider

*note: trails are signed
for direction of travel*

downtown Prince George

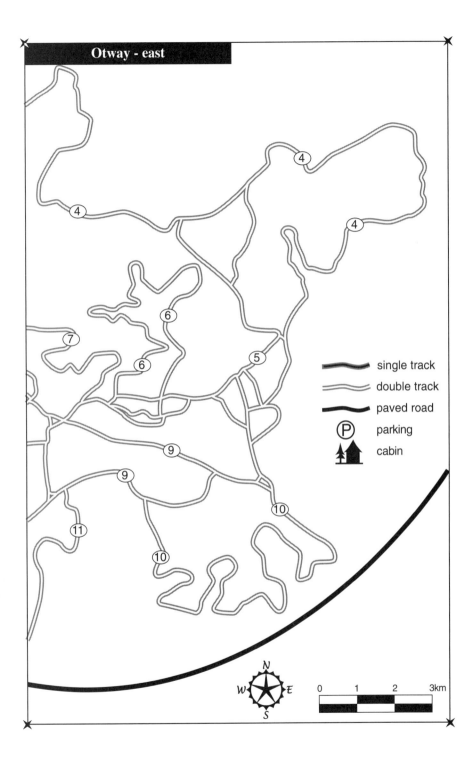

Otway - east

single track
double track
paved road
Ⓟ parking
cabin

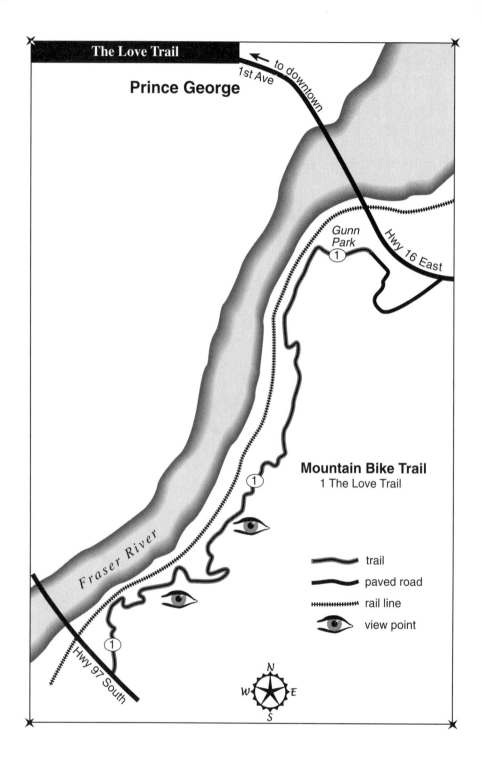

The Love Trail

Prince George

to downtown

1st Ave

Gunn Park
①

Hwy 16 East

Mountain Bike Trail
1 The Love Trail

Fraser River

①

①

Hwy 97 South

trail

paved road

rail line

view point

N
W E
S

trail head is 10 minutes from downtown along 1st. Ave. East. Climb across the Hwy. 16 bridge, and look for the trail entrance 50m past the end of the bridge. Return on Hwy. 97.

local knowledge

tasty bites & frosty pints
Buffalo Brewing Co. Pub - 564-7100

campsites
There are plenty of provincal and private campgrounds all around Price George ranging from remote wilderness sites to full service RV parks, and all types in between. Contact Tourism Prince George for a complete list of sites in the area at (250) 562-3700.

off the bike in prince george
Llama trek anyone? What are these South American native quadrupeds doing in BC's north? Carrying your packs through the moutains, of course. If that freaks you out a little too much, ensconce yourself in the rich history that surrounds the area and visit a native burial ground (no, really, you can). Or climb all over an authentic steam train at the Railway & Forestry Museum, (250) 563-7351. Crank it up a little and have a pant-filling ride on a River Jet Boat Safari, (250) 962-8913.

smithers

what to expect

Smithers is way up there when you're looking at the BC map, but hey, look how much further it is to the Arctic Circle. This town is a little gem of BC's north. The laid back Bavarian style, with heaps of charm and European flavor along with the ripping fast singletrack make a trip to Smithers worth rolling your odometer for.

Much of the riding in this area is on beautifully maintained trails that link old mining and logging roads as well as through ranchlands; all historical remnants of Smithers' past. The town sits in the middle of three mountain ranges and therefore has some of the most spectacular mountain scenery of all the trails in this book. You could search for years and not find a ride with the views that the Telkwa Pass trail has.

trail descriptions

PERIMITER TRAIL (EASY)

This is an excellent family ride or a good "healer" if your body is in need of some re-coop time. Circumnavigating the entire town, it's 9.4 km length has many access points, a good one being Riverside Park, on the east side of town along the Bulkley River. It is a multi-use recreation trail consisting of crushed gravel and paved paths, so you should keep your be aware of other hikers, bikers and horses.

CALL LAKE TRAIL (EASY)

Created by a bunch of benevolent, forward thinking cows, this 5 km trail winds through Call Lake Provincial Park in a loop that skirts the lake and has sweet veiws of Hudson's Bay Mountain. Take Hwy. 16 east from town for about 2 km an turn left on Viewmount Rd. Turn right on Van Gaalen and follow to the last left turn on the top, wher it turns into Montainview Rd. Take this left and follow to its end. Park near the signs to Call Lake. The trail head is at the sign. Be sure to close the gate, i'm sure Ed Walton's cows would love to wander through the valleys creating pleasant singletrack for miles, however, Ed wouldn't.

MALKOW LOOKOUT TRAIL (INTERMEDIATE)

This trail takes you to a former Forest Service lookout, making the views of the town and surrounding mountains superb. This one is a great singletrack climb, so make sure your granny ring is working. To reach it, head east of Hwy. 16 and turn left on Old Babine Lake Rd. After about 4.5 km, turn left on McCabe Rd, following it for about 1.5 km to a small parking area on the left. Voila! The trail starts here. Please ensure you close any gates you open, the horses tend to stroll into town if given the opportunity in the form of an open gate.

Photo: Wendy Perry

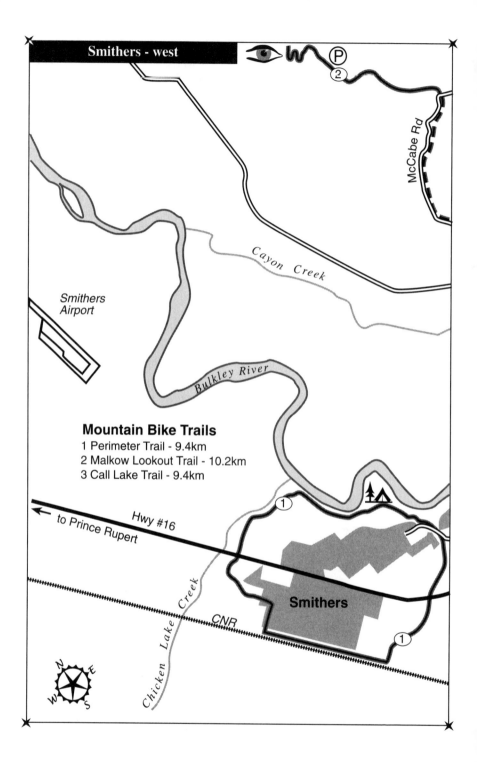

Smithers - west

McCabe Rd

Cayon Creek

Smithers
Airport

Bulkley River

Mountain Bike Trails
1 Perimeter Trail - 9.4km
2 Malkow Lookout Trail - 10.2km
3 Call Lake Trail - 9.4km

Hwy #16
to Prince Rupert

①

Chicken Lake Creek

Smithers

CNR

①

N
E
W
S

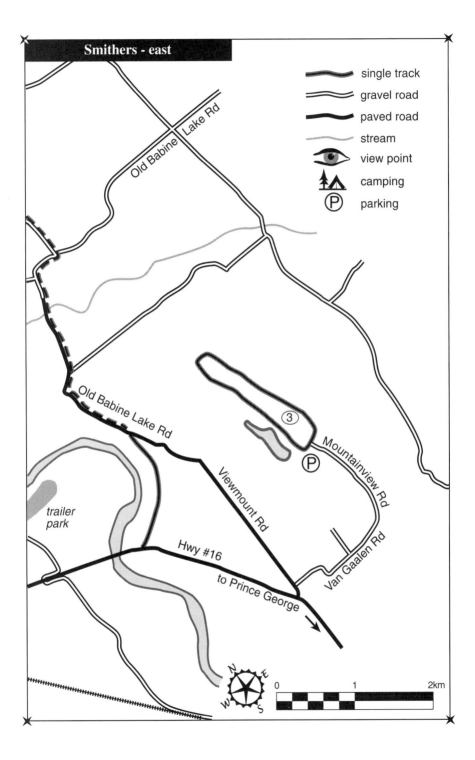

SILVER KING BASIN TRAIL (INTERMEDIATE)

It's a trail like this that puts the 'mountain' in mountain biking. In a short 7 km, you can reach the basin and sub-alpine meadows. In the basin is the Joe L'Orsa Cabin, an idyllic place for an overnight stay($5 fee).

To access this trail, head east from town and turn left on Old Babine Lake Rd. and follow it to the intersection of Telkwa High Rd. Turn left and travel 2 km to reach Driftwood Rd., turn right. After 4 km, you'll see Driftwood Canyon Provincial Park and the fossil beds. The Driftwood Parking Lot is the best place to park on this road and it's a further 7 km or so north along the road. The parking lot has a picnic area and toilets. About 1.4 km after the gate at the parking lot, you'll cross the Sunny Point foot bridge, turn right and start up the moderate, yet constant climb to Silver King Basin.

CRONIN PASS (INTERMEDIATE)

The Cronin Pass trail is a very scenic ride into the alpine meadows of the Babine Mountains. This ride combines the full spectrum of mountian biking trail types and will include a minimum of 1 to 2 hours of climbing. Expect good wildlife viewing possibilities (espessicaly if you duct tape some bacon to your buddy's pack).

To access the trail, take Hwy. 16 east for about 6 km to Eckman Rd. Turn left and follow Babin Lake Rd. for about 33 km, you should see the turn off to the Cronin Rd. parking area just before the 33 km sign. From here, pedal about 7.5 km to the trail head on the left side of Cronin Rd. There is a sign and a registration box.

TELKWA PASS ROUTE (DIFFICULT)

Requiring slightly more "huevos" than most trails in the area due to its commitment factor, the Telkwa to Terrace route, or the Telkwa Pass, is a serious backcountry trek. If you're ambitious enough, you can ride it in a 120 km, point-to-point fashinon, or simply grind your way up to the pass and turn around to head back. At the top is the appropriately named Top Lake, a good rustic spot to camp.

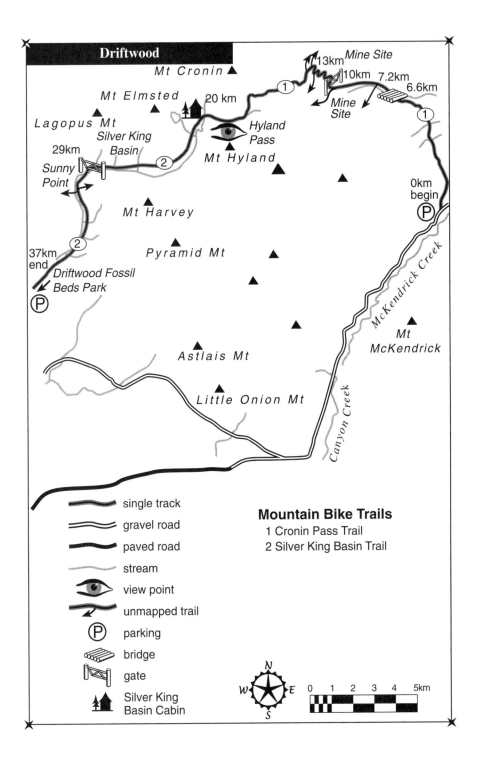

Driftwood

Mt Cronin ▲

13km Mine Site

10km

Mt Elmsted ▲   20 km   1   7.2km   6.6km

Lagopus Mt ▲   ▲   Mine Site

Silver King   Hyland
Basin   👁 Pass   1

29km   Mt Hyland ▲

Sunny   2
Point   ▲

0km
begin
Ⓟ

Mt Harvey ▲   ▲

2

37km
end   Pyramid Mt ▲   ▲

Driftwood Fossil   ▲
Beds Park
Ⓟ   McKendrick Creek

▲

Mt
McKendrick ▲

Astlais Mt ▲

Canyon Creek

Little Onion Mt ▲

〰〰 single track

══ gravel road

━━ paved road

〜 stream

👁 view point   **Mountain Bike Trails**
1 Cronin Pass Trail
➤ unmapped trail   2 Silver King Basin Trail

Ⓟ parking

🪵 bridge

⊠ gate

🌲🌲 Silver King
Basin Cabin

N
W E
S

0 1 2 3 4 5km

smithers

To access the route, turn off Hwy. 16 at the flashing light in Telkwa and cross the bridge to Coalmine Rd. After 6.3 km, take the right fork, follow along until a left fork onto Telkwa River Forest Rd. at 9.9 km. Stay on this road, passing some Forest Service Recreation sites, keeping left at the junction at 36.1 km and climb the steep right fork when you reach the junction at 41.1 km, descend the steep grade and take the left road after the bridge at 44.4 km's. Follow along to the top of the hill above Mill Creek. Descend down to Mill Creek (46.6 km) and begin to climb up to the Telkwa Pass (el. 945m) at about 51 km. Top Lake is reached soon, a great rest spot and possible camp site. Enjoy the ride through the rolling alpine and the wicked descent down the other side of the pass.

local knowledge

tasty bites & frosty pints
Alpenhorn Pub & Bistro – (250) 847-5366

camping
Tyhee Lake Provincial Park – (10 KM east of Smithers) (250) 846-5511
Beautiful lakeside campsites with all the amenities, located in the beautiful Bulkley River Valley. There are many other campsites available in the Smithers area, contact Smithers Visitor Info. Centre, (250) 847-5072. Talk to the nice folks at McBike in town and they might have some more options for you, (250) 847-5009.

off the bike in smithers
Rest days in Smithers can be almost as much fun as riding. There are several provincial & regional parks in the area that have some incredible camping and hiking. There is also some wicked fun to be had on the rivers in this valley. If the supercharged singletrack only gave you a taste of adrenalin, the kayaking and rafting in the canyons will give you a few heaping helpings of it. For more relaxed and mother-approved activities, try canoeing, fishing or horseback riding, and if you're still stuck for something to do contact the Smithers Visitor Info. Center. If that doesn't help you, you're either too picky, you've been grounded or you're dead.

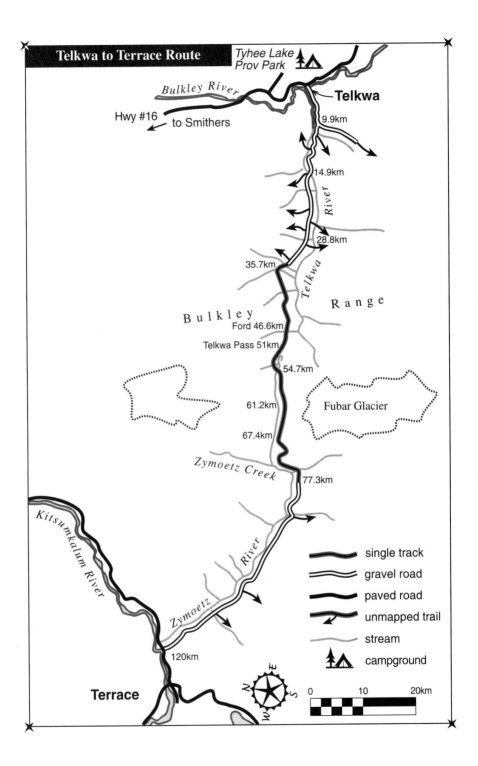

Telkwa to Terrace Route

Tyhee Lake Prov Park

Bulkley River

Telkwa

Hwy #16
to Smithers

9.9km

14.9km

River

28.8km

35.7km

Telkwa

R a n g e

B u l k l e y

Ford 46.6km

Telkwa Pass 51km

54.7km

61.2km

Fubar Glacier

67.4km

Zymoetz Creek

77.3km

Kitsumkalum River

River

Zymoetz

120km

Terrace

N E S W

single track
gravel road
paved road
unmapped trail
stream
campground

0   10   20km

306

The Sanctuary Foundation

Everyone deserves a bike. There are people out there who dedicate their lives to making this happen. The purpose of the Sanctuary Foundation is to provide services and programs that will assist individuals in achieving educational, employment and personal goals through bicycle-related training. Through esteem-initiatives such as the Sanctuary Training Centre and E-Teams the Sanctuary Foundation, which is a non-profit organization, takes a proactive approach toward reducing the likelihood of Family Violence, which is one of the Foundation's primary concerns.

The training centre offers courses to youth on probation, youth in care and individuals on BC benefits. Courses offered include Bicycle Mechanic Technician and Ski Technician Work Experience Programs.

As well as training troubled youths locally, The Sanctuary Foundation is engaged in a number of environmental and bicycle projects both locally and abroad. The Cuba Project aims to create the infrastructure for developing the bicycle industry for the people of Cuba, as well as recycling donated bikes for the country. The BC "E" Team is another Sanctuary project. The idea behind the program is to bring young people together with employers, so that they may gain work experience and training on environment-related projects. The "E" Team provides bike patrol for the Greater Vancouver Regional District, as well as participating in the Sanctuary Foundation's Cycle Recycling Project.

This organization thrives on the generosity of people like you. The Sanctuary Foundation accepts the following donations:
- Bicycles or bicycle parts in good condition for the Cuba Project
- Computers or computer parts in good condition for the Cuba Project
- Clothing books or other donations
- Cash, cheque or credit card donations

Please visit the Sanctuary Foundation website for information on other projects as well as how to donate.

www.sanctuary.bc.ca

Steve Dunn is a transplanted Cape Bretoner from Sydney, Nova Scotia who's had a long love affair with mountain biking. Steve began off-road cycling in Cape Breton in the early 80's, during those early days of the sport, when flat bars, wool socks and cantilever brakes were king and six inches of travel was just a bad holiday. He has been exploring his creative side while writing articles for magazines and hosting an adventure travel TV show called *"Treks In A Wild World"*. Steve has a BSc in Kinesiology from Dalhousie University, a Masters in leisure time management and is currently working on his PhD in life.

Darrin Polischuk is the author of the first edition of *Mountain Biking BC*. Since 1996 he has had three knee operations, which got him off the bike and into the world of sporting media. He founded and currently produces *16mm- "beyond the action"*, a TV series currently seen on The Outdoor Life Network in Canada and in over 30 countries abroad. His simple desire to tell stories and encourage an active lifestyle is still the central focus of Darrin's work and life. Darrin finds peace riding with Bean on easy trails throughout BC, surfing south of the border in warm water or rock climbing.